This Nest of Vipers

This Nest of Vipers

*McCarthyism and Higher Education
in the Mundel Affair, 1951–52*

Charles H. McCormick

UNIVERSITY OF ILLINOIS PRESS
Urbana and Chicago

This book is printed on acid-free paper.

Library of Congress Cataloging-in-Publication Data

McCormick, Charles Howard, 1932–
    This nest of vipers: McCarthyism and higher education in the
Mundel affair, 1951–52/Charles Howard McCormick.
        p.   cm.
Bibliography: p.
Includes index.
ISBN 0-252-01614-9 (alk. paper)
1. Academic freedom—West Virginia—Fairmont—History—20th
century.   2. Communist college teachers—West Virginia—Fairmont—
Dismissal of—History—20th century.   3. Anti-communist movements—
West Virginia—Fairmont—History—20th century.   4. Mundel, Luella—
Trials, litigation, etc.   5. Trials (Treason)—West Virginia—
Fairmont.   I. Title.
LC72.3.W4M38   1989
378'.121—dc 19   88-30129
                                                                      CIP

For Margie

Contents

Acknowledgments

I incurred many large debts and obligations in the pursuit of this topic. The faculty personnel committee and administration of Fairmont State College kindly granted me a semester's sabbatical leave for research. Librarians and archivists were uniformly kind and helpful, especially those at the West Virginia and Regional History Collection of West Virginia University. Fairmont State College librarians Ruth Ann Powell and Dr. Janet Salvati shared with me their expertise in locating obscure publications and knowledge of local history and its sources.

I am grateful to the American Association of University Professors and especially to Associate General Secretary Jordan E. Kurland and to Committee H on the History of the Association for granting me access to their Mundel case file, and to Elizabeth Miller who took the considerable trouble to variously photocopy, retype, or copy by hand the contents of the two-inch-thick file in order to save me a trip to Washington, D.C. Harold D. Jones's continuing interest in the Mundel affair after more than three decades and his willingness to share with me his very valuable cache of letters, clippings, and miscellaneous items about it was extremely helpful as I tried to reconstruct events. So was his vivid recollection of what happened then and his undiminished passion for righting a wrong. Although, as mentioned below in the Note on Sources, I have relied heavily on contemporaneous documentary evidence to buttress the narrative, many persons were kind enough to speak or correspond with me about one or another facet of the affair and/or to offer suggestions to guide my research. Some of these contacts involved no more than a letter, a phone call, or a brief conversation. Others were extensive interviews. All were polite and helpful and I thank them. They include: Jack Sandy Anderson, L. O. Bickel, James Brooks, Peggy Edwards, Edward Fleming, Eleanor N. Ford, Dr. and Mrs. George H. Hand, Dr. Harry B. Heflin, Edgar Jaynes, Harold D. Jones, Ann Holbert, Victor Lasky, Regis Larkin, Anne B. Morgan, Dr. Luella R. Mundel, Judge Richard Neely, Emily Nichols, Richard Parrish, and Helen C. Whitney. I am also grateful to Ms. Whitney for providing me with a videotape for study purposes of the 1983 ABC Television documentary, *The American Inquisition.*

I thank those who have taken the time to read this study critically at one stage or another, especially the referees and editorial staff of the University of Illinois Press. I owe a very special thanks to Richard M. Fried, who read and commented kindly and expertly on two different drafts and who was unfailingly enthusiastic about the topic. So, too, was Margie K. McCormick, who in addition to helping to improve and refine my manuscript had to endure my often tiresomely repetitive trepidations and ruminations about the project over several years.

Of course any errors of fact or interpretation are mine alone and not the responsibility of anyone named above.

Luella Raab Mundel, in the late 1950s. (Courtesy Mayville State University.)

George H. Hand at his office door in 1950. (Courtesy Fairmont State College.)

Luella Raab Mundel, from the Fairmont State College yearbook. (Courtesy Fairmont State College.)

Fairmont State College campus c. 1950. *Aerial view:* administration building (foreground) contains administrative offices, art department (third floor), and library and cafeteria (wing at left). (Courtesy Fairmont State College.)

Fairmont State College campus c. 1950. *Left to right:* gymnasium, classroom building, and administration building. Note the unpaved roads and rural setting. (Courtesy Fairmont State College.)

Introduction

The nation never before has been faced with an external enemy of such danger.... Moreover, it is not only an external enemy; through ideological infection, thousands of its agents have been planted in our midst. It has a shocking — almost unbelievable — way of converting individuals born, reared, and educated in America to its fold. Not only that but converts are often difficult to identify — lying like serpents in ambush in an industrial firm, labor union, school, or church, waiting for the opportunity to strike.

— John Edgar Hoover (1952)

E Pluribus Unum — From many persons one nation, and from many peoples one world — indivisible, with liberty and justice for all. A strong and dynamic national community intertwining in harmony and unity of purpose an infinite variety of individual talents and careers, and in time a strong and dynamic world community, embracing in brotherhood and mutual respect a rich and enriching diversity of national cultures. These are the twin goals which America, and therefore its institutions of higher education must strive to attain.

— The President's Commission on Higher Education (1947)

This is the story of Dr. Luella Raab Mundel's unsuccessful fourteen-month struggle in 1951 and 1952 to keep her job as head of the art department at Fairmont State College, a small, changing teachers college in a minor Appalachian city. It is about the few who tried to help her, the few who hounded her, and the many who ignored her. It has melodrama, interesting characters, and sensational revelations. It has perjury and posturing and principled courage (although one cannot always tell them apart). It does not have, invective and vituperation all around to the contrary, many black-hearted villains or heroes of spotless raiment. It is about a period in the lives of a number of decent but ideologically and culturally diverse men and women who found themselves caught up in a confusing and frightening dispute that seemed to threaten their careers and some of their most private and deeply held values. It is not a simple story and the chapters that follow attempt to reveal its complexity and make some sense of it as a conflict among individuals, institutions, and interests over a wide range of national, state, and local issues.

The Second Red Scare or the Age of McCarthyism,* a domestic manifestation of the Cold War, was a mid-twentieth-century national crusade against real and imagined Communist internal subversion. It is the most severe and, to many living Americans, the most familiar in a series of related periodic occurrences that lie like smudges on the timeline of American history. In British colonial America, French- or Spanish-influenced "papists" or wretched women accused as witches were the outsiders within the community upon whom fell the blame for things gone awry (along with such perennial victims as blacks and American Indians). In later times the same unwelcome mantle fell upon others — Freemasons, Mormons, Roman Catholics, Jews, atheists, and the advocates of radical political ideologies, usually of the Left.[1]

However different the circumstances and the times of each, the functional similarities of each of these episodes are evident. Robert Wiebe offers a useful distinction between society and culture. The latter, he suggests, represents the values and habits that condition our everyday choices in such areas as family governance, work, religious belief, friendship, and casual interchange. Society combines culture, or in the modern United States, cultures, into broader, more systematic behavior such as the organization of a community's life, the structure of a profession, a religious denomination, or a formula for apportioning economic rewards.[2]

Changes in a society often force painful adjustments in the culture of one or more of its parts. This in turn may cause stress and occasion resistance and reaction from the affected parts. At certain times, such as the decade after World War II, the accumulating pressures for change invade the cultural arrangements of many segments of society. The result can be widespread fear of losing one's culture. From this perspective discrete episodes of apparent witch-hunting, irrationality, and intoler-

---

*These terms are used interchangeably throughout this work. I had intended to eschew "McCarthyism" entirely, but it has become so generally accepted there seems to be no way to avoid it. The problems with "McCarthyism" are several. First, although Sen. Joseph R. McCarthy's famous 1950 Wheeling speech was given less than eighty miles from the site of Luella Mundel's travails, I have found no evidence that he played any part at all in the events described here. Second, and more important, the complex of political, social, economic, and cultural factors involved in the Second Red Scare transcends the influence of any individual, even McCarthy, and both pre- and postdate his national prominence. Finally, to personify this phenomenon is implicitly to assign its responsibility to a single individual and to absolve by obscuration the countless others — politicians, bureaucrats, businessmen, educators, journalists, civic leaders, plain citizens, conservatives, and liberals — who by rights should share the responsibility.

ance toward vulnerable groups and individuals in American history have conformed to a pattern.

But historically witch-hunting episodes seem to be less the fruit of mass hysteria driving leaders willy-nilly before it than the result of political disarray among elites in times of societal crisis—a sort of anxiety-ridden thrashing about of the body politic unbridled by coherent, responsible directions from its head. At such times, in the absence of an elite consensus, leaders or would-be leaders of disaffected elements of the population have sought to heal a society under stress from rapid political, economic, and/or social change or at least to relieve its anxiety. Their method was to identify the carriers of contagion, ascribe to them great (often exaggerated) powers, project upon them the blame for social ills, and build a consensus that they should be purged from society. Often projecting their own cultural agenda to the whole, the exorcists assumed that society had lost the true way, or was in imminent danger of doing so, and that to regain the correct path required a high degree of social uniformity. The conditions that produced an anti-Catholic crusade, an outburst of anti-Semitism, or a Red Scare are, as John Demos points out, highly specific and circumstantial, but the common thread that runs through them all is "broad, generic, even trans-historical." Over time the prevailing paradigm, the worldview by which Americans interpret their experience, has changed. To take an obvious example, the generally accepted seventeenth-century Protestant cosmology that included magic and witchcraft as functional explanatory devices for evil and otherwise inexplicable happenings has long since lost its potency. But social dysfunction and cultural disruption have, if anything, increased. So has the need felt by many for cathartic social purge.[3]

Reading the late FBI Director J. Edgar Hoover's words quoted above, can one doubt that in the post–World War II era communism became the most powerful American metaphor for anxieties stemming from uncertainties and impending changes in the nation's public and private life?* Or that the secret Communist supposedly living in the people's midst personified its evil agency? Or that fear at the bottom was encouraged from the top? Many Americans succumbed to the notion that cultural and religious conformity was the litmus test for loyalty to the nation and that by extension a nonconformist was a risk to national security. To the degree that certain specific groups and individuals felt their cultural arrangements threatened—their values, habits, and everyday choices—

---

*To be fair one should point out that Hoover publicly insisted that civil liberties should be scrupulously protected even as Communist Party USA (CPUSA) members and fellow travelers were exposed.

they responded positively to radical anticommunism. Insofar as individuals and groups were culturally different from the majority, in some fashion "outsiders" in a troubled part of society, they became its potential victims. Thus, many of the victims of Red hunting were in a sense surrogates for the national elites who championed social change and who appeared to reap the major rewards of the American system. Unable to strike effectively against powers greater than their own, disaffected groups turned on those in their midst who were weaker. Few were truly weaker than teachers and single women.

So it was that the smear "Communist" became for some a sort of *cri de coeur* against the pain, while for others it was an effective, all-purpose metaphorical tool to advance their political interests by using unpopular individuals, ideas, and policies, including those in academe. With regard to higher education, Isaac Asimov put it graphically in one of his early works, a fictional mystery set in a university. Discussing the job security of professors, he wrote: "After all, a professor might drink himself into a stupor every night; might bumble out lectures no one could understand; might bathe only during Lent; might be unbearably rude; intolerably boring; intensively obnoxious and [with tenure] all would be forgiven. . . . But two levers could always remove him, tenure or not. One was disloyalty (a comparatively modern crime) and the other was moral turpitude."[4]

One authority calculates that from 1947 to 1955, 600 supposedly disloyal teachers at all levels of education lost their jobs in the United States, about half of them in New York City.[5] Just as at Salem in 1692 some of the accused were witches—that is they believed in witchcraft and practiced it—so were there practicing Communists in the United States in the 1950s, including some in the schools. With the advantage of hindsight, even accepting the most inflated estimate of the number of party members and fellow travelers in American classrooms, such as that of Red hunter J. B. Matthews, they now seem to have been a very slight threat to the educational system. But that was not the general perception of the time. A broad consensus existed that a Communist should not be permitted to teach in a college or university.[6]

Although professors at prominent universities were their most publicized targets, Red hunters did not ignore the lower end of the academic hierarchy—public schools and teachers colleges remote physically and intellectually from the centers of national power. Controversial faculty members at the latter seem to have been particularly vulnerable, but there were probably fewer of them in the generally more conservative or nonintellectual atmosphere. It is difficult to know how many were dismissed or intimidated because of McCarthyism. Yet, as Allen Weinstein has noted, precisely here may be found not the martyrs, but the clear-cut victims of the "age of suspicion . . . remaining to be rescued by historians from among the human debris of the McCarthy era."[7]

In their 1955 analysis of the effects of McCarthyism on higher education, *The Academic Mind,* Paul Lazarsfeld and Wagner Thielens, Jr., gathered data from 2,451 social science faculty at 165 institutions. They isolated teachers colleges in a separate category and concluded that the educational quality of such places was low. They also found that compared to all except Catholic institutions, teachers college faculty members ranked generally low in academic achievement and tolerance for controversial or new ideas. They found that such faculty also tended to be less liberal than colleagues elsewhere and less interested in academic freedom. Interviewers from the study met with cold receptions at many such institutions from both faculty and administrators. The interviewers' assessment was based upon their assumptions about the nature and purpose of higher education, which were informed by the powerful twentieth-century intellectual construct of relativistic materialism. Many teachers colleges were resistant to this worldview as it was expressed through the modern university curriculum, clinging instead to a sort of late McGuffeyite Newtonianism. In part this clinging to the past was a defense thrown up by some faculty at former teachers colleges against the conversion of their institutions to a comprehensive curriculum and against what they perceived as an invasion of their teacher-training monopoly by liberal arts professors—an invasion that became most threatening in the postwar era. In their struggle they found allies in small-town elites who interpreted educational change as a threat to the status quo. The Second Red Scare made the "security" issue available and, one suspects, almost irresistible to opponents of the new worldview as a weapon against change. All of this fuels speculation that many teachers college instructors whose "crime" was to represent advanced academic thinking may have lost their jobs or, more likely, been silenced in the McCarthy era unnoticed by the press or their peers at more exalted institutions.[8]

Such may have been the case. At many teacher training institutions budgets and institutional survival depended on the whims of legislators, the attitudes of insecure local elites, and volatile and uninformed public opinion. Here ideas of academic freedom and education as inquiry and knowledge-gathering took a backseat to the preservation of local interests and vocationalism. Here instructors earned substantially less than assembly-line workers and worried much more about keeping their jobs.

It was at such a place, one groping for the proper way to respond to postwar ideals and realities, that Luella Mundel, an advocate of the new ideas, fought her battle to keep her livelihood and her academic freedom against the wholly specious accusation that she was a leftist and a security risk. It was a battle that affords the historian a rare opportunity to observe in painful detail the playing-out of an anticommunist episode in a single community. Three decades of fruitful scholarship on McCarthyism have taught us much. Yet there remain unresolved a number of questions. It is obvious that multiple fears and grievances energized and sustained the movement. Widespread if vague anticommunist feeling intimidated even wise political and social leaders into going along with some of its excesses. It imperiled those who spoke against those excesses. Conversely, some political and social leaders used public fear of or, at the very least, public indifference to dissenters' civil liberties for their own purposes. We know much more about McCarthyism at the national level than we do about its workings at the grass roots. It is hoped that this case study will help us to understand the process by which national issues and policies can become entangled with state, local, and personal matters and so be transformed.[9]

CHAPTER 1

Luella Mundel, the Friendly City, and Democracy's College

[For] more than 19 centuries mankind has had three unfailing sources of inspiration to heroic efforts, great accomplishments, and sublime attainments. . . . These . . . are "Jesus," "home," and "mother."

—Sen. Matthew M. Neely (1951)

They have started to clean out this nest of vipers which has made Fairmont State College a hissing and slander and humiliation for the last four years.

—Sen. Matthew M. Neely (1952)

Luella Raab Mundel came to West Virginia in September 1949 to head the art department at Fairmont State College. Born in 1913 to a German-Austrian family in Waterloo, Iowa, she was the daughter of a Roman Catholic potter and his Lutheran wife. Enduring economic hardship to earn a Ph.D. in art psychology and art history at the University of Iowa at the age of twenty-five (1938), she was highly regarded by her mentor there, psychology professor Norman C. Meier, who rated her among the top three or four of the twenty graduate assistants who participated in the Spelman-Carnegie research program (1929–39) on the nature of art ability. In this program she worked with artists, child psychologists, educationists, and other art psychologists and in 1939 had published an article, "The Effect of Lectures about Art Principles upon Art Production at the Fifth and Sixth Grade Levels."[1]

In 1938, newly married to an industrial engineering graduate student, New Yorker Marvin E. Mundel, Luella Mundel obtained her degree, taught briefly at a college in Ypsilanti, Michigan (1938–39), and audited an art class in New York City (1940). Otherwise her academic career languished. In 1942 her husband joined the engineering department at Purdue University, where he remained through the 1940s and early 1950s, rising to become department chairman. They divorced in September 1946, and after years as the wife of a rising professor on a large, sophisticated university campus, Luella Mundel now found it necessary to reconstitute her career in art education.

The month her divorce became final she took a job at Park College in Kansas City, Missouri, and after two years moved on to Phoenix College, Arizona, apparently attracted by a higher salary and a new scene. After only a semester Mundel quit Phoenix in order to take graduate courses in art at the University of California at Berkeley. After a semester there, she came to West Virginia. Mundel was well traveled and had spent much of her adult life in the bosom of one university or another. It was an atmosphere at once removed from and, to outsiders, contemptuous of and condescending toward the "real world" beyond its gates. Mundel had never been long in a small public college in a small provincial town and nothing in her academic experience had prepared her for what she was to encounter in Fairmont, West Virginia.[2]

Fairmont, the seat of Marion County, owed its development to its location in the western foothills of the Appalachians on the Monongahela River at the confluence of the Tygart Valley and West Fork rivers. It lay in northern West Virginia, a region scarcely distinguishable from adjacent areas of Pennsylvania and Ohio. Its dominant economic and cultural influence was Pittsburgh, eighty-five miles down river to the north.

A modest marketing and manufacturing center near the rich Pittsburgh and Sewickley bituminous coal deposits, Fairmont was a small, prosperous city with a population close to 30,000 in 1950. The population had grown nearly 28 percent in the 1940s in response to the World War II–based boom in coal and local industries such as glass, coke, and mining equipment.

Between the 1890s and the Great War, the key period in Fairmont's economic history, a small group of locally based entrepreneurs had built fortunes from the coal lands. They had intermarried with descendants of the largely Scotch-Irish and German early settlers, "Old Fairmont," to create an economic, social, and cultural elite. From 1910 until the mid-1920s, during the heyday of the coal barons, Sonnencroft, the twenty-eight-room stucco and tile mansion of the coal baron Clyde E. Hutchinson, was the jewel of the east side of town. On the west side Sen. Clarence Wayland Watson maintained his internationally famous show horses on a sprawling stuccoed Spanish mission–style estate known as Fairmont Farms. Even more splendid stood nearby James E. Watson's family seat, High Gate, where ex-President William Howard Taft was once a guest. There gorgeous peacocks graced the grounds of an enormous ersatz Tudor palace where the annual tennis tournament for the $1,000 Tiffany Cup was held. It is said that on one weekend the Ziegfeld Follies cast was brought from New York City by rail to entertain the master of the estate. Less elegant evidences of prosperity and conspicuous consumption were the plenitude of illicit liquor and drugs, the gambling dens, the brothels, and the "cablines" of prostitutes who beckoned to customers from the curtained windows of autos on Main Street. It was a time, according to longtime Fairmont journalist Clarence E. "Ned" Smith, when "a coal miner who did not own a 15 dollar silk shirt was a humble citizen, indeed."[3]

The garishness was an obvious manifestation of an *arriviste* aristocracy without an existing regional model to guide its behavior. One of the special features of West Virginia society from its beginnings was the lack of a significant upper class or even an upper-middle class. In the absence of the more typical American leadership groups the standards of the rural lower-middle class prevailed and became the values of the politicians who were the state's functional leaders. Janet B. Welch has listed the principal West Virginia cultural values as traditionalism, individualism, pessimism, fatalism, fundamentalism, religiosity and puritan morality, familialism, love of home, and isolationism. One might quibble with Welch's emphasis, but her categories echo generations of scholars. The point here is that this cluster of values is essentially defensive and antimodern — a means of keeping out the ever-intruding present.[4]

By 1950 Fairmont's coal baron aristocrats were on their uppers. Whatever the reasons — the 1920s collapse of the coal market, the Great Depression, the folly of the rich, greener pastures elsewhere, changes in the structure of the coal and steel industries — the great wealth was gone. Corporate boardrooms in New York, Pittsburgh, Cleveland, and other distant metropolises had long since grasped control of local mines and industries. Old Fairmont, its big money mostly gone, hung on to what power it could. This was true especially in cultural affairs, where it sought to preserve its superiority through promoting a rather sterile gentility. A community orchestra, concerts, decorous churches, and orderly schools were means to this end. Still, because the town lacked enough substantial old wealth, it could not provide the large-scale philanthropy necessary to nurture strong cultural institutions or a well-developed sense of *noblesse oblige* in local leaders.

Sixty-two clergymen served the community. One was a rabbi, four were Catholic priests, and the rest were Protestants of various stripes. Among the white Protestant majority denominations the social hierarchy was topped by the Presbyterians, with the United Methodists and mainstream Baptists a notch below. The position of the Episcopal church was ambiguous. In eastern Virginia it was of course *the* church. But western Virginia had been settled in the eighteenth century by dissenters against the Church of England, among whose descendants it remained suspect.

The political and cultural impact of Fairmont's Protestant churches in the 1950s is difficult to assess. Ministers had little discernible political influence and seldom spoke out on social issues.

Fairmonters in the mainstream churches clearly shared the core assumptions of American Protestants that there was a universal moral law and that Americans more than any other people were God's people. In terms of its overall influence in formal thought, public policy, and the daily affairs of the nation, this once-dominant progressive Protestant vision of a Christian America had sharply declined in the 1920s and 1930s. But, according to Robert T. Handy, for a decade or so after World War II, this "second disestablishment" was masked by a surge of popular and public interest in religion. Documenting the revival was the growth of nominal church membership nationwide from about 50 percent to nearly 70 percent along with a comparable attendance increase. Other evidences of the surge were the popularity of White House prayer breakfasts, record-breaking sales of religious publications, and the addition in 1954 of "under God" to the Pledge of Allegiance. Because West Virginia church membership was well below the national average and the state usually lagged behind national trends, it is hard to estimate the degree to which these conservative cultural, as opposed to theological, developments affected the the Fairmont community-at-large, but they surely affected the events described below.[5]

Although the great wealth was gone, the city seemed prosperous and bustling, stimulated by the economic activity that carried over after the war's end. It had two hospitals, several department stores, a handful of manufacturing plants, and many small businesses. Two radio stations, two daily newspapers (which shared facilities and put out a combined Sunday paper), and six movie theaters were its eyes and ears to the larger world. The average age of Fairmonters was just over thirty-one, the average income just under $3,000, and the mean level of schooling a little higher than the tenth grade.[6]

The population, income, and education figures for Fairmont suggest a more sophisticated and urban setting than actually existed. Narrow, winding, steep roads limited travel, and the virtual absence of chain stores diminished the influence of the national commercial culture. Dotting the surrounding countryside among the ridges were numerous small to minuscule communities in the "hollers"—hamlets or former coal camps that were home to a large, poor, rural nonfarm population. Such places would seem models of the ideal community on a human scale—no larger than one could shout across and be heard. But nothing was ideal about coal camps. The educational level in these hamlets and the breadth of exposure to the modern world were as low as the suspicion of outsiders was high. It was from these areas that Fairmont drew much of its population and its social attitudes.

Hard times were coming to the county in the early 1950s. The rapid mechanization of the coal industry and a declining coal market would reduce employment in West Virginia mines by more than one-half during that single decade. While the national population grew, Marion County's population shrank by over 11 percent. More than 3 percent of the loss occurred during the years of the Mundel controversy, 1950–52.[7]

Measured by its educational and cultural resources, the region was ill prepared to cope effectively with the impending changes. Just over 31 percent of the Marion county population had finished high school. Typically the regional male culture relished chewing tobacco and bloody and violent sports, particularly deer hunting and football. It was as if uncouthness and the catharsis of grisly frontier or gladiatorial rituals could give a feeling of physical mastery to the otherwise powerless. The laboring majority preferred what was then called "hill-billy" music and hellfire and damnation revivalistic religion. Although formal church membership in the state was well below the national average, ubiquitous, tiny, mostly white-frame independent community churches (many of them Pentecostal) were the vital centers of rural culture. Appalachian children were reared permissively, critics said, growing up without the positive adult role models and self-discipline typical of the middle class. Yet this permissiveness was mostly in mother-child relations, for the father was often a harsh disciplinarian, an outsider in the family. Women were encouraged to work outside the home where possible because it made life easier when the husband was unemployed, a not infrequent occurrence. A sense of powerlessness was reflected in lives that seemed unplanned, that just happened. Life was about "being," not "becoming." Education is of course about "becoming" and so there was no real, broadly based commitment to quality schools or scholarship. A negative value attached to intellect or high culture. There was little appreciation of beauty or art. Humor was not highly developed and it tended toward the crude and physical. The greatest of glee derived from the embarrassment of authority figures and the misfortune of others. In many cultures humor is a psychic defense against life's hardships. Here fatalism and pessimism largely served that function.

In this world kinship assumed great importance, as did personal relationships that depended on oral communication and face-to-face contact. The family was the fortress against the world, the survival safety net. Those outside the family were treated with courtesy and suspicion. Neighborly contact and house-to-house visiting were minimal and people were expected to mind their own business. True respect for authority was weak but fear of authoritarian power was great. En masse, unionized coal miners were notoriously truculent, particularly toward their employers. But individual miners dared to express their independence in only small (but to employers irritating) ways. Fairmont area mines have taken a heavy toll of lives. So it was not surprising that men who performed heavy labor in the mines with death perched on their shoulders rarely showed up for work on their birthdays or the first day of hunting season.[8]

Reflecting its position as a market center in a blue-collar culture, Fairmont boasted forty-eight beauty shops, four bowling alleys, four tap-dance studios, and twenty-five places serving beer (liquor by the drink was technically illegal except for those who belonged to private clubs). There remained a small, now rarely mentioned, red-light district. But no shop was devoted exclusively to the sale of books, no gallery to the display of art, no museum to the preservation of local history. Only by torturing the meaning of language could one call Fairmont a college town.[9]

The town population was about 5 percent black and the schools and other public facilities were legally segregated. Local black youths were prohibited by law from attending Fairmont State. If they wished state-financed higher education they had to travel to one of the two distant "colored" colleges, West Virginia State or Bluefield State. One local beer establishment advertised "Separate Dance Halls—Colored and White." Amateur minstrel shows were still common. As late as 1949 the college drama group, the Masquers, presented, apparently as a humorous melodrama, *Uncle Tom's Cabin*.[10]

The sharpest ethnic divisions and economic conflict in the town and county were between the longer settled, largely Scotch-Irish and German Protestant majority and more recent arrivals whom the coal barons had brought to the area a generation or two earlier from southern and eastern Europe to work in local mines. Mostly Italian Roman Catholics with a strong admixture of Poles and Balkan peoples, this group was making substantial economic and social progress in the face of the predictable discrimination and resentment. In 1950 the process of assimilation of the newcomers was far from complete.

John Gaventa's description of the social structure of the Cumberland Gap region coal culture appears at least loosely to fit north-central West Virginia. He describes a society characterized respectively top to bottom by: (1) absentee owners and managers; (2) local business, white-collar, and professional elites; (3) the miners; and (4) the poor (working and nonworking). For the Fairmont region one would have to factor in a cohort of industrial workers on a level close to that of the miners. With that exception, Gaventa's analysis of the role of the local elites is instructive.

He labels the businessmen and professional groups "gatekeepers" who act as brokers for jobs and political favors in their communities and as mediators of culture and power between the inside and outside worlds. There was not enough wealth in the state's colonial economy to make everyone in West Virginia prosperous, and Gaventa's gatekeepers or those whom John Alexander Williams calls a narrow middle class owed their position and status to serving directly or indirectly the interests of the absentee corporate rulers. Therefore they inclined to resist social change, to control who entered their ranks, and to guard their place. One important way to do so was by controlling public schools and limiting educational opportunity for blue-collar folk.

The stratified nature of American higher education before World War II is well documented. While virtually all local leaders publicly professed enthusiasm for public education, many were in fact disinclined to pay taxes to support it if to do so meant addressing obvious deficiencies in the educational system and thereby affording groups below them a means to rise in the socioeconomic hierarchy. As an example, in the 1950s when many public schools were staffed by unqualified teachers while qualified teachers fled in droves to more progressive states and the high-school dropout rate was 40 percent, double that of neighboring Ohio and Pennsylvania, a Morgantown newspaper editor and former state board of education member characterized the need for more money for schools as "unadulterate piffle of the first water." In Fairmont Luella Mundel collided with the gatekeepers, and college president George Hand paid with his job for challenging their powers.[11]

Politically speaking, in 1951 Fairmont was a Democratic town in a Democratic county (since 1941) in a Democratic state (since 1933). True, the local afternoon paper, the *West Virginian,* featured a conservative Republican slant, much of the small business-professional establishment remained Republican, and the city's governing commission was comprised of two Democrats and two Republicans. These anachronisms echoed the pre–New Deal days when Marion County had been a Republican stronghold. In 1950 much of the white-collar professional cohort remained Republican and hostile to the New Deal, but county Democrats outnumbered Republicans eight to five and they had controlled the key county offices—sheriff, prosecuting attorney, and assessor—since 1932. Thus, the GOP no longer held much local influence, except at those times when Democratic infighting became self-destructive. The greatest power lay within the Democratic party coalition of prominent local families, the United Mine Workers (which included a cross-section of ethnic groups), and political job holders. Despite obvious cultural and economic differences, all factions shared a commitment to advancing coal and associated industries. In the abstract, if coal prospered, land values, miners' wages, and business activity would rise and all would benefit. All three groups had generally supported the economic programs of the New Deal, despite John L. Lewis's difficulties with several Democratic presidents. The most visible symbol of this political alliance was U.S. senator, ex-Fairmont mayor, ex-governor of West Virginia, Matthew Mansfield Neely.[12]

All the groups were socially conservative. The work of miners has traditionally separated them from most other men and contributed to an observable clannishness and cultural separateness. Adding to this sense of separation from and hostility toward outsiders was the recent immigrant status of many mining families and the long cultural isolation of the established majority. The region's political style was tailored to the culture of its people. Although the turnout for elections was usually high, voters were cynical toward candidates and toward the efficacy of the political process. The key to a successful political career was to develop a folksy style, to be known by the voters, to deal effectively with the personal problems of constituents. West Virginians were far more willing to reelect a known sinner than an unfamiliar saint. Voters did not require politicians to be scrupulously honest, but they did expect them to be discreet in their transgressions and to stand publicly for traditional regional norms and received values.

Although some were educated, well traveled, and sophisticated, leaders of the local squirearchy were socially conservative, nonideological, and much attached to their own security. As elsewhere in Appalachia, they had learned, as Gaventa suggests, that power can be exercised by mobilizing popular biases through the use of symbolic resources such as the fear of "troublemakers," "outsiders," "atheists," and Communists (usually pronounced "ca'-mon-is"). This tactic, which was applied through the invocation of myth and rumor, was made all the more effective in preventing unwanted change because of self-fulfilling, fatalistic popular attitudes, conditioned by hard experience, that reform efforts were bound to fail.[13]

In a time of a shaky local economy, national social turmoil, and generalized political anxiety such as the early Cold War years, this natural conservatism was intensified. New political, economic, and religious ideas or an influx of outsiders were potential challenges to the cultural status quo which reflected the values and prestige of dominant local interests. Few institutions incorporated and vivified these values more visibly than the local college.

Fairmont was not a college town, but Fairmont State was a town college. It was a typical American special-interest college of its time. As Christopher

Jencks and David Riesman point out, before the twentieth century most American colleges had been more like high schools than universities. Typically, they were founded in the nineteenth century by hometown boosters, often with a religious affiliation, to serve local interests and to extend opportunities for higher education to local youth. If they survived it was by rooting themselves in one or another local subculture. In the case of Fairmont the special interest was teacher education, the sort of uplift that appealed to the post-Victorian progressive and genteel elements of the town's middle class. The element of localism at the college was magnified by the rugged terrain, mountaineer individualism, a virulent strain of Protestant moralism, and a populist disdain for intellectualism. Public education, including higher education, had long been politicized in West Virginia and in some parts of the state was considered to be a special concern of various Protestant home missions.

Across the nation by the 1940s the rise of meritocratic job requirements and a growing national economy and culture had blurred and diminished regional and local differences, stimulated mobility, and challenged the hegemony of small-town elites. And, often as not, community leaders discovered too late that their colleges had been "taken over by academicians with no local roots or commitments"—outsiders who carried the contagion of unfamiliar and unwelcome moral and cultural values. The Mundel case arose in part from the efforts of a local elite to maintain its hegemony.[14]

Before 1945, Fairmonters counted themselves lucky in that respect. Although funded by the state, the college changed slowly and remained a bastion of dominant local values. From the enrollment of its first class of thirty students in 1867 through World War I, it developed into a normal school offering the equivalent of a high-school diploma to public school teachers. Between the world wars it followed the national trend by becoming a four-year teachers college.[15]

The key figure in the between-the-wars history of the college was Joseph Rosier, its president from 1915 to 1945. "Uncle Joe" was a local boy. Born in neighboring Harrison County of an old stock West Virginia family, he spent his working life, excepting two short excursions to Washington, in northern West Virginia. His formal education was at Salem College near his boyhood home, and he had little respect for high academic degrees or "intellectual snobs." (His doctorate was an honorary LL.D. bestowed in the 1930s by Marshall College.) Rosier ascended the career ladder rung by rung from teacher to Fairmont public school superintendent, then college president, then president of the National Education Association (1932). In 1941–42 he served briefly as United States senator.

Typically for his time and place, success came partly from talent and hard work and partly from political and family connections: Rosier married a woman affiliated with the powerful Randolph and Meredith families; and as an instructor at Salem College in the 1890s he began a friendship with student Matthew Neely that endured for half a century. Given the educational realities of the Mountain State, it is no criticism to say that he was remembered more for his political skills than for his erudition. In the 1920s and 1930s Rosier was considered to be one of the "West Virginia Education Triumvirate" along with West Virginia University education dean J. N. Deahl and Marshall College president M. D. Shawkey. Charles Ambler, historian of West Virginia education, puts it diplomatically when he credits Rosier with "a keen sense of the politically expedient and the educationally possible."[16]

This meant in part that Rosier accepted the supremacy of politically potent West Virginia University, which lay only twenty miles to the north, and understood that the university would brook no competition for curriculum or students from the Fairmont school. It also meant that he understood the importance of keeping on the good side of state and local politicians. So, although he was a political liberal for his time and place, Rosier maintained a secure niche for his college by avoiding the freethinking of a liberal arts emphasis and by restricting its development to teacher education. He used his political savvy to steer the college toward training teachers for jobs throughout the state and yet, by stressing self-help, character, morality, and community participation, to keep it closely and safely identified with local interests. It was a difficult balancing act. He understood the importance of public relations and made good use of the local newspapers through college staff members who were adept at singing his praises and those of the college. His survival for three decades as president testifies to his political skill.[17]

Rosier's "friendly college in the friendly city," "college on the hill," or "Rosier's Knob," as some called it, was respected and popular with the people who counted. The president liked to chat with townsfolk about "our college." And they approved of the way he ran the place. The small, relatively homogeneous student body hardly caused a ripple in town affairs. Through the depression and war years the enrollment gradually fell from over 1,800 (1931) to fewer than 1,300 (1939) to about 600 (1944), about half of them full-time students. All were Caucasian, almost all were West Virginians, and according to a 1937–39 survey, more than 50 percent lived at home, 25 percent within one and a half miles of the college, and more than 75 percent within a radius of thirty-nine miles. A few women lived in a dormitory, but most students commuted on foot, by streetcar, or by automobile.[18]

The 1941–42 faculty numbered forty-five, of whom five held the doctorate and more than forty had at least a master's degree. Columbia University Teachers College graduates dominated the teaching ranks by filling eleven positions, four more than West Virginia University, whose graduates placed the next highest. Conforming to the national norm, the faculty was middle-aged and was either native to or long resident in Fairmont. Its members owned homes and participated noncontroversially in town life. Most belonged to the service clubs, lodges, and churches, and several were prominent and visible local boosters. Campus public relations director Medora Mason wrote a column in the *Fairmont Times* which combined gossip with institutional PR. Another teacher wrote regularly in the same paper on gardening. Others called square dances or promoted such activities as birdwatching. Few belonged to national professional academic associations or pursued scholarly activities. Alcoholism was a problem for some of the teachers, and old-timers recount tales of campus eccentrics and absentminded professors who were, naturally, harmless and charming.[19]

To hear the old-timers tell it, student-teacher relationships were warm and paternalistic in the Rosier years. Waxing nostalgic, some tell humorous stories of student pranks and youthful exuberance. They remember that the college was like a family, and for some, friendships made then still bloom.

Rosier and his staff were training schoolteachers to survive if not prosper in isolated West Virginia districts and to spread genteel middle-class values in rural, hardscrabble coal country. To do so they stressed practical political skills, citizenship, and the social graces. Observers described the atmosphere at the college as "professional" and dedicated to "teaching." Social life, athletics, band, and debating were fostered for their conservative and utilitarian worth in promoting school interests. In this process of refinement, fraternities and sororities had a prominent place and there were many teas, parties, and receptions. The official historian of the college uses the apt phrase "good breeding" to describe this aspect of the approved regimen.[20]

Absent from these recollections is the intense joy of the mind set free, the electricity generated by active minds engaged in intellectual discovery, or the excitement of a good argument about things that matter. This was no accident. Community leaders viewed the college instrumentally as a means to socialize the young and to train those responsible for socializing the young—an institution to perpetuate and spread the middle-class culture, which they regarded as the expression of tolerant and liberal democracy at its best. College was to shelter and inoculate the young against strange ideas and unseemly behavior.[21] College officials knew well that the price of good town-gown relations was a decorous avoidance of controversy.

Wonderful as Rosier's school of the 1930s may have seemed, by 1945 it was by no means certain that the septuagenarian president could master the challenges and opportunities of the post–World War II era. Returning GIs would claim a college degree as a right and most would not want to be teachers. As President Truman's Commission on Higher Education would report in 1947, *"American society . . . is . . . failing to provide a reasonable educational opportunity to its youth"* (italics in original). It blamed the unequal access upon a variety of factors that could be applied to the situation in West Virginia. Along with the more widely publicized racial and religious barriers, these included economic hurdles, variations in quality from region to region, and a restrictive curriculum. Like many educators long before the Truman Commission's report, Rosier acknowledged the need for change. He advocated the expansion of campus facilities, the postwar enlargement of some programs such as physical education, and the addition of a nursing program and special courses for local retail and industrial employees. But he insisted that teacher training must remain the college's main mission.

In 1943, in anticipation of the demands of hordes of returning veterans and a growing sentiment favoring overhaul of the educational establishment, the state government shook the status quo. That year it designated Fairmont and the four other state normal schools as colleges, which presumably meant that they must expand and change to serve a broader population. The new designation opened the door to a major reorganization . . . or did it? The enabling legislation left the state colleges under the control of the board of education and stipulated that "the function of these colleges shall continue to be the preparation of teachers." And yet, if the legislators did not envision a broader mission for Fairmont and the other colleges, why did they bother to change their names?[22]

Rosier's answer to that appeared in the 1944 college catalog and in his annual report to the board of education. He dismissed the notion that the war would be followed by an educational revolution and rejected "visionary schemes for the future." Instead, he reemphasized that Fairmont would eschew a broader curriculum and would remain "glad to be considered a teachers college."[23]

That same year the state legislature commissioned retired Columbia Teachers College professor and pioneer in educational administration and statistical surveys George D. Strayer to study and report on public education. In his report Strayer, who was publicly and prominently identified with progressive education, found much amiss at all levels.

The document described higher education as underfunded, uncoordinated, and atomistic. It reported that various institutions often worked stubbornly at cross-purposes and characterized them as not only "mountain-locked" but "mind-locked" in placing local interests above those of the state. It cited dismal statistics showing that West Virginia ranked well below the national average for high-school graduates, college attendance, and years of teacher preparation. It showed that fully 25 percent of college-bound West Virginians chose to attend out-of-state institutions.

The report urged "drastic" and "courageous" remedies. Recommendations included depoliticizing college and university governance, assigning specific educational tasks to each institution, and using funds more efficiently. To end institutional balkanization and to strengthen West Virginia University as the capstone of the system, separate nonpartisan governing boards were proposed, one for the university and one for the other state colleges.

Strayer's report contained several notable passages about Fairmont State. A statistical table showed its student body to be the most narrowly recruited of any in the state. A summary of accreditation revealed that unlike several sister institutions, the college was unaccredited by the North Central Association of Colleges and Secondary Schools. In order to make more rational use of system resources and to avoid wasteful duplication, Strayer recommended that Fairmont should develop a major liberal arts and vocational curriculum. The report was never fully implemented and West Virginia higher education has remained captive to generations of unimaginative politicians, but the Strayer recommendations fueled the reform efforts that brought on the Mundel affair.[24]

Serious reform was unlikely as long as Fairmont State remained under the control of the West Virginia state board of education. The board was underfinanced and understaffed, had too many diverse responsibilities, and its legal charge was too general to provide clear and firm oversight. It was composed of nine members appointed by the governor to overlapping five-year terms plus the elected state superintendent of schools (Democrat W. W. Trent) who acted ex officio. By law no more than two of the nine appointees could be graduates of the same college or university, none might be public or political party officials, no more than five could be registered in the same party. Each of the state's congressional districts must be represented and (since 1947) at least one member must be "of the Negro race." In practice one board member was usually a woman and the majority were Democrats. Only the governor could remove board members and only for "official misconduct, incompetence, neglect of duty or gross immorality." They served without pay and the only full-time permanent staff member was a secretary at $5,000 per year for salary and expenses. This post was filled at midcentury by Herbert K. Baer, who acted both as the administrative glue that held the board together between its meetings and as a lightning rod to attract the criticism and resentment of the college officials who had to deal with the board through him. The fact that Baer came to his job by way of the public schools rather than higher education was a sore point with some of the college presidents.[25]

The Fairmont resident on the board was Thelma Brand Loudin. Born and reared in the nearby small town of Barrackville, of respectable family but not of Old Fairmont stock, she had attended West Virginia University in the late 1920s to study the violin but left after two years without a degree. Married to a Fairmont storekeeper, Loudin was a housewife who part-time gave piano and violin lessons. Although a devout Baptist, since 1945 she had served as organist and choirmistress at Fairmont's former Southern Methodist Church, now Central United Methodist. Her association with local Democratic politics brought her to the state board of education. In May 1941 then-Governor Matthew M. Neely appointed her to the woman's seat, and his successors, whose selection he greatly influenced, renewed the appointment. Loudin considered herself to be an educator, but she lacked even a bachelor's degree, and one could ask if she was qualified to judge the academic abilities and performance of college professors.[26]

Loudin and the eight men who made up the 1950–52 board were decent, responsible, public-spirited citizens. Most were well-to-do small businessmen and/or erstwhile party activists. Like Loudin, none was professionally trained in higher education administration. The board president in 1951, Garland Dunn, was a woolen manufacturer.

The board had too many responsibilities and too little time. Fairmont State was only one of eleven institutions for which it was responsible. Meeting officially every two months for a day or two, the board had to hurry through an overloaded agenda that allowed little time for the problems of specific schools. Without a staff to gather detailed information or to provide a range of higher education policy advice, its members sometimes seemed not to understand the particular problems raised by individual college presidents or to be able to provide them with clear directions or explanations of the board's educational goals. In dealing with the problems of a particular institution the board tended to defer to the member who lived nearest. In the case of Fairmont State College the board was likely to vote as Thelma Loudin suggested.[27]

In the summer of 1945 the board seemed determined to remove the deadwood from Fairmont State. It enforced the mandatory retirement age of sixty-five and forced Rosier and six of his faculty members from their posts. By September it had hired a new president, George Henry Hand.

Hand proved to be a dynamic and controversial president (1945–52). A native of Wheeling, he had starred in three varsity sports at West Virginia University. After graduation in 1928 and a brief stint as a high-school teacher, he moved to Ohio to be a professor of economics at Denison College (1934–37) and Ohio Wesleyan College (1937–41) and head of the economics department at the University of Vermont (1943–44). He had attended Columbia University graduate school and completed his Ph.D. in economics at Princeton (1939).[28]

Despite his West Virginia roots, Hand had built his career outside the state. By his association with two of the country's major graduate training centers, one of them given over to an urban liberal outlook and the other a bastion of Ivy League elitism, he became a representative of the national academic community. A virtual subculture, the national professoriate included those recruited meritocratically nationwide. They were trained at one of the dozen or so university graduate schools that effectively monopolized the production of Ph.D.s, influenced their job placement, and often even determined their status and prestige within the higher education hierarchy.[29]

Hand risked the dead-ending of his academic career by accepting the presidency of the undistinguished former teachers college at Fairmont. Teachers college administrators do not usually advance to comparable posts at more prestigious schools. But he had seized an opportunity. To mold Fairmont State progressively into a comprehensive up-to-date institution would be a triumph and a stepping-stone to greater things. But it would not be easy. To succeed, the reform-minded president would need the support of an energetic, loyal faculty; a sympathetic state board of education; and, at the very least, the tolerance of community leaders. Only then could he rescue the college from its long thralldom to the politics of provincialism, localism, and social and aesthetic conservatism.

From its beginning Hand's tenure was marked by controversy and tension, some of which was unavoidable and typical of the entire state system. After the war, state college presidents were obliged to expand their institutions very rapidly. It was imperative to train many more public school teachers in light of the apparent baby boom. It was vital to hire more instructors with doctorates and to offer courses in the newer, more research-oriented fields in place of more traditional subjects in order to gain accreditation. This was particularly true at Fairmont State, which was seeking to develop from a teachers college into a comprehensive state college. Implementing this policy rubbed raw the frictions between the pedagogically-oriented established education faculty and the new liberal arts instructors of specialized subject matter. This was a nationwide problem in postwar state colleges which was noted by Truman's Commission on Higher Education in 1947 and one that became acute at Fairmont.

Hand's policies in fact followed the generally progressive and controversial guidelines of the commission, which proposed using higher education instrumentally to prepare American youth for world citizenship, ending discrimination against minorities, and breaking down regional and provincial barriers to equal opportunity. Among its recommendations, the commission advocated federal involvement, financial and regulatory, in state and local education and essentially tuition-free higher education through two years of college for the 49 percent of the population it believed to be academically qualified. It proposed a full four years of free college for the 32 percent it believed capable of doing the work for the bachelor's degree.[30]

To complicate matters in the short term, the so-called GI bill brought veterans who swelled college enrollments and made new and forceful demands. They were older, perhaps more vulgar, certainly more practical and less tolerant toward the paternalistic authority and the more precious aspects of traditional campus life. An extreme version of their demands was expressed in a controversial 1947 article in *School and Society* by University of Nevada forensics professor S. M. Vinocour. He claimed to have traveled more than 7,000 miles over a year talking to ex-GI students. Based on their complaints, he called for a "house cleaning" of the nation's faculties. Professors were too old and had lost touch with the young. Ninety percent were over thirty-five and only 6 percent had earned their highest degrees in the last ten years. Veterans had special needs which must be addressed. They wanted specific job training, more practical course work, more classroom concern with current events, more democracy for students, and above all to be treated as mature adults.

The article was certainly hyperbolic. Gratuitously insulting terms— "ossified," "senile," "mummified," "doddering," "antiquated," and "ineffectual"—were sprinkled throughout. But overstated as it may have been, Vinocour's litany of ex-GI gripes was real. West Virginia students complained loudly about the state's system of higher education. For example, in 1947 the American Legion post commander at West Virginia University wrote to all other post commanders in the state urging them to support legislation to provide independent governance for the university so that it might better serve veterans. He complained that the campus suffered from inadequate housing, funds, classroom facilities, and teaching staffs. He blamed the problems not on the university administration but on the "educational system of this State which is incompetent, poorly administered, and disorganized." Hand's reformist regime at Fairmont State was a response to these pressures.[31]

It is hardly surprising then that resentment of the invaders welled up among those still loyal to the memory and goals of the prewar college. Although Hand had no part in forcing Joseph Rosier's retirement, and furthermore was well connected by marriage to prominent local families, he lacked his predecessor's folksy public style, instinct for politics, and gift for public relations. Some perceived him as an interloper and a stranger, and he had to endure sullen resentment that occasionally erupted into open opposition. As the historian Charles Ambler puts it, "To those sympathetic with the former regime, . . . [Hand's] program involved the uprooting of cherished traditions and the abandonment of equally cherished objectives." As early as 1946 "Dame Rumor had it that the president would not be sustained."[32]

The uprooting of which Ambler writes was the deliberate effort to make Fairmont State a comprehensive state college, which Hand described in 1952: "Since practically none of the students . . . could afford a college education if they could not attend the local institution, we changed the emphasis of the academic program from a single purpose teacher training to [one] of offering A.B. and B.S. degrees in many fields."[33] He established core course requirements for the B.S. and B.A. degrees and began a business-economics department. He vigorously reshaped the curriculum, adding programs in business and retailing, industrial arts, philosophy and religion, recreation, office administration, and nursing. He strengthened the liberal arts and preprofessional programs. He enlarged the campus by a third, added thousands of shrubs and trees, oversaw the construction of several new buildings, including a library, an industrial arts building, and what some considered an overelaborate president's house. By 1951 the student body had doubled in size and grown more cosmopolitan by the addition of a number from out-of-state. Hand had raised the highest nine-month faculty salary from its 1945 level of $2,700 to $4,700 and increased the base salary to $3,000. During the same period he had reduced the average faculty teaching load from more than eighteen credit hours per week to just over fourteen. (The required teaching load varied from department to department to produce fractional averages.)

Tirelessly preaching the need to create a democratic college as a foundation of a free society, Hand put his words into action by setting up a number of faculty committees to share in decision-making and instituting a form of student government. His policies paid off in 1947 when the college earned the coveted accreditation by the North Central Association of Colleges and Secondary Schools. In all of this he enjoyed the apparent support of the superintending body, the state board of education, and of its local member, Thelma Brand Loudin.[34]

Hand assiduously, if in the end fruitlessly, cultivated community relations. Like Rosier before him he was an enthusiastic Rotarian, frequent community speaker, and faithful member of the First United Methodist Church (situated only a block away from Loudin's Central Methodist and formerly affiliated with the northern Methodists). He continued the college radio program on local station WMMN and hosted the annual high-school basketball tournament at the college gym. He started a "merchant's fair." A little theater, a college-community chorus, a concert series, and a municipal symphony orchestra were all town-and-gown collaborations. He encouraged the general public to attend campus cultural functions.[35]

The author has spoken formally or informally with dozens of people about their impressions of Hand's regime at the college. They included townspeople, former students, current and former faculty members. It was not a scientific sampling, nor after more than three decades was its factual accuracy to be trusted. But it did reveal lasting impressions and attitudes. In general it showed that those who had opposed Hand still found fault with his stewardship. Those who sided with him then continued to defend him. Those who had remained on the sidelines then were still ambivalent about his presidency. Members of this last group made the most interesting assessments. Several declared that George Hand was "the best [or best damn!] president the college ever had, but. . . . " They felt that he had shaken the sleepy college from its lethargy and provincialism and almost made it into something greater than it had ever been. He assembled an articulate, interesting, talented, and diverse faculty. It was an exciting time. But in the end he failed.

It is clear that his failure was not due to a lack of drive or energy. Hand was thoroughgoing, almost ruthless. Neither was it due to insincerity, for he tried to make the college respond to the needs of liberal democracy. His trouble began with the fact that he was perceived by some as an egoist and an autocrat who was bent upon hurriedly reshaping the college precisely according to his own plan. It may be necessary to break eggs to make the proverbial omelet, but they need not be overbeaten. Hand's colleagues noted that he emphasized democratic governance and held frequent meetings to allow the faculty to express its will by majority vote. But they add that if the majority seemed disinclined to vote as he wished, the meetings might go on and on until he could convert the majority to his view. Hand was frank and aggressive at times to the point of tactlessness and insensitivity. These personal traits were exacerbated by the times and by his status as a newcomer and an outsider. How much his failure stemmed from insufficient preparation for the job, local bigotry, or his own hubris is hard to tell.

Whatever the causes, the potential for disharmony between Hand and powerful community forces was evident from the first. At his formal inauguration as president in 1946, Hand and state school board member Loudin laid down different policy priorities. The new president offered a liberal elitist interpretation of the college mission. The college, he said, should periodically survey the needs of its service area and then plan its programs around "an active, realistic guidance service to satisfy those needs." The implication was that the college administrators were the experts and that in accordance with national academic standards they rather than local business and political leaders would determine community needs and the appropriate educational responses.

Board member Loudin, following Hand to the podium, seemed to put it the other way around. She warned that the future of the college depended upon the new president. "This community," she emphasized, "has the right to expect the 'college on the hill' to fulfill its needs. In other words, Fairmont State must serve."[36]

By 1947 Hand's policies had begun to raise eyebrows in the town. To establish his independence and underscore the break with the past, Hand refused to grant Emeritus President Rosier office space on campus. This was not a sound political move. Rosier was so highly regarded by the public school establishment that in January 1950 state schools celebrated his eightieth birthday as Joseph Rosier Day. Adding to the controversy, Hand forced the retirement of several older staff members associated with Rosier and his regime and with earlier ideas of teacher education. The college continued to turn out schoolteachers, but in a move that symbolized his broadened concept of the college, he transmogrified the college sports teams from "Fighting Teachers" into the "Fighting Falcons."[37]

Occasionally he irritated local businessmen when, as an economist, he offered free public advice. For example, when inflation raged in April 1947, Hand announced that as a remedy Fairmont merchants ought to follow the lead of a group in Newburyport, Massachusetts, by cutting retail prices by 10 percent. This brought an irritated public reply from a Chamber of Commerce spokesman who testily explained that merchants could not lower their prices unless manufacturers first lowered theirs.[38]

The tone of Hand's administration was Democratic liberal and on most social issues apparently to the left of local leaders of both political parties. So, too, was its dominant attitude toward the growing national fear of communism. As an academic liberal anticommunist, Hand spoke to local groups in opposition to Soviet policies. But in his actions toward the American Legion and his later written report and courtroom testimony on the Mundel affair, he made clear that he perceived the anticommunism of the Right to be an ill-disguised attempt to discredit New Deal liberalism and limit free inquiry. Hand advocated rational opposition to Soviet aims based upon understanding and did not think Communists should teach in the schools. However, he did not support the quasi-religious emotional crusade that portrayed communism as the Antichrist and excited nothing less primitive than the fight-flight response. (In this he was not different from his predecessor Rosier, who in 1950 wrote to Sen. Harley Kilgore comparing McCarthy's hunt for Communists to the Salem witch trials.) During his tenure anticommunist speakers such as George S. Counts and Holmes Alexander and antifascists such as William L. Shirer and Adm. Ellis M. Zacharias were brought to the campus. In 1947 and 1948, when Hollywood was beginning to turn out Red-baiting propaganda movies, Fairmont State presented a film festival including three on Russia: *Peter the Great*, *The Eagle* (a 1925 epic with Rudolph Valentino as a Russian Robin Hood), and the 1943 Sergey Eisenstein–Sergey Prokofiev collaboration, *Ivan the Terrible*.[39]

If the shift of mission and intellectually open style of the Hand administration weakened the traditional pillar of support for the college from the local elite, it was Hand's selection and handling of personnel that ground it to dust. In retrospect his personnel actions seem well-intentioned efforts to improve the institution. He tightened up administrative procedures and bucked a twenty-year tradition by seeking to curtail instructors' non- or quasi-professional outside activities, particularly those that involved lodges, fraternities, and service clubs. Even at West Virginia University such activities had become substitutes for learned society membership. In 1950 Hand could boast that collectively his faculty had published a book and five articles and had attended ninety-six professional meetings.

But in 1947 his "housecleaning" of longtime staff members identified closely with the former president exhausted the treasury of merit that previous good works had earned him. Twenty-one faculty members left that year by means of resignation, retirement, or removal. It was the departure of three in particular that brought the heaviest criticism. First, in July Hand forced the retirement of campus fixture Oliver Shurtleff, who had been acting president during Rosier's brief sojourn in the U.S. Senate and was well known locally. This produced a scolding editorial in the *West Virginian* that praised Shurtleff, a witty, humorous, and much beloved local after-dinner speaker and radio personality.[40]

More damaging was Hand's firing that summer of Medora Mason and Blanche Price. Price had worked for fourteen years in the college business office and given her time to chaperoning the college band on its trips. She was well known downtown and was very active in community and charitable affairs. Mason, for eighteen years public relations director and journalism instructor, was closely identified with the Rosier administration and with the college, for which she had tirelessly beaten the drum. A sympathetic local journalist claimed that her writings had won the "admiration and love of everyone," and that "gracious and charming[,] ... [she] was a popular member of the [Fairmont] social set."[41]

Details of the dispute between Hand and the two women, especially Mason, were never made public, although rumors abounded. The editor of the Fairmont afternoon paper commented that "it was patent for some time that either these two women would not return this fall, or the president of the college would not." Hand later explained that Mason's personal and political attachments to Rosier prevented her from working for the goals of his administration. She spent more time at work on projects such as her "Mary Chatter" gossip column for the *Fairmont Times* and her Sunday series, "This Passing Town," than at her duties as college public relations director. Whether or not the firing was justified, it was not good local politics. Clarence "Ned" Smith, Mason's superior at the *Times,* was so moved by her firing that he wrote a wry appreciation of her, resorting to quotations from *Cyrano de Bergerac, Gunga Din,* and Whittier's *Maud Miller.*[42]

Hand's dismissal of Mason in 1947 was as unpopular in the Fairmont business and professional community as his refusal to dismiss Luella Mundel in 1951. But the results were strikingly different. In the Mason-Price case the state board of education and its Fairmont member, Thelma Loudin, sustained his action. The board, meeting in May 1947, refused to intervene in the dispute. It simply agreed to dismiss the women "because of the obvious lack of harmony ... between the parties, ... [and because it recognized] the right of the President to have a staff with whom he feels he can work efficiently."[43]

The board's action was to have a bearing on the Mundel case. For the moment it strengthened Hand's position. A local newspaper editorial reflected the frustration of conservative efforts to influence the college, noting gloomily that there was never any real doubt that the board would support the president. The editor was relieved that no public hearings had spread scandal and controversy and that the board had agreed to pay both Mason and Price for the rest of the fiscal year. The college, he hoped, could now rise above the dispute.[44]

In the long run, however, the Mason-Price case hurt Hand and Mundel. On the crest of North Central accreditation that summer, Hand seems to have let victory in the personnel dispute make him too certain of the support of the board of education. Thus, he underestimated the deep resentment in the community over the 1947 firings, which remained much alive in 1951. Indeed, several veterans of the anti-Hand campaign in Fairmont brought it up to the author as soon as the Mundel affair was mentioned. Local indignation intensified when the state auditor refused to honor the board's commitment to pay the women the remainder of their salaries, citing a state law that he interpreted to forbid payment unless actual services were rendered. This resentment carried over from 1947 and was expressed in the feeling that Mundel's firing was proper retribution against Hand and that as a matter of principle she should be dismissed.[45]

The principles of academic freedom and tenure took a beating in the Mason-Price affair from both Hand and the board. Without a hearing, published cause, or substantial notice, Hand simply dismissed the two employees, one of them a journalism faculty member, despite the fact that they had accumulated fourteen and eighteen years continuous full-time employment at the college. The board affirmed that it could dismiss longtime employees at will. In the light of the Mason-Price precedent, the later public identification of Hand as defender of AAUP tenure guidelines in behalf of Dr. Mundel, who had completed only two years at the college, appeared incongruous.[46]

In line with his policy of hiring faculty members with diverse background and training to give students the enrichment of exposure to many points of view, Hand had by 1951 assembled a complement of sixty-one instructors and administrators. In his five years as president he had hired no fewer than thirty-four of the fifty instructors and six of the eleven administrators. Even for those turbulent postwar years these figures suggest an unusual turnover and tend to validate contemporary student complaints that they hardly knew any of the teachers.

The forty men and women on the 1951 faculty brought to the college by Hand were by local standards a diverse and cosmopolitan group. Along with the graduates of the regional feeders, such as West Virginia University (nine) and the University of Pittsburgh (three), were graduates of the national Ph.D. mills: Harvard (one), Yale (two), Chicago (one), Columbia (five), and Iowa (five), and universities as intellectually and geographically distant from Fairmont as Texas, Oregon, Northwestern, Minnesota, Syracuse, and Tübingen.[47]

Along with diversity of background, Hand wanted youth and research degrees. There had been five Ph.D.s at the college in 1945. By 1951 there were sixteen, many of them with little teaching experience. To attract and retain the young and the bright, the president established an incentive pay schedule that decisively favored degrees over experience. Although training, experience, and merit all counted, the salary formula offered no added pay for experience beyond five years. Coupled to the absence of a rank system at the college to endow seniority with some kind of prestige (there were only "instructors" and "department heads"), the pay schedule provided real disincentives to veteran teachers to identify with Hand's regime and its goals.

As this salary schedule actually worked by 1951, for example, Boyd Howard, Ph.D. and head of the education department hired by Hand in 1948, earned $4,700, the top salary among instructors. But Paul Opp, Ph.D. and instructor in English hired by Rosier in 1923, earned $4,000, and C. Moore Roberts, M.S. and head of the botany department hired by Rosier in 1926, earned $3,700. One cannot tell if these seeming inequities were justified, but the fact remains that eighteen of the twenty highest salaries for instructors went to men and women hired by Hand who averaged less than three years at the college. It is therefore not hard to understand why some veteran faculty members with strong local connections who had survived the Hand administration purge became his enemies. Neither is it surprising that in May 1951 board of education member Thelma Loudin questioned Hand sharply about the salaries of Opp and Roberts.[48]

More than salary disparities, Hand's cultivation of diversity caused divisiveness. Cleavages among faculty members opened and widened along several axes: religious, political, pedagogical, cultural, and personal.

A small but rich literature about academic life in the 1940s and 1950s testifies that Fairmont State's internal conflicts were unusual only in that they were aired so publicly. Ranging across space, time, and style are such notable examples of fiction as Mary McCarthy's *The Groves of Academe* and Isaac Asimov's *A Whiff of Death.* Nonfiction works include Logan Wilson's sociological study of *The Academic Man* and Jacques Barzun's classic *Teacher in America.*[49]

Despite their great differences, all of these books portray the pervasive insecurity in American higher education. Back of the tweedy urbanity and wry campus humor there ached in many a professor woeful feelings of insecurity, hostility, and isolation bred by the nature of the profession. The unavoidable failure to live up to impossibly high professional standards or to advance one's career as one had hoped was the lot of most, particularly those employed at the low-prestige colleges—such as Fairmont State.

Some liberal arts doctors fresh from graduate school found college teaching uncongenial and depressing. At graduate school they had ingested the idea of a status system that condemned public school teachers and teachers college instructors as intellectually inferior. They had been taught that research was superior to teaching and universities ranked high above colleges. Colleagues who were mere teachers were one's professional inferiors. But their feelings of self-confidence and superiority suffered by an obvious paradox. If Ph.D.s were truly superior and research was the highest academic pursuit, what were they doing at a college that devoted itself to teaching? Since their training equipped them to train other Ph.D.s, why were they facing classrooms of inattentive and bored undergraduates? Compounding the insecurity of many was their lack of teaching experience. Were they to be judged on their weaknesses instead of their strengths? Could it be that they lacked the right stuff for university work? Was Harvard or Penn or Iowa burying a mistake in northern West Virginia?

Veteran teachers wrestled with their own demons. Their scholarship was rusty, their career hopes had been dashed, and they were growing old. The Great Depression and Fairmont's remoteness from graduate schools had deprived many of the chance to earn doctorates. Threatened by the faculty newcomers, they behaved defensively. They froze out the newcomers from their long-established cliques. To the wonder of many of the newer Ph.D.s, the older instructors seemed positively to revel in their own professional deficiencies and provinciality, to be proud to be considered anti-intellectual. But their insecurity was deep.

Uncertainties gnawed, making teachers in all categories anxious to know where they stood with administrators, colleagues, students, and the public, and to have their work validated. Asimov put it insightfully in his whodunit about murder in a university biology department when he wrote of a professor's desperate search for "inner tenure," and Mary McCarthy brilliantly captured the interplay of Cold War political ideology and the struggle for job security in a small eastern Pennsylvania college. Such a climate in the best of times and among the most congenial staff can produce gossip, backbiting and jealousy. At Fairmont State in the Cold War among a diverse crew of relative strangers, it caused exaggeration, viciousness, and extremism.[50]

The beginnings of the internal feuding came not from the Rosier regime veterans but from among the new people hired by Hand. Until 1951, Hand effectively neutralized the remnants of the old regime. His appointees, mostly political liberals, controlled or had strong influence in the art, sociology, political science, psychology, history, mathematics, and social science departments and the campus AAUP chapter. Only the teacher-oriented Association for Higher Education chapter remained outside the fold. What the president did not anticipate was the rise of vindictive and destructive behavior among the newcomers.

Among the new academicians were ideologues, eccentrics, and bohemians and some like Dr. Mundel who were shy and somewhat ill at ease at social gatherings. This was not surprising. In 1942, Logan Wilson had cited widespread national grousing by older faculty against younger colleagues for "faulty speech, bad dress, boorish manner, and general uncouthness." A 1938 AAUP study of several thousand college professors revealed that most came from the lower-middle class and had been selected for their scholastic aptitude rather than for their congeniality or gentility. Many had struggled long and hard to achieve upward social mobility and professional status in graduate schools dedicated to the idea that scholars were a guild removed from the general population by their special knowledge and their responsibility to think critically and speak truthfully. All of this did not bode well for relations between Fairmonters and the new faculty. In a national poll sponsored by the Fund for the Republic in 1954, Samuel A. Stouffer found that the rural and small-town South, in which he included West Virginia, was the region least tolerant of individual nonconformity. Polling data identified churchgoers, women, and the less educated as those who tended to be most suspicious of outspoken behavior and unusual ideas. Fairmont, then, was filled with people likely to be offended by the newcomers.[51]

Remembered as the most eccentric of the new professors was the brilliant, independently wealthy psychologist Spaulding Rogers, who came to the college in 1947 from Mount Holyoke. Knowledgeable sources swear he kept goats, lived in a rude dwelling on the edge of town with a wife many years his junior, and experimented with behaviorism (it was said he put his toddlers in a Skinner box).[52]

To genteel townsfolk, the behavior of several of the women Ph.D.s was unacceptable. Self-styled "good" women of the town, spiritual cousins of e. e. cummings's Cambridge ladies with "furnished souls and comfortable minds,"[53] took offense because some of the new women smoked cigarettes, ignored church and other social activities, were unmarried or divorced, and pursued "masculine" careers. As we shall see, the unschoolmarmly Mundel became a symbol for the composite behavior of all of the unorthodox women at the college. Beyond that, she and the others would find themselves falsely suspected of transgressions that must have occurred only in the minds of some of the townsfolk.

No persuasive evidence was offered during the entire Mundel affair that there was a Communist or fellow traveler on the faculty of Fairmont State College. It is difficult today to find anyone on either side of the dispute who feels certain that Mundel or any of her associates were Communists, in the sense that they were members of the Communist party or agents of an international conspiracy. But to some people, what they were—sophisticates, internationalists, bohemians, agnostics, and liberals, some shaded to the left of the political spectrum—was bad enough. One faculty member, sociologist Eric Barnitz, was a graduate of North Carolina's fabled radical Black Mountain College. Librarian Harold Jones, with degrees from Swarthmore and Columbia, came from a Quaker background that emphasized freedom of expression and social conscience. University of Chicago–trained theologian Thomas Bennett II, chairman of the religion and philosophy department, stirred up local bigots by proposing that blacks should be permitted to attend public events at the college. Mundel herself had come to town directly from Berkeley, a reputed center of left-wing activity and an object of House Un-American Activities Committee (HUAC) concern.[54]

As befitted a community of young scholars, there was disputatious and, to some, irreverent and shocking talk at campus dinner parties, cafeteria lunches, and faculty meetings. Luella Mundel, shy and reticent though she was, paid dearly for occasional off-the-cuff remarks on such occasions. As might be expected, some of the new teachers belittled the town and its leadership, the old faculty, and the abilities of the students. This could be condemned as a display of arrogance and an assertion of superiority by the critics. But it could also be justified by the community's mindless rejection of "outsiders" and by the objectively demonstrable deficiencies of the objects of the criticism. It was solidly in keeping with the ideal that a college is a community not of like minds but one of minds alike only in their commitment to free expression and thought.

In the time-honored American tradition of Comstockery, colleagues and townsfolk often projected their darker and more delicious fantasies onto the strangers. To bowdlerize Richard Hofstadter, opposition to liberal new faculty became the pornography of local puritans. This became apparent at Mundel's slander trial, but it manifested itself earlier. Gossips spread rumors about the new teachers. One had it that they engaged in mixed-gender nude parties. A principal offender was reputedly a female English teacher who smoked Fatima cigarettes. Another story told of the existence of a Communist cell on campus. Yet another held that various new faculty, including Mundel and her friend librarian Harold Jones (who were also rumored to be heterosexual lovers), were homosexuals. Still another, which eventually reached the state board of education, alleged that a middle-aged female faculty member and a much younger male colleague were cohabiting. The accused bachelor was suspect in part because he wore his hair long in an age of crew cuts and liked to spend time alone listening to his prized classical record collection.[55]

Shocking and unforgivable to many who saw them were paintings of nudes that from time to time graced (or disgraced) the walls of the corridor outside Mundel's art department on the third floor of the main building. Was it possible, impressionable students wondered, that some flesh-and-blood female had actually posed for them? Probably not, for live models were never used at the college. Some of the offending pictures were the work of Mundel's colleague Fridtjof Schroder, who, according to an interview in the college newspaper, eschewed bohemianism and taught art as a trade. His nudes, it was said, were painted from imagination. Mundel experimented with abstract expressionism and analytical cubism, by most accounts rather pedantically. Based on newspaper descriptions of them, student art exhibits sound more clichéd than risqué. True there seems to have been a certain amount of social realism. In their spring exhibits in 1951, students displayed paintings of a matador, a steel plant, a sand and gravel facility, two "men gossiping," several nudes, a still life with teacup, a starry night, and a variety of nature scenes. Still, there were nudes, and the college newspaper even printed a photo of one and advertised its display.[56]

All of these elements and some from the Mundel trial eventually merged in local lore into a composite myth, a hodgepodge interpretation reflected in the 1983 ABC–TV documentary. According to this tale Mundel and those associated with her were somehow linked to Communists at Antioch College in Yellow Springs, Ohio, and indulged in sex orgies. In order to become sexually aroused, they brought paintings of naked women to their parties.[57] The most obscene of these paintings were abstractions, which it was evidently assumed were more satanic than representative canvases because they were filled with mysterious but surely dirty symbols. It is interesting to note the catalog of taboos in this story against female nudity, nontraditional female behavior, and homosexuality. It is also worth noting how little the story squares with Communist reality. The popular myth, which for example held without evidence that Communists regularly engaged in "sex orgies," contained nothing that suggests even a rudimentary acquaintance with Soviet or more general Communist ideology or reality.

The facts out of which Fairmonters' fantasy of the college "Communists" is woven are mundane. Many of the newcomers were only behaving as they had at graduate school by affecting varied styles of intellectual searching—bohemianism or political dissent or avant garde cynicism. In Fairmont, which must have seemed to them an intellectual Sahara, these behaviors were surely exaggerated strategies to retain professional identity and to resist sinking beneath the surface of the encircling morass of mediocrity. Despite major differences in background, outlook, training, and personality, many of the outsiders were drawn together like colonizers among the colonized, their "odd" behavior as ritualistic and as important to their sense of identity as a British civil servant's high tea in darkest Africa at the Empire's zenith. We should remember that to them the local behavior and mores often seemed hopelessly narrow and reactionary.

Given time, the old town and the young gown might have adjusted to each other. But certainly most of the adjustment would have fallen one-sidedly upon the newcomers. Those unwilling to give in to the local culture would have moved on to greener, or at least other, pastures. Those who surrendered to it partially or totally would have settled down and somehow coped. For some of Hand's teachers there was to be no time. Events of 1951–52 brought matters to a head and to an abrupt conclusion.

In 1952 Hand reported to the American Association of University Professors (AAUP) and other educational organizations that his problems with local state board of education member Thelma Brand Loudin had begun in January 1951. The issue was public use of the college gym. At that time, while Hand was absent from the campus, Loudin intervened in behalf of local sports fans. She persuaded college administrators to override Hand's guidelines to the contrary and allow a high-school basketball game to be played at the gym. When Hand returned and learned what had happened, he became angry at the school board member's meddling in administrative affairs. On January 15 at the end of an unpleasant meeting in Hand's office Loudin left in tears. But she had the last word the next day when *Fairmont Times* sportswriter Bill Evans publicly praised her in his column for obtaining the use of the gym. It was a petty incident, but one that obviously bruised the egos of both Loudin and Hand. Relations between the two would never be the same.[58]

Soon after the public dispute between Hand and Loudin, a private feud flared up between Mundel and her art department colleague Fridtjof Schroder. Their differences were philosophical, professional, temperamental, artistic, and political.

The son of religious missionaries, Minnesotan Schroder in his published writings championed tradition, order, and deductive reasoning. He was a self-proclaimed evangelist for classic Greek idealism and medieval Christian spiritualism and was opposed to "bohemianism," to "secularism, negativism, Freudianism, and relativism." He felt alienated from the intellectual mainstream. The academic world, he claimed, was in the hands of phony intellectuals "who made the radical ideas of the early Twentieth Century into the stifling orthodoxies of 1950." "Our colleges and universities," he wrote in 1952, "are cluttered with pseudo-liberals who . . . see themselves as an elite, isolated from what they feel are the insensitive, materialist bourgeoisie...[and the masses who] will not understand their esotericism[,] for as the psychologists monotonously insist the average level of intelligence is but 12 years."[59]

Schroder never directly linked Mundel with communism or disloyalty, but in a series of Fairmont newspaper articles in May 1952 he did suggest that liberals were aiding communism. He claimed that in their zeal to separate themselves from conservatism they gravitated toward leftish attacks on the American social and economic system. "Like Moscow, they grind away at faults." Although he granted that American society should tolerate pseudo-liberals, "yet the discovery of Communists in governmental research and scientific research projects has given us cause to examine carefully any expressions of sympathy for the Communist cause."[60]

The background of Schroder's argument was a conflict within the art world that was linked to anticommunism. At issue was modern painting in its various manifestations—cubism, futurism, dadaism, expressionism, and surrealism—that began before World War I, raged through the 1920s and early 1930s and broke out anew after World War II. Illustrators, commercial artists, and representational painters felt threatened by the practitioners of nonrepresentational modes. Exemplified by Michigan Republican congressman George A. Dondero, some anticommunist politicians, dubbed by one scholar "cultural fundamentalists" and undeterred by suppression of modern art in the USSR, saw modern art as a key element of the international Communist conspiracy. They claimed that by rejecting established ways of seeing form and space modern artists undermined traditional worldviews and invited moral chaos to replace tried and true norms and values. Influencing the attack on modern art was the attackers' extreme discomfort with the increasingly influential scientific relativism and psychological worldview, particularly the ascendancy in the latter of Freudian emphasis on the unconscious and the irrational. Tied to the attack was the reactionary notion that modern art was foreign, elitist, undemocratic, and un-American.[61] So here was Schroder with his disdain for modern art and psychology in the college art department yoked to psychologist Luella Mundel who dabbled in abstract expressionism and analytical cubism.

Added to Schroder's political and intellectual alienation from Mundel was his trouble with George Hand, which antedated Mundel's arrival in Fairmont. In 1947 Hand hired Schroder fresh from the University of Iowa with a master's degree. In Fairmont he joined another Iowa grad, art department head Ernest Freed. When Freed departed in 1949, Schroder expected to become department head. That year he had paintings on exhibit in New York City and Youngstown, Ohio. Instead, to his chagrin, Hand hired Dr. Mundel. In his report to the AAUP, Hand explained that although Schroder was "a good teacher and a good artist," the consensus of college department heads and administrators was that the art teacher was too "pessimistic, gloomy, [and] uncooperative" to lead the department. As if to rub salt into the wound, Hand gave Schroder a talking-to and even criticized his wife's alleged public statements "about the college, the community, and the people."[62]

Powerless to confront the president directly, Schroder evidently transferred part of his hostility to Luella Mundel. Artistically, she had achieved less than he, and she represented ideas he opposed. With little more teaching experience and less seniority and only because of her Ph.D., Mundel became his higher-salaried superior. He fumed against college hiring and promotion practice where the doctorate represented the highest order. He complained that Ph.D.s merely learned to soak up and regurgitate secondhand information. To him they were intellectually so all alike that they might as well be "selected from the files of teachers' agencies as seeds are ordered from a seed catalogue." Given his opinions, Schroder's relationship with Mundel became increasingly strained. There were disagreements over teaching styles and control of student assistants. She thought him sullen and uncooperative.[63]

From the time of Mundel's appointment, in Hand's words, Schroder told "people, including faculty members that the president was persecuting him and had insulted his wife." Finally after two years, in the spring of 1951, Schroder denounced Hand, Freed, and Mundel in a missive filled with hastily jotted and overwrought notes to Thelma Loudin. The extraordinary action was evidently triggered by Schroder's fear that he would lose his job. At a faculty meeting Hand had warned that the enrollment decline caused by the graduation of the first wave of GI bill students and mobilization for the Korean War necessitated a staff reduction. The fear seemed well justified. Total enrollment in West Virginia's colleges fell from 18,000 in 1949 to 13,000 by 1952.[64] When Schroder asked Hand about his employment prospects in light of the anticipated reduction in force, Hand had told him that he "would probably be going" in spite of his seniority. In early May 1951 Hand decided to renew Schroder's contract and may have told him so. But Schroder distrusted the president and decided to go over his head by seeking a meeting with state board of education member Loudin. She refused a face-to-face meeting and asked him instead to put his complaints in writing.

The result was a strange communication from Schroder to Loudin, which eventually found its way from her desk into print on the front page of Fairmont's Republican newspaper, the *West Virginian*, on August 15, 1951, without signature or attribution. (It was conveyed to Loudin by an intermediary, Dr. Robert L. Carroll of the physics department, who was one of her choristers at Central Methodist.) The note consists of an outline of real or alleged grievances against Hand, Ernest Freed, and Luella Mundel. Mainly taken up with castigating Hand, it lacks coherence in places, and its numbered short sentences and fragments give it a jumpy, stream-of-consciousness quality. Less than 10 percent of it relates to Dr. Mundel. Under the heading "Complaints against Dr. Mundel" were these items:

1. She cannot teach.

2. She is supposed to be in charge of art education but puts it all in one oversized class and then teaches painting and sculpture which she knows nothing about.

3. Dislikes students. Always talking about how poor they are and stupid. Gives harsh tests after reading dull lectures. Does not really understand her subject matter.

4. Jones [the librarian] constantly after me to teach her education courses.

5. Would not take responsibility and I had to do much of the departmental administrative work. I had to organize the student assistant's work. Dean Pence has to ask me for information he could not get from her. He had to send her repeated notes for curriculum material. Art department untidy.

[6?]

7. Mr. Jones is actually is [*sic*] now the department head.

8. She is subject to tantrums. If I disapprove of something she blows up and threatens to run to the administration.[65]

These charges are general and undocumented. Even if they were all true, excepting the charge that she could not teach, they are hardly grounds for dismissal.[66] Why, then, did Loudin choose to credit them? Obviously she was predisposed to believe the worst about Dr. Mundel and/or she wished to use them to damage George Hand (and probably Harold Jones). That she neglected to take them up with Hand or Mundel and the way she did use them reinforce this view, as does her own subsequent court testimony. Before receiving Schroder's complaints in early May 1951, Loudin had already compiled a dossier on Mundel. It included four items.

First, on April 1 the American Legion Post 17 commander, whose wife sang in Loudin's choir at Central Methodist, told her that Mundel had "heckled" Americanism speakers sponsored by the veterans' group (see chapter 2). Second, that same month Loudin had heard from C. Moore Roberts, another church member and the college's longtime botanist. Roberts was a solid citizen who had served on the city planning commission, had worked to create a local arts center, and was the town's best-known birder. He had recently suffered a heart attack but, although unable to teach, kept up with college gossip. He said he had heard that Mundel admitted publicly that she was "probably a communist, but for convenience called herself a Socialist because the other term is in ill repute."

The third item had come to Loudin even earlier, in January or February of 1951, when another of her choir members, the physicist Carroll, told her that Mundel remarked to him that "a belief in God is not socially acceptable."[67] Carroll was personally close to Schroder, had grown up in Fairmont and graduated from Fairmont Teachers College, and was connected by marriage to Old Fairmont. He had joined the faculty in 1946 with advanced degrees from West Virginia University in mathematics (M.S.) and mathematical physics (Ph.D.). Carroll made no secret of his resentment toward Hand, his ambition to become president of the college, or his deep, pietistic, antimodern religious feelings. Neither did he react gracefully to the rejection of his theoretical work by leading physicists and by most of Hand's new faculty.

Carroll contended that Einstein's theory of relativity was flawed and had publicly said so in letters to Einstein himself and to President Truman. In a 1949 script prepared for a local radio audience he stated that he had tried to get the truth to the secretary of defense and government scientists, but could not even secure an interview. He believed the failure of his theories to make headway in the scientific community was because he based his science on the premise that God had created the universe. Modern scientists, he claimed, had closed their minds to the truth by refusing to accept the revealed truth of God. Being a devout Christian had made Newton the greatest of all scientists, for basic truth was revealed to humankind by God through Christians.[68]

Mundel earned Carroll's ire by ridiculing his religious beliefs. As Mundel later described it, at a party at the Schroders' Carroll announced, "I have seen God." Which brought from Mundel the response: "Some people who are hallucinated only hear voices."[69]

Finally, Loudin had completed her file condemning Mundel with the gripes of three night-school students about Mundel's teaching. They came to her to complain that Mundel had said to them in class "I don't know who you are and I don't want to know." The remark was easy enough to explain had Loudin bothered to ask. On the other hand, it fitted neatly into her catalogue of Mundel's unprofessional behavior.[70]

By May 1951 most of the ingredients for an open rebellion against Hand's stewardship were already stewing in the pot and near the boil.

Standing by ready to abet Schroder, Carroll, and Loudin or at least not to come to Hand's defense were the remnants of the previous regime. Should controversy spill off campus into the town, as it surely would, Old Fairmont, the newspapers, and others who disapproved of the changes at the college might enter the fray against Hand.

Up to now it was an all too typical intracollegiate dispute. Like the Schroder-Hand imbroglio, almost half of the cases investigated nationwide by the AAUP before 1954 were mainly personal conflicts between president and professor stemming from jealousy or the need to economize.[71]

But lurking in the background of this one was another faction with another issue. The faction was the Red-baiting element of the American Legion and the issue was the alleged association of liberalism with communism, subversion, and disloyalty, which some thought threatened Fairmont State College.

CHAPTER 2

Kindling on the Pyre: The Legionnaires and the "Reducators" of Fairmont State

> I think this is a period in which you kill dragons: That is so-called communists, to raise yourself in public esteem, and if you can root out some so-called communists, you become a great hero or heroine to the public.
>
> —Luella Raab Mundel (1951)

> With the ascendancy of Dewey in the classroom, Teachers College of Columbia became the Mecca to which thousands of American teachers made pilgrimage to kiss the blackened stone of progressive education as reverently and superstitiously as any Moslem.
>
> —J. B. Matthews (1953)

The influence of Fairmont's American Legion Post 17 in the Luella Mundel affair is difficult to evaluate. It is certain that responding to national Legion policy, local Legionnaires tried to censor college library materials, donated $2,500 to defend Thelma Loudin against Mundel's slander suit, and attended her trials in force. Remarks made by imported anticommunist speakers at Legion-sponsored "antisubversive seminars" in 1950, 1951, and 1952 helped to create an atmosphere of hostility toward noncomformity. Throughout the affair recurrent rumors assigned Mundel's troubles to her indiscreet remarks at the March 31, 1951, seminar. After that meeting the Legion supposedly carried on an organized campaign to discredit her and drive her from the college. It is most difficult to prove or disprove these charges. One suspects the whole story may never come to light.[1]

Several scholars have found the Legion to have been a powerful anticommunist force in the postwar years. Dale Sorenson presents the veterans' organization in its headquarters state, Indiana, as a major architect of the anticommunist consensus. Daniel Whiteford cites a 1962 *Redbook* poll of congressmen that ranked the American Legion just below the AFL–CIO in lobbying power. In his study of the Second Red Scare in Texas, Don E. Carleton shows the Legion as an active anticommunist agent and molder of public opinion. But both Sorenson and Carleton describe the Legion's limitations. In Texas, its message gained little support until it was picked up and extended by right-wing activist groups such as the Minute Women of America and the Committee for the Preservation of Methodism. In Indiana, its power, never total, declined after 1952. Unquestionably, except for specifically veterans' issues, the Legion did not win the allegiance of ex-GIs as it had of the doughboys. In West Virginia it achieved mixed results in its anticommunist battle.[2]

If one may question whether or not the Legion was the decisive influence in the Mundel affair, one cannot deny that it was a major player. Neither can one deny that Legion leaders believed in a Red conspiracy to undermine American society and sought to combat it. Of course Soviet agents operated within the country and some American citizens supported or sympathized with the aims of the Communist Party of the United States (CPUSA). But it is clear that anticommunist zealots in the Legion and elsewhere greatly exaggerated the danger of internal subversion and exploited public fears for partisan ideological and political ends.

Fear of conspiracy or what Richard Hofstadter denominated the "paranoid style of American politics" is a hardy perennial in the nation's history. From colonial times, groups and individuals exotic to Protestant America have been accused of seeking to destroy the American way of life.[3] Since the late nineteenth century, left-wing radicals had been so identified and after the First World War and the Bolshevik triumph in Russia, communism had acquired connotations of evil that usually exceeded its apparent capacity to harm capitalist, Christian, individualist society in the United States. But to many defenders of the status quo, the open, individualistic nature of the American republic seemed safe from subversion only as long as Christian morality, small-town values, and the middle-class nuclear family prevailed. As American society became increasingly urbanized and pluralistic, no single morality, ethos, culture, or ethnic identity described all Americans. With the coming of the New Deal in the 1930s government became increasingly centralized, distant, and intrusive. Instead of defending the status quo and the interests and values of middle-class white America, as often as not, it abetted unwanted change.

Since its inception in 1919 at a meeting of anti-Bolshevik American military officers, the Legion had fought communism with "100 percent Americanism," a term that comprehended opposition to all forms of Marxism, anarchism, and pacifism, which it assumed were linked in an international plot to destroy the American way of life. Communists were believed to be inherently rational and immoral and to operate covertly, so danger lurked both abroad and at home. To the anticommunist true believer, subtle, seemingly innocent changes in national or community life might actually be the visible signs of a hidden design that would end by enslaving the American people to a dreary, godless dictatorship. To combat the evil, it was the duty of patriots to encourage Americanism and expose and eradicate all that was "un-American." Amid the tumult of the thirties and early forties, few listened.[4]

World War II amplified the voice of veterans' organizations. The American Legion was the largest and most powerful lobbyist for ex-GIs. Its combination of conservative politics, community service, patriotic ritual, and adolescent male camaraderie attracted a nominal membership of about one quarter of the approximately twenty million World War II and Korean veterans. Its committed, active membership was of course much smaller.[5]

The Legion claimed many influential members and supporters. Politicians and celebrities from Adlai Stevenson to Norman Vincent Peale, from Walter Reuther to Richard Nixon were gratified to address Legion conventioneers. In 1950 nearly 200 United States representatives, forty-four senators, five cabinet members, and three Supreme Court justices wore the overseas cap. Extrapolated to state and local government officialdom, the figures for Legion membership showed a deep penetration of the national infrastructure. But the organization's real strength was in smaller American communities where Legion posts were as familiar as the corner drug store. Fairmont's Post 17, for example, celebrated its thirty-second anniversary in 1951. And Legion baseball leagues and school oratory contests seemed as American as cherry pie. So sacred was the American veteran and so strong was the Legion's claim to custody of the national iconography that few dared publicly criticize the organization.[6]

It is questionable whether the Legion's distinguished membership list and secure place in the American landscape permitted it to impose its conservative ideology on government policy. To be sure it was good politics for a legislator or public official to pay court to veterans through Legion membership. But outside strictly veterans' issues the Legion point of view was one voice among many in the national political discourse. More than it shaped public policy, the Legion was a conduit, a bully pulpit used by federal officials to sway grass-roots opinion or by Legion leaders to affirm their own patriotism, usually by wrapping controversial policies in the flag. From this perspective the Legion's early Cold War anticommunism was partly an expression of the agenda of the House Un-American Activities Committee (HUAC), which provided the staff experts to conduct the campaign against internal subversion, and of J. Edgar Hoover's FBI. In the late 1940s and early 1950s, each for its own reasons, the Legion, the HUAC, and the FBI combined to promote

Americanism. To a degree Legion influence was magnified by the competition of the two federal entities for the affections of its large membership.[7]

Both publicly and secretly the Federal Bureau of Investigation encouraged Legion anticommunist activities. It was no secret that the bureau provided information on subversives and on anticommunist policy to Legion officials. It "educated" the veterans about the evils of Communist subversion so that they might alert their communities. But it was a secret that the FBI maintained a large network of Legionnaire covert informants intermittently from 1940 to 1966 through what it called the American Legion Contact Program.[8]

The program was begun in 1940 at J. Edgar Hoover's direction with the reluctant acquiescence of then Attorney-General Robert H. Jackson. It was undertaken to head off American Legion officials who were threatening to create what amounted to vigilante groups reminiscent of World War I's American Protective League. The APL had used private citizens to investigate slackers, "unpatriotic" trade unions, and antiwar activities in their communities. The idea of the World War II Contact Program was to avoid the APL's excesses and abuses, but it, too, became a source of abuses. By 1943 the FBI, working through its field offices, had engaged some 60,000 "reliable" Legion members at 11,700 local posts as confidential informants. The task assigned to these "listening posts" was to watch over defense plants and other important institutions near their homes and to report suspicious activities to the bureau. The main value of the Contact Program proved to be in helping the FBI to locate Selective Service delinquents. This was not so much accomplished through the secret informants as by the simple expedient of reading out the names of draft dodgers at local post meetings and asking members to be on the lookout. In 1945 when World War II ended more than 10,500 Legionnaires received FBI certificates of appreciation for having provided useful information, and a flattering account of the program was prepared by a public relations firm. Then it was deactivated without being technically discontinued.[9]

On July 13, 1950, in response to the emergency created by the outbreak of the Korean War, top FBI officials met to consider reactivating the ALCP. They weighed the probable disadvantages: the program would use up much valuable time of both administrators and field agents; experience showed that the number of valid cases reported would not justify the effort; and the Veterans of Foreign Wars and other similar groups might "take umbrage" at being left out. But these counted less in the minds of the FBI leaders than the apparent advantages of reactivating the program. First, the Legion was a large, powerful group active in the affairs of the country. From the "standpoint of public relations alone and having the backing of such a group, the time and effort involved in the program is well worthwhile," they decided. Second, the program would prevent the Legion from embarking on its own investigations.[10]

On July 24 President Truman in a one-page directive giving the FBI jurisdiction over sabotage, espionage, subversive activities, and related matters added: "I suggest that all patriotic organizations and individuals likewise report all such information relating to espionage, sabotage and subversive activities to the Federal Bureau of Investigation."[11]

In August 1950 under the aegis of the presidential message and the guidelines of Bureau Bulletin no. 43 (1950), the program was reactivated. The Special Agents in Charge (SACs) of the various FBI field offices met with Legion Americanism Commission and district officials to explain the details. They told the Legionnaires not to conduct investigations or act as vigilante groups. But they also told them that the bureau needed Legionnaires as: "reliable sources of information in industrial plants, public utilities, and communications and transportation facilities *as well as in groups or settlements of persons of foreign extraction and un-American sympathies in order to combat sabotage, espionage, and subversive activities. . . . No one but the Post Commanders and Adjutants should be aware of the identities of the legionnaires selected"* (italics added).[12]

After overcoming some initial organizational difficulties the program expanded dramatically during the heyday of McCarthyism, 1950–54, when the names of more than 110,000 persons associated with the nation's 16,700 American Legion posts were on FBI contact lists.[13]

As a device for gathering useful information in the Cold War, the program never worked very well and FBI field officials complained that it wasted scarce agency time and labor. But from the FBI director's point of view it remained useful. It helped to maintain good public relations with the Legion, "a numerically strong and powerful militant group," and deterred it from embarking on "security-type investigations." According to Athan Theoharis it helped to give Hoover freedom of action by winning him a politically potent constituency.[14]

Although the ALCP did not formally end until 1966, it had declined sharply by the mid-fifties. And in 1957 FBI field offices were told to destroy their American Legion files and no longer record Legion contacts.[15] This order of course would have included the Fairmont resident agency of the FBI. With the paper trail obscured one cannot prove beyond the shadow of a doubt that Luella Mundel and her "clique" at Fairmont State College were in any way incidental victims of the ALCP. Yet the declassified FBI–ALCP files lend strong circumstantial support to that hypothesis.

Summaries of quarterly reports on ALCP activities to Director Hoover show that the most active period in the program's life was from the early months of 1951 until mid-1952. Prior to January 1, 1951, the Pittsburgh field office, whose jurisdiction included western Pennsylvania and all of West Virginia, had contacted a total of only 303 Legionnaire informants from the 540 local posts for which it was responsible. During the first three months of 1951 that number more than doubled to 680. In the next three months, March 20 to June 20, during which time Luella Mundel was attacked as a security risk and denied reemployment by the West Virginia board of education, the number of ALCP contacts reported by the Pittsburgh SAC soared from 680 to 1,732. By the time Mundel's slander suit went to trial in December 1951 the number of Legion contacts in the Pittsburgh region totalled 3,725. In 1953, the program would top out at 4,204 contacts, but the increment was small compared to what had occurred in 1951.[16]

We do not know how many of these hurriedly recruited FBI "listening posts" were from Mundel's nemesis, Fairmont's Post 17, but there must have been some. SACs were to see that every post was contacted and Fairmont's coal mines and coke and other manufacturing plants gave it more than run-of-the-mill significance. It is hard to imagine that the FBI field agents in Fairmont would have failed to establish contact with a post only a few blocks from their desks, especially when the post commander in 1951 worked for the IRS in their own building.

We know from the scattered and heavily censored remnants in the FBI–ALCP documents that the kind of information the FBI sometimes received from its Legion informants was precisely the sort that brought Luella Mundel to grief. Examples in the director's office file (not from the Pittsburgh office) include information from a New York City post commander who named eleven members of his own post as Communists. From the Philadelphia region came allegations that several persons exhibited Communist sympathies, particularly a druggist who had been "talking against the United States and in favor of Communism." From the same region, a Legionnaire reported on a woman: "one [deleted], whom he advises is presently teaching children of [deleted]. [She] was formerly a teacher in the [deleted] school system and [he] had heard that she had Communist leanings."[17] The FBI evidently took no legal action against the accused individuals. That their names reached the director's office files based upon Legionnaires' hearsay is disturbing.

The zeal for service of some Legionnaires, the high level of anxiety accompanying the darker moments of the Korean War, and McCarthyite rhetoric came together at the same time in 1951. On top of all this the ALCP by its very nature encouraged the "listening posts" to inflate offhand remarks and simple gossip into threats to the national security.

That this was an unanticipated consequence rather than the intent of the ALCP is beside the point.

Unlike the "invisible" ALCP was the Legion's public involvement in the community, its anticommunist "education," and its defense of conservative social and economic values. Some of its officers, including a few West Virginians, used the American Legion as a springboard to prominence and prestige. In 1951 nearby Clarksburg's Don Wilson became the first World War II veteran to be elected national commander. His appointment followed the earlier success of Louis A. Johnson, another Clarksburger, who had climbed the ladder of Legion politics to succeed James Forrestal as Truman's secretary of defense. Until his career-shattering firing from that post in 1950, Johnson dreamed of winning the Democratic presidential nomination based upon the support of conservatives, Legionnaires, and the business community. Thus patriotism merged with personal ambition and state pride to motivate Fairmont Legion officialdom to support Don Wilson's regime as national commander. They would vigorously promote programs such as Americanism and its companion, "Back to God."[18]

The Legion mirrored certain local political attitudes, and membership could be a sturdy strand in the web of community affiliations. But typically the Legion Hall was a place for casual socializing, an alcoholic oasis, and little more. It loomed larger for those careerist state and local officers who were ambitious to ascend through the ranks or to improve their positions in the local pecking order. Legion officers were usually small businessmen, white-collar professionals, or politicians who combined multiple community affiliations, of which the Legion was one, to exercise power and win prestige. But small-town power and prestige, based as they were on intense competition among individuals and fickle group opinion, were ever shifting and insecure. In the fluid, status-conscious middle class, the struggle to define and maintain one's position ended only at death when the town finally passed judgment on the cost and appropriateness of one's tombstone.

Main Streeters were therefore acutely sensitive to what they perceived as threatening changes in the status quo. By 1950 many had long felt squeezed by the proliferation of New Deal–inspired government regulations and taxation. Despite the prosperity, economic growth, and business opportunities of the postwar years, they were ill at ease with the ambiguities and uncertainties of the postwar era.

From 1948 to 1951, into this disturbed world of the small town intruded national and international shocks like the ever louder footsteps of a creeping barrage. At least that is the clear perception one gains from reading the Democratic *Fairmont Times* and even more from the Republican *West Virginian.* The loss of China to communism, the abrupt end of the United States' atomic monopoly, the undeclared limited war of ambiguous purpose in Korea, and the revelations of espionage high in Western governments cumulatively sapped national confidence. Nothing seemed sacred. When college basketball players shaved points and even West Point cadets cribbed on examinations, could one believe in anything?[19] As Don Wilson told delegates to the 1951 Legion national convention: "The confusions, the contradictions, the unexplained and disturbing situations with which we seem to be officially unable to cope, have created a fog of disillusionment and apathy which has seeped across the entire nation."[20]

To allay such fears, the Legion executives promoted "aggressive Americanism"—a slogan that appealed to those who revered "our concept of life."

Some of the political positions taken by the national Legion hierarchy agreed with those of many liberals. It supported the Truman Doctrine, the Marshall Plan, and foreign aid. Matched to its internationalism was the Legion's advocacy of racial and religious tolerance. And yet when Legion national policy was translated into local action, it could sometimes become little more than a vigilante version of McCarthyism.

By simplifying complex issues for the bewildered many, Americanism offered an enemy to fight, a set of simple values to defend, and an exciting course of action to pursue. It provided a solid ideational structure in an uncertain and changing world. Again to quote Wilson, patriotic Americans were to work aggressively against forces seeking to "attack, smear, and undermine" "traditional standards." No longer should they "tolerate the deliberate insults which subversive malcontents offer us as demonstrations of 'free speech.'"[21] Above all, Americans should stop being confused and afraid "to light a light for fear of seeing a [Russian] Bear." They must become "lusty, practical, hard-headed" like their forefathers in fighting Communism to insure that the nation's children did not grow up afraid. They must defend and promote national traditions, the Holy Bible and the Constitution.[22]

Wilson delivered this speech in 1951 at the most fevered time in the Legion's Americanism crusade. By that time its professional anticommunist strategists had targeted the "anti anticommunist."[23]

In 1949 some CPUSA leaders had gone underground and the FBI had hamstrung the party. The process of "cleaning out" Communists and "Fifth Amendment Communists" from American institutions was well under way. But many believed great danger remained. J. Edgar Hoover claimed in 1952 that there were still 500 fellow travelers for every FBI agent. The Legion's way of coping with so many disloyal citizens was to promote the idea that everyone must ritualistically and publicly *affirm* the status quo, as if repeating an oath or patriotic saying enough times inoculated one against subversive influences. Any sign of doubt about traditional American values as defined by the Right made the country vulnerable to the Red conspiracy. By this line of reasoning, those who did not support Americanism must be opposed to anticommunism (thus anti anticommunist) and by logical progression must be procommunists or fellow travelers.

By emphasizing political conformity the Legion program showed it valued personal liberty less than capitalist enterprise and social unity. Legion spokesmen frequently denied any intent to impose "thought control," to interfere with true academic freedom, or to silence political and social liberals. But, they added in the same breath, boys were dying in Korea and that left no room in America for any "ism" except Americanism.[24]

Communism, for the extreme advocates of Americanism, became a symbol of all worldly evil and a metaphor for a Pandora's box of irresistible and unwelcome intrusions into their personal worlds. Racial strife, some said, was caused by Communists carrying out their threat to set class against class. Or agnosticism was a Communist-inspired doctrine because its denial of a divinely inspired morality promoted Red materialism. Welfare advocates were aiding communism when they sought to prevent poor individuals from accepting responsibility for their own failure. Taxation was potentially communistic for it embodied the radical notion that property is theft. Even criticism of city police might be part of the Communist plot to destroy law and order. Placing its faith in symbols, the Legion Right personified the real Soviet military and economic threat as the immanent Antichrist, the evil in opposition to which all good must be defined.[25]

Fearful of losing control of their lives and families to a dangerous and mysterious conspiracy in a society where already everyone had to depend more and more on strangers and outsiders, zealous conservatives grew hypersensitive to the content of the mass media, the arts, and education. In conventions, official publications, and post meetings Legionnaires heard thunderous right-wing jeremiads against subversive entertainers and educators. The Legion lauded and honored the florid patriotism of entertainment figures such as Cecil B. deMille, John Wayne, and Ward Bond and turned its wrath on a host of suspect celebrities including composer Roy Harris; a popular singing group, the Weavers; actors and writers; and even a play, Arthur Miller's distinguished *Death of a Salesman.*[26]

Viewed from the Legion Right, the nation's schools were a primary battleground because the nation committed its youth and future to the care of teachers and professors. And the education establishment was suspect. One Legion ideologue feared that some professors and teachers promoted a depraved and distorted view of the American political system to the point where "old fashioned patriotism is a thing of scorn and derision in our best academic and intellectual circles."[27]

Legion-sponsored writers and speakers orchestrated the natural concerns and even guilt felt by parents who daily surrendered their children to strangers in the schools into a symphony of fear. There was no gainsaying that the explosive postwar expansion of public education generated widespread unease. The GI bill and the baby boom, World War II veterans and their children, set off a chaotic, expensive, and often disturbing growth in educational bureaucracy and school populations.

It is axiomatic that at such unsettled times true educational innovation is most likely to occur. As a creative movement, the heyday of the "child centered" progressive reformers was long past by 1951 and the Progressive Education Association was dying. Yet in the years after the war progressivism had its greatest practical influence in the schools through sympathetic teachers and pedagogues who were by then positioned to implement some items of their agenda.

Playing upon the public's suspicion of educators, extremists on the right were quick to label every form of educational change that they opposed as "progressive." To Irene Corbally Kuhn, writing in the *American Legion Magazine,* child-centered education was the subtle plot hatched by totalitarian progressive educators, the teachers college "brain trust," to "capture the 'whole child,' usurp parental authority, and so nullify moral and spiritual influences." J. B. "Doc" Matthews (a sometime staffer or advisor of HUAC, the Hearst papers, and Sen. Joe McCarthy, as well as the Legion) alleged widespread Communist infiltration of the universities. And it was progressive education that made the schools vulnerable to Red subversion. Matthews claimed that first Darwinism, then William James's pragmatism and John Dewey's instrumentalist philosophy had produced moral chaos on American campuses. It was not that progressive education and communism were the same. They were in fact opposites. But progressive education prepared the way for communism by destroying traditional American standards and values. Teachers colleges were especially guilty, because, according to Matthews, they focused not on *what* to teach but only on *how* to teach. Thus prospective teachers were not imbued with traditional values. The moral vacuum fostered by the progressive educators, "the relaxation of the old intellectual standards and moral disciplines and loyalties, encouraged by Dewey's progressive education, became *Communism's opportunity*" (Matthews's italics).

Such analyses of progressive education appealed to many Americans. Whichever way one viewed progressivism's response to the needs of individuals and mass public education in a pluralist, industrial democracy, the inevitable sins and stupidities sometimes committed in its name over more than a generation had alienated and puzzled much of the public. So had the secularized and scientific approach to human problems promoted by the elitist university professoriate. Against this background, educators' advocacy of academic freedom was to traditionalists nothing more than an arrogant and unjustified demand by teachers to be free to act irresponsibly, and to do so in front of the children.

Free speech within reason might be all right in ordinary times, but these were not ordinary times. Conservatives reasoned that the community hired the teachers, who should be role models for youth and guardians of patriotic traditions. As an HUAC report put it in 1953: "The molding of a young mind becomes the total responsibility of the teacher, and, in the selection of subject matter and by precept and example, the Communist teacher can and will distort the facts of American life into a hideous mockery of its true reality." Communism was said to be everywhere and the schools and colleges, run by impractical idealists, eccentrics and agnostics, seemed a fertile medium to nourish Communist indoctrination of impressionable youth.

Not surprisingly, the creators of Legion anticommunist policy questioned the soundness of education in the Cold War years. Were the professors really teaching *about* communism as they should, or were they promoting it indirectly by criticizing American values and institutions and leaving patriotism, Christianity, and character-building out of the schools?[28]

The strength of the Legion lay in its multitude of local posts across the land. Its weakness was the independence of its local post commanders. Therefore, its national officers and particularly those on its thirty-nine-member Americanism Commission had to work hard to get out their anticommunist message. In December of 1947 Legion post commanders received copies of the attorney-general's list of subversive organizations with a cover letter from Seth Richardson of the President's Loyalty Board. At Legion headquarters in Indianapolis the file on alleged subversives, procommunist organizations, and suspect publications grew from 5,000 "old cards" in 1947 to more than 200,000 in 1951 — their contents available upon request to Legion post commanders. Indianapolis furnished free lists of anticommunist publications and compilations of alleged procommunist materials from which the Legion hoped to shield a naive and unsuspecting public. It offered subscriptions, mainly to post commanders, to *Summary of Trends and Developments*, which abstracted and condensed materials relating to communism from seventy-five publications. Companion periodicals were *Red Channels* and the *Firing Line* newsletter. The latter was dedicated to "exposing members of the Communist conspiracy and other sympathizers to Communism." In addition occasional publications were distributed free at Legion conventions or in conjunction with such organizations as the Chamber of Commerce. Notable among these was *The Key to Peace* by Notre Dame Law School dean Clarence Manion, who urged a return to the principles of free enterprise, individualism, organized religion, and national divine guidance—a solution he claimed to be "as simple as the little red school house problem in primer arithmetic."[29]

Aimed more at the average family than the committed Legionnaire was the *American Legion Magazine,* a monthly resembling in format *Field and Stream.* In 1950–51 in its pages stories about the dangers of Communist subversion vied for space with those on other topics such as small-arms home defense ("The Mighty .22"). Article after article by professional anticommunists such as Louis Budenz, Victor Lasky, Irene Corbally Kuhn, Howard Rushmore, Freda Utley, Clarence Manion, and Eugene Lyons revealed new faces of evil. Lurid titles—"Do Colleges *Have* to Hire Red Professors?" "Your Child Is Their Target!" and "Academic Hucksters"—provided variations on the recurrent theme that Reducators, or Reds in the schools, threatened the nation.[30]

In 1950 the Legion joined fifty-eight other associations in the "All-America Conference to Combat Communism," a loose arrangement embracing the spectrum from the AFL–CIO to the National Association of Manufacturers, to reach "Main Street U.S.A." The working core of the alliance was made of grass-roots organizations: the Legion itself, the Chamber of Commerce, Daughters of the American Revolution, Kiwanis, Lions, Masons, and the Improved Order of Red Men.[31]

Bringing teams of anticommunist writers into local communities was a dramatic and popular expression of the Americanism crusade. The effect of the meetings varied from place to place but they seem to have stimulated both community interest and mischief-making. Apparently to protect the community, in May 1950 Fairmont Legion Post 17 sponsored the appearance of nationally prominent experts who were riding the Legion's cross-country Americanism circuit.[32]

Their first antisubversive seminar generated noisy controversy at the college and in the town papers. Combining some of the aspects of a traveling medicine show, a revival meeting, and a lyceum, the meeting was an all-day affair on Saturday, May 20, by invitation only for 100 or so "representative" Fairmonters. Five speakers told the assembly about the menace, or, as a local journalist hyperbolized, "five experts tore the mask off that insidious, implacable enemy of free men and revealed him as a growing giant who must be halted now or never." Leading off was Karl Baarslag, American Legion Americanism Commissioner. He was followed by former HUAC researcher Benjamin Mandel; media producer Vincent Hartnett; former *Daily Worker* reporter Howard Rushmore; and ex–fellow traveler, ex-professor J. B. Matthews.[33]

Matthews had compiled the Dies Committee (HUAC) fellow-traveler files before leaving its employ in 1943 to work for William Randolph Hearst, the American Legion, and other patriotic organizations as an expert on Reducators. At the Fairmont meeting "Mr. Anticommunist," as his followers apotheosized him, denounced Far Eastern affairs expert Professor Owen Lattimore, who had been charged by Senator McCarthy with ties to communism. Warming to the subject of Red professors, Matthews charged with pseudo-precision that twenty-nine of the top 100 Communists in the United States were college professors and that 3,000 professors on 700 campuses were involved in Communist front activities.[34]

Matthews's claim that the nation's campuses and the intellectuals who inhabited them were the "scene and source" of much Communist advance in the United States caused the gorge to rise in President Hand and several Fairmont State College faculty members in the audience, which did not include Luella Mundel. In the question-and-answer session that followed the prepared remarks, Hand, college business manager Regis Larkin, librarian Harold Jones, and others challenged Matthews's assertion that professors "as a class" were suspect, that college people were ignorant about communism, and that the colleges and universities had done nothing to fight against it. Matthews had given few facts to support his sweeping charges, they noted. Furthermore, they claimed he was not really hunting Reds but smearing liberals. To which Matthews riposted, "This is the type of college mentality I have referred to." According to Hand and a companion, Hartnett later told them in the hotel lobby that he could tell by the questions that faculty members had asked in the meeting that there was a Communist cell on the campus.[35]

The Legion speakers advanced the partisan Republican claim that Franklin Roosevelt, New Deal liberalism, and by logical extension the Truman administration were all soft on communism. Democrats in the audience reacted to this as an attack on their party. The Democratic *Fairmont Times* agreed and labeled the meeting an "anti-Truman" and "pro-McCarthy" "witch hunt."[36]

Predictably, the Republican *West Virginian* lauded the Legion speakers, endorsing and amplifying their message in an editorial by directly linking higher education to New Deal liberalism. Many academicians, wrote the editor, had made Franklin Roosevelt their "patron saint." It was Roosevelt, he added, who had allowed communism an American foothold and then at Teheran and Yalta had sold out to Soviet expansionism. Beating the GOP drum, the *West Virginian* proclaimed "Let the people be aroused!" "Let's have some real Anti-Communist sessions in this city."[37]

When the dust had settled on the first Legion antisubversive session, the town appeared divided along political party lines. Liberals and Democrats, both town and gown, backed by the morning paper, disputed the arguments of the professional anticommunists. The afternoon paper and conservatives supported the antisubversive speakers. Each side agreed to disagree. There were no apparent sanctions or repercussions against those who had debated Matthews and the others, although probably grudges were deepened.

From the standpoint of advancing the Americanism program, Legionnaires could not rest content. In overwhelmingly Democratic Fairmont, it would not do to have the cause of the nonpartisan Legion identified as a GOP issue. Few could have guessed that ten months later the local political atmosphere would have changed so drastically that liberals would find themselves political outcasts.

Those ten months produced the outbreak of the Korean War in June 1950, the subsequent intervention by Communist China, the Great Debate over the permanent deployment of U.S. troops in Europe, strenuous arguments over a proposal for universal military training, and, contemporaneous with Fairmont's second antisubversive meeting, Truman's firing of MacArthur and its political aftermath.

The growing national shock over the bloody Korean War fueled Senator McCarthy's charges of subversion in government and gave the Republicans a major theme for the 1950 elections—alleged liberal Democratic softness toward communism. The Republicans did not win control of either house of Congress in 1950 but the Red Scare tactic appears to have worked rather well. Richard M. Nixon won a California Senate seat from Helen Gahagan Douglas using it to perfection, and Millard Tydings, after being targeted for political oblivion by McCarthyites, went down to defeat in Maryland. And Senate majority leader Scott Lucas of Illinois was defeated by conservative Everett Dirksen. All told, the Democrats lost five seats in the Senate and twenty-eight in the House.[38]

A few Democrats saw a silver lining in defeat. West Virginia's liberal Ken Hechler argued that the twenty-eight-seat debit was less than the average off-year loss for the House majority since 1914.[39] In his *Men against McCarthy* Richard Fried shows that the 1950 election results indicate that the grass-roots appeal of the McCarthyites was less than overwhelming. Moderates, liberals, and orthodox conservatives survived politically. So did most of the political opponents of the McCarran Internal Security Act. However, at the time politicians in both parties read the entrails and pronounced the elections a "mandate for McCarthy." Truman aide Hechler writes that the 1950 election was a "preview of the 1952 defeat for the Democratic party, when the Republicans capitalized on the issue of 'Korea, corruption and communism.' "[40] As the military crisis deepened in Korea it became necessary to woo Southern conservative Democrats in order to mobilize the country's resources. At the same time the administration had to confront the difficulties of winning public support for sending men to die in Asia so soon after VJ Day. By early 1951 after Chinese intervention had snatched apparent victory from the grasp of United Nations forces and turned it into near military disaster, the war was settling into a bloody stalemate.

As the costly police action dragged on in the spring of 1951, it became imperative to try to explain what to many Americans was unexplainable— that the Korean conflict was a limited war to *contain* communism, not to defeat let alone destroy it. In the face of the surging Red Scare, liberal Democrats and government officials understandably felt vulnerable to the "soft on communism" charge, became defensive, and went to great lengths to demonstrate that they were just as anticommunist as conservatives and Republicans. They appeared to believe that they must ride the juggernaut or be crushed by it. The tightening of the Federal Loyalty-Security Program and Democratic campaign materials designed to show that it was their party that had brought the Communist Party USA to its knees were symptoms of the trend. But they neither silenced conservative critics nor restored public confidence.[41]

Against this background, on Saturday, March 31, 1951, Luella Mundel went with her friend Harold Jones to the second Legion antisubversive seminar held in the ballroom of the Fairmont Hotel, a large, red-brick pile overlooking the Monongahela River proximate to the town's rail depot, central business district, county courthouse, and Legion Post 17. Evidently she did not especially wish to go, but Jones prevailed with his argument that she should get out more. She said later that she understood that President Hand had wanted faculty members to go to the meeting to help restrain the antiliberal tendencies of the speakers.[42]

So she went to the meeting and soon found herself listening to a team of speakers imported under the sponsorship of the Legion's Americanism Commission. Unlike the one ten months earlier, this meeting was open to the general public and had been well promoted in advance by the Democratic-leaning *Fairmont Times*. The crowd was half again as big as the one in May 1950, and among the estimated 150 in the audience were at least a half dozen others from the college. Jones pointed out to Mundel a woman he thought was Thelma Loudin. He may have been wrong, for it was never proved that Loudin was there. The mistake is easily forgiven, for Mundel and Jones were upset by the atmosphere at the seminar and neither knew the school board member well.[43]

The scheduled roster of speakers at this second antisubversive meeting differed from that of the first and was further changed when two speakers did not appear.[44] There were three sessions—morning, afternoon, and evening—and Mundel and Jones attended only the morning and after-noon meetings. The morning session began at nine o'clock and consisted of talks by former HUAC official and soon-to-be McCarran Committee research director Benjamin Mandel and ex-Communist party member Paul Crouch. Mandel spoke about "The Communist Party: What It Is and How It Works" while Crouch described the "Soviet Underground USA." In the afternoon Rabbi Ben Schultz discussed "Communism and Religion" and stated explicitly that "this fight against Communism is a fight against atheism and a fight for God." According to the *Fairmont Times* he asked, "How many clergy, teachers, professors, editors, writers, commentators, and others who help to form public opinion are aiding the Commies by taking an indifferent attitude?"[45]

How Dr. Mundel and the other college liberals reacted to all of the speakers is not recorded, except that Mundel objected to one speaker's characterization of the good, gray *New York Times* as a "pink sheet" and she questioned Benjamin Mandel about his assertion that the colleges were full of Communists. A controversy remains about her exchange with Victor Lasky. A well-known journalist and coauthor of *Seeds of Treason,* a study of Communist espionage in the United States, Lasky discussed the infiltration tactics and techniques practiced by Communists, including references to then-current espionage cases. According to the Fairmont Sunday newspaper, he said: "There are still Soviet agents who are active in all walks of life—even in government. The Hisses, Coplons, and Remingtons were caught. But how many of their counterparts are still holding high and trusted positions is problematical. But that they are there is beyond dispute."[46]

As far as one can tell from contemporary accounts and what the principals said later, during the question-and-answer period following Lasky's talk, several faculty members questioned him sharply, claiming as one said that he was "calculatingly linking liberals with Communists and their sympathizers with the intention of discrediting liberalism" and limiting civil liberties. Supposedly Dr. Mundel asked if Lasky believed that an audience such as he was addressing could be expected to detect Communists on the basis of what they heard at the Legion seminar. She then suggested, as Harold Jones recalled, that the association of liberals and Communists in some minds might threaten the civil liberties of noncommunists. When Lasky asked what civil liberties had anyone lost, Mundel suggested (in the most plausible of several versions of her remarks) that what Lasky advocated smacked of totalitarianism and fascism.[47]

Exactly what was said next is in dispute, but there certainly was some shouting. The antagonists may have hurled the terms "Communist" and "Nazi" at each other. In testimony given in connection with Lasky's suit against ABC in 1988 Harold Jones remembered that Mundel had said to Lasky words to the effect, "If I'm a Communist, you are a Fascist." A Fairmont resident who was at the 1951 meeting told viewers of ABC–TV's documentary that Lasky called Mundel a Communist. Lasky has adamantly and publicly denied the charge. In a conversation with the author, he remembered her vaguely as a woman who made an emotional attack on the Legion speakers.[48]

In November 1951, six and a half months after the incident, Harold Jones wrote to Lasky and to Mundel's lawyers recalling the exchange. Mundel herself gave similar testimony on December 20, 1951, during her slander suit against Thelma Loudin. Context is important here. Vincent Hartnett's assertion to Hand at the 1950 meeting that he could tell by questions from the audience that there was a Communist cell at the college must have been on Mundel's mind. According to both Fairmont newspapers (and the different accounts of the reporters for each paper, Logan Carroll and William Evans, Jr.), Mundel said on the witness stand that she had asked Lasky how he could identify a Communist by looking. But Lasky, probably missing the reference because he had not been present at the 1950 meeting, replied, "Well maybe I can. I know you're not one because you 'shot off your mouth.'" The *Fairmont Times* quoted her as testifying later that school board member Loudin was the "only one who had accused her of being a Communist or anything of that nature."[49]

No matter what the exact words were, the situation is clear. Remembering the May 1950 Legion meeting and the words of Matthews and Hartnett, the college liberals went to the March 1951 meeting on the alert against attacks on academic liberalism.[50] But it was a different cast of Legion speakers. Hartnett, Matthews, and Baarslag were absent and the focus of the seminar shifted away from partisan McCarthyite rhetoric of internal subversion to a more general anticommunist line. Of all the speakers, Mandel and Lasky came closest to expressing the view that the college people had come to challenge. To add to the tension, some in the audience found Lasky's style abrasive. Lasky became the target of the college faculty in part because of what he said, but more because of the ongoing Legion Americanism campaign and what had been said by antisubversive speakers at the 1950 meeting. It is important to remember that Mundel later sued Thelma Loudin, not Mandel or Lasky or the American Legion. The premise upon which Mundel's suit rested was that the whole fault for blackening her reputation lay with Loudin.[51]

In the wake of the second meeting what is most striking is the attitude of Fairmont's Democratic press. In contrast to the reports of the previous year's meeting, this time no partisan debate enlivened the Democratic and Republican papers. The Sunday *Fairmont Times–West Virginian* was content to summarize the remarks of each speaker without comment or direct allusion to the liberal criticism of the proceedings. Those who had been there of course knew what the reporter meant when he wrote that "many interesting questions were asked of the speakers, particularly of Victor Lasky." But the paper offered no suggestion that the Legion speakers had engaged in McCarthyism.[52]

Obviously reflecting the mood of the country and the strategy of the national administration, the local Democratic establishment observed a prudent silence in the face of the Legionnaires' attack on alleged subversives. In so doing it left college liberals isolated and vulnerable to opponents on campus and in the town. This retreat was evident in April and May when the national and local anticommunist tide rose. Following the antisubversive meeting, in cooperation with local clergymen, Legion Post 17 organized "All Faith Week," designed to bring Protestant, Catholic, and Jew together "in an appeal for divine guidance at this difficult time in American history." Concurrently the Legion launched the "Go to Church" movement to bring families together in worship to reinforce community and national ties. Both programs were part of the Legion's Back to God movement.[53]

On April 12 Post 17 brought from Pittsburgh Matt Cvetic, a former Communist party member and paid informer for the FBI, whose story was the subject of a book and a motion picture, *I Was a Communist for the F.B.I.* He told a crowd of Fairmont citizens that there were two ways to fight communism in the United States. First, every citizen must help to expose Communists, who, he said, would "bore from within"—that is, infiltrate trade unions, industry, schools. Second, communism could be defeated "through the education of youth." American young people must be taught "what communism is about." As if to underline the danger, Cvetic predicted that the Communists would liquidate one-third of all Americans if they ever took over. Among those doomed would be all Kiwanians, Rotarians, Lions—in short most of those in his Fairmont audience.[54]

That colleges served to carry on Communist indoctrination and that women were most often their dupes and followers was an argument made in the Republican *Fairmont West Virginian* on April 4. Far-right syndicated columnist, FBI conduit, and sometime Legion anticommunist expert George Sokolsky made precisely this point in a review of popular novelist Helen MacInnes's latest novel, *Neither Five nor Three*. This tale of impressionable college students and radical ideas offered Sokolsky the opportunity to rail against colleges that produced unhappy young women who divorced themselves from God, turned to radical ideas, and destroyed everything around them. Lamenting the plight of these "tortured souls" who reflected "the ugliness of a degenerate spirit," he complained that these "so-called liberal women" had become national "pests." They upset a community by "injecting alien ideas, and insisting upon having their way." They were dopes and dupes.[55] Sokolsky's misogyny was of course not aimed at Fairmont, and it would be impossible to gauge his influence or that of any other political columnist in a given community. Nevertheless here was timely ammunition for those who believed there was evil afoot at the college. It reinforced resentments that festered against Mundel, a woman who appeared to flout local behavioral norms and traditional gender roles.

At the same time, Sokolsky's column linked the spread of Communist subversion in the colleges with the "woman question." What William Chafe defines as a paradox resulted at mid-century from women's increased role in the American economy and the cultural lag which could not assimilate that change into the institutional fabric. While the war had produced unprecedented opportunities for women to join the labor force, it produced no comparable reduction in discrimination against them. "Rosie the Riveter" was praised and women flew planes, held commissions in the armed forces, and thoroughly penetrated the wartime job structure, but such behavior was tolerated only as a temporary phenomenon. At the war's end a woman was expected to return to her traditional place as mother and homemaker. The sexual double standard remained the norm as did inequality in hiring and wages, access to professional and business training, and legal rights.[56]

Although the postwar baby boom was evidence that many women did return to domesticity, female participation in the economy continued to grow and the Korean emergency renewed the national need for women to serve in the armed forces and the work place. In September 1951 *New York Times Magazine* published a laudatory profile of women who built jet fighters in a Burbank, California, plant, an article comparing the modern "developmental" family favorably with the traditional patriarchal family, and a report that a federal task force was considering conscripting women for the armed forces.[57]

But women, especially articulate, educated, middle-class women, received mixed signals, felt cultural contradictions, and experienced role confusion that stimulated an extended debate on the nature and purpose of their education. Mirra Komarovsky, writing in 1946, had set forth the apparent dilemma. Should a female college senior set her sights upon becoming an "ideal homemaker" or a "career girl?" The illogical but practical answer of course was that she should pursue both, but in a feminine manner. The girl with a "middle of the road" personality was best adjusted to the current historical moment.[58] "She is a girl who is intelligent enough to do well in school but not so brilliant as to 'get all "A"s'; informed and alert but not consumed by an intellectual passion; capable but not talented in areas relatively new to women; able to stand on her own feet and to earn a living but not so good as to compete with men; capable of doing some job well (in case she does not marry or, otherwise has to work) but not so identified with a profession as to need it for her happiness."[59]

Komarovsky, a feminist, believed that role conflict for women would persist until culture caught up with modern society and women could approach their lives with the same autonomy as men. But others believed with Freud that anatomy is destiny and that women could not be happy or "fulfilled" unless their education prepared them for a traditional life of nurturance, which was assumed to be in harmony with woman's true nature. Conservatively oriented social scientists used the modern jargon of their discipline to preserve traditionalism. For example, in a study of sixty unmarried Alabama career women, Evelyn Ellis concluded that in women ambition was an illness. "Upward social mobility is likely to be an outgrowth of basically neurotic drives resulting from unsatisfactory early primary group relations and ... mobility leads to a continuation of superficial, impermanent primary group relations and other overt manifestations of emotional maladjustment."[60] In a more comprehensive and less cautious 1947 work, *Modern Woman: The Lost Sex,* Ferdinand Lundberg and Marynia Farnham declared feminists neurotic and "masculine women" a threat to the future of the nation.[61]

In 1951 even moderates, such as college presidents Lynn White, Jr. (Mills College), George Stoddard (University of Illinois), and Anne Parnell (Sweet Briar College), wrote in separate publications urging a special curriculum for women that trained them for home and motherhood. Each was committed to equal education for men and women, but on separate tracks.[62] White went so far as to suggest that only women, the survivors of impending military catastrophe, trained to kill, could save civilization: "When disaster descends on civilian communities, not only ancient tradition but also an understanding of the psychology of little people will lead women in general to huddle guarding the children in what safer places may be found, while men fight fire and peril. Even bacterial warfare will probably slay fewer women than men; for . . . the blood of women makes them somewhat more resistant than men to infection."[63]

A major defect of modern education for women, White added, was that by "a major perversion of the constitutional provision separating church and state, systematic study of religion has been discouraged in tax-supported colleges and universities." Professors of art and philosophy were giving short shrift to the importance of religion and religious values. And their best students often entered the rapidly enlarging professoriate only to pass on religious illiteracy to new generations of students.[64]

Thus, in 1950 the rise of secularism in the colleges, the threat of nuclear war, women's changing socioeconomic position, the belief that female ambition led to neurosis, and women's education all could be considered as part of the same syndrome—modernism. Many conservatives associated modernism with subversion and communism. Fairmont State had long been a teachers college principally educating women to educate children. Luella Mundel was a very modern woman and her presence there disquieted conservative traditionalists.

Perhaps by accident, the Fairmont State College administration itself fanned the anticommunist fires. On various occasions Hand had denounced leftists on the nation's campuses. In 1949 he had told students at Waynesburg College (Pennsylvania) that while the number of Communists on American campuses was not large, it was a "vicious minority" when its effects were considered. He also upheld the then-recent firing of "communistically minded" professors at the University of Washington.

On April 13, 1951, the social science department brought in George S. Counts of Teachers College, Columbia University, to speak on Russian communism. Counts, who had in the thirties embraced the radical Left, was an anticommunist liberal progressive educator and social scientist who remained best known for a 1932 speech to the Progressive Education Association in which he advocated "imposition" of progressive social ideas upon school children as a means of reforming American society. Although he had visited the USSR in the late 1920s and admired much about its education system, he was a dedicated enemy of international communism. The gist of his Fairmont remarks was the need to study communism and the USSR soberly and carefully.[65]

Despite Counts's anticommunist message, his visit could not have pleased Legion officials. He was no Communist, but he was exactly the type of educator they meant when they spoke of subversive influences in the colleges. He had been strongly influenced by the controversial explanation of American history advanced by his friend Charles A. Beard, who emphasized economic conflict in the nation's past. An instrumentalist pragmatist in the tradition of John Dewey, Counts was a prolific author, a central figure in the despised Progressive Education Association, a onetime major figure in the American Labor party, a former president of the American Federation of Teachers and, in 1952, he would be the Liberal party candidate for the U.S. Senate in New York.

A longtime critic of One-Hundred Percent Americanism, he was the sponsor of a 1938 Teachers College monograph (according to its title page) that savaged the American Legion's educational activities. Legion spokesmen had attacked the book and blamed its findings on the influence of Red professors. Interestingly enough, it was not until 1950, just a month after President Hand and Librarian Jones among others had debated J. B. Matthews, that the Fairmont State College library acquired this book. Above all, Counts represented the most aggressive wing of the professional education establishment, which, its critics charged, had proclaimed itself the new mandarin class destined to reform society by reshaping the schools. This view was much resented throughout the country, particularly by the local small-business elites for whom the Legion often spoke. Who better than Counts embodied Matthews's charge that from "Morningside Heights, there spread across the entire land the intellectually envenoming and morally disintegrating view" represented by progressive education? And the local college already numbered several Columbia Teachers College graduates on its faculty. The invitation to Counts as well as the growth of the anti-Legion collection at the college must have seemed provocative to the Legionnaires.[66]

Had it not been for the national and international situation in April and May 1951, none of this would have mattered much. But at the very time when Luella Mundel was incurring the wrath of the local anticommunists, the front pages of the Fairmont newspapers were covered with both lurid scare headlines and truly bad news. It would be helpful to know exactly how the radio news was interpreting the information flow, for Fairmonters probably got most of their news from that source. It would be helpful, but not necessary. To a degree the same wire services supplied both radio newsrooms and newspapers. If anything, radio news reports were capsules, resembling newspaper headlines and affording much less detail.[67]

Objectively, the situation on the ground in Korea had been reduced to fierce, inconclusive ground battles near Seoul and the 38th Parallel. Headlines warned that "CHINESE REDS RECEIVE 3000 RUSSIAN

PLANES," "18 NEW CHINESE DIVISIONS MOVE INTO NORTH KOREA," "REDS BELIEVED MASSING 40 FRESH DIVISIONS FOR OFFENSIVE," "REGROUPING ENEMY HAS POTENTIAL OF 63 DIVISIONS," "FANATIC REDS HALT ALLIED ADVANCE," "UN FORCES . . . TO MEET EXPECTED MAY DAY ATTACK AND PERHAPS BIGGEST BATTLE OF THE WAR," and "RUSSIA HAS 400 HEAVY BOMBERS, ATOMIC BOMBS."[68] During April at least three local men died in Korea. By the end of the month Fairmont readers learned that U.S. casualties since June 1950 had reached 62,799, including 1,055 in the previous week.[69] Forty thousand men were drafted nationally during the month and there was talk from the administration of making it more difficult for young men to receive deferments.[70] The papers also covered the disturbing proposal for a new law requiring all young men to submit to universal military training—until it was dropped in mid-month. Several West Virginia National Guard outfits were mobilized for duty in Europe and nineteen Charleston area Air Force men died in an operational accident.[71]

Concerning internal security, the press reported of Ethel and Julius Rosenberg in early April, "HUSBAND, WIFE SPY TEAM GETS DEATH PENALTY," and, later, "CONFESSED SPY GETS 15 YEARS." Actor Sterling Hayden inspired such headlines as "HAYDEN ADMITS BEING COMMIE," and it was reported that American citizen Robert A. Vogeler and his wife arrived in the country after a harrowing seventeen-month imprisonment in Communist Hungary.[72]

The biggest and most disturbing story of the month was without doubt Truman's dismissal of Gen. Douglas MacArthur as commander of forces in Korea on April 10. It revealed a deep split in the national leadership over the war and related problems and daily it was a front-page story well into May. First came the shock recorded by the *Fairmont Times* in the banner headline "MAC FIRED!" Then came the charges and counter-charges, MacArthur's slow, triumphal return to the States and eventually to Washington. Finally, after political maneuvering, came Senate hearings.[73]

This partisan issue played differently in the Democratic *Times* and the Republican *West Virginian*. The former supported the administration, reporting that Europeans were pleased with the ouster, that Eisenhower hoped it would not cause national dissension, that "MOUNTAINEERS BACK TRUMAN," and that the United Nations now looked to the United States for a new Korean policy. The paper featured Truman's version of what had transpired at the Truman-MacArthur meeting at Wake Island and portrayed West Virginia senator Matthew Neely favorably for his ridicule of the adoration heaped on MacArthur by the

Republicans. The Fairmont native was widely quoted as having said, "If the second coming of Christ had happened, there could not have been any more hysterical, emotional uprisings than there have been in this country over MacArthur."[74] He likened the fuss to a Barnum and Bailey promotion and conjured up analogies to Babylon, Nebuchadnezzar, and the Roman Hippodrome. For good measure, he recalled how as a soldier in the Spanish-American war he, a Democrat, had obeyed the Republican president, old "Bill McKinley" and that the Roman general Scipio had kept a slave to say to him " 'Remember O great Scipio, thou art but a man.' "[75]

The Republican *West Virginian* rallied behind MacArthur. It played up the possible impeachment of Truman, ridiculed the thought that the firing had a historical analogy in Lincoln's dismissal of George B. McClellan, and condemned the "communist" British government for urging MacArthur's removal. It called Truman's secret notes of the Wake Island discussions with MacArthur "outrageous" and derided the president's proposal for a negotiated settlement of the war as appeasement. The afternoon paper gave prominent coverage to the public release of Lt. Gen. Albert C. Wedemeyer's 1947 report that had warned of a Communist attack on South Korea. Commenting on Neely's proadministration stand, a local columnist quoted a neighboring paper, the *Clarksburg Telegram,* to the effect that the senator's statements had been "mad," and that he was no more than a sacrilegious "Bible quoter" tied to the "men who gave us Dean Acheson, 'Deep Freeze' Vaughan, and a few others of similar standing."[76]

Despite their political differences, the two papers relied exclusively on the same source for their world and national news, the United Press. This gave both front pages a doomsday flavor, for the UP, locked in a struggle for survival with the much larger Associated Press, often resorted to sensationalism in its coverage and was quite vulnerable to McCarthy's manipulation.[77]

But even without sensational coverage, the situation in April 1951 was surely grim enough. At least it was if one believed the rhetoric emanating from administration spokesmen and Democratic members of Congress who were variously trying to light a fire under a war-weary public, defend Truman's dismissal of MacArthur, and convince many doubters that the Democrats were not the "Commiecrats."

Charles E. "General Electric" Wilson, head of the Office of Defense Mobilization, was the source of one gloomy pronouncement after another. He warned of impending rubber and steel shortages, urged tighter controls on food prices, and raised the possibility of rationing, if only to deny its immediate necessity. Meanwhile, producers predicted a meat shortage. In early May newspapers announced Wilson's claim of "G.I. LIVES IN KOREA MENACED BY PUBLIC'S APATHY." House Speaker Sam Rayburn went farther when the headlines reported "[RAYBURN] SAYS NATION IN TERRIBLE DANGER," "U.S. MAY BE ON BRINK OF WORLD WAR III" and "[RAYBURN] BEGS US TO AWAKEN TO WAR DANGER."[78] While MacArthur demanded the bombing of Manchuria and a showdown with the Communists, the papers reported nonjudgmentally Tennessee Democrat Albert Gore's proposal to end the war by spraying a belt of radioactive waste the breadth of Korea near the 38th Parallel. This "death sand" would "dehumanize" the zone so that all enemy soldiers attempting to cross it would face "certain death or slow deformity."[79] So May began in a charged atmosphere.

At the end of the first week in May 1951, the state board of education was scheduled for its annual session to renew teachers' contracts for the first time since the Korean War had begun. In light of the more urgent meaning internal security had now taken on, the time must have seemed ripe to elements of the local Legion to strike against what they thought to be improper goings-on at Fairmont State College. Mundel's outburst at the Legion meeting had drawn attention to her and, given the political climate of the moment, the Legion could coalesce with other community interests to cast her out.

CHAPTER 3

A "Security Risk": Fired for the Good of the College

> In defiance of all reputable lexicographers—living or dead—
> ... the word "security" or the term "security risk" includes such
> wholly unrelated abominations, frivolities, and misfortunes as
> communistic contamination, gossiping indulgences, or child-
> birth with fewer than nine months after the ... mother's marriage.
> ... I am unalterably opposed to the ruinous slandering of any
> innocent American by calling him or her a Communist either
> directly or by innuendo.
>
> —Sen. Matthew Mansfield Neely (1954)

Every year at the May meeting of the West Virginia board of education, college presidents submitted their budgets for the next fiscal year. Approval was usually routine, and Fairmont's George Hand expected no surprises when he presented his personnel recommendations on May 7, 1951. Unbeknownst to Hand, Fairmont board member Thelma Loudin, armed with complaints against Luella Mundel, came to Charleston determined to do something about them.

Hand's audience with the board began smoothly. But the budget hit a snag when board members reached the name of Dr. Helmut Schoeck on the proposed salary list. The refugee scholar held a Ph.D. in sociology. But the board wanted him to teach only German. In September 1950 Schoeck had come directly from East Germany to Fairmont State, saying that he had been denied employment in his homeland for speaking out against communism. Despite this, board members evidently doubted his loyalty. They ruled that he must not teach "American History, Social Studies and other related fields." Then Loudin challenged several more names. Why, she asked, had Hand not proposed salary increases for English instructor Paul Opp and botanist C. Moore Roberts, who had between them fifty-three years of experience at the college? Hand answered that Opp was about to retire and Roberts had been ill and away from the college for part of the year. Then she asked why he proposed to give Dr. Mundel a raise, let alone to rehire her?[1]

No formal transcript records exactly what Loudin and Hand said next, but both later offered their own versions. In most particulars Loudin's July 1952 court testimony and Hand's April 1952 written report agree. It was not the words uttered so much as their context and implications that stirred controversy.

The two concur that Loudin objected to Mundel's reemployment. She remembered saying to Hand: "Are you sure she is the type of person you want?" When Hand inquired what she meant, Loudin asked if he had not heard criticism of Dr. Mundel. He admitted that he had heard "something" about her actions at the American Legion seminar. In Loudin's version, Hand mentioned Mundel's alleged atheism, but the president denied he discussed that. At the climax of what must have been a tense exchange Loudin said, according to her testimony, "Dr. Hand you are building a long term faculty, to work with you for years. Is she [Mundel] a good security risk?" When Hand asked if "security risk" meant "Communist" Loudin said (and she was later backed by the court testimony of six board members) that she demurred: "Oh, George I didn't mean that. I'm not making accusations, just asking questions."[2]

Loudin's demurral aside, the term "security risk" had sinister connotations in 1951 that are now impossible fully to appreciate. Under the Federal Loyalty-Security Program, which had been developing since the late 1930s and was greatly expanded by Executive Order 9835 in 1947, millions of federal employees were screened, thousands were investigated in detail, and several hundred, most of them lower echelon, were discharged.[3] Unsubstantiated charges damaged the reputations of thousands. Even if the charges against one were eventually dismissed, one's civil service career might be left in shambles. Investigative policies and procedures initially hedged by protections of a citizen's due process and First Amendment rights were frequently reinterpreted to curtail those rights because of the presumed threat of internal subversion.[4]

By 1951, following the lead of conservative Republican federal Loyalty Review Board chairman Seth W. Richardson, the boards, commissions, or other entities responsible for employee loyalty in the various states adopted the position that public employment is a privilege, not a right. Therefore state governments could discharge employees at will without hearing or explanation.[5] Such entities tended to treat employee *loyalty* and *suitability* as synonymous. In the words of scholar Eleanor Bontecou, suitability in public employment encompassed such matters as "sobriety, conventionality in sex, veracity, criminal record, and general reliability."[6]

West Virginia had no loyalty-security board. It had no Tenney Committee as did California or Feinberg law as did New York. Like more than twenty sister states, it required teachers to take a loyalty oath. But the West Virginia oath dating from the Civil War era required only that a teacher must uphold the state and federal constitutions, "honestly demean himself in the teaching profession and to the best of his ability execute the position of a teacher."[7]

Possibly because of the absence of strong state anticommunist legislation, Loudin's action suggests that she believed that the West Virginia state board of education was a de facto loyalty board whose task it was to pass on the loyalty and "suitability" of state college employees. Less than ten days before the May board meeting several well publicized developments in the loyalty-security field brought the issue to the foreground and might have encouraged her to take that position.

On April 28, President Truman issued Executive Order 10241 to permit the discharge of federal employees if "reasonable doubt" existed as to their loyalty. This supplanted the requirement that "all the evidence" must provide "reasonable grounds . . . for the belief" that employees were disloyal. It further shifted the burden of proof from the government, which had previously been required to establish employees' disloyalty, to the accused workers, who must now convince investigators that they were loyal.[8]

On April 30, just a week before the board meeting, the United States Supreme Court announced its findings in four cases bearing on the employee loyalty program. In the key case, *Bailey* v. *Richardson,* the court affirmed the principle that there was no constitutional right to federal employment and therefore no right to due process for a discharged worker. Despite the court's profound internal disagreement over the issues as reflected in eight separate opinions totalling 40,000 words, the decision was widely accepted as support for the "reasonable doubt" standard of dismissal for public employees.[9]

Loudin's action cannot be considered apart from the national political and emotional climate. State governments tend to follow the federal government and the federal civil service was a model for state employment. Loudin later admitted as much by claiming that her duties as a board of education member were to: "help ascertain the qualifications of all professors and teachers, including their ability, education, character and loyalty to the United States and its form of government and their freedom from atheistic, communistic, or any anti-religious or unamerican taints or infirmities."[10]

The board's actions must also be understood with reference to the line of defense being thrown up across the country by academic institutions against outsiders' efforts to purge them of alleged subversives. According to the chronology suggested in a recent study, Mundel's dismissal came in the trough between two waves of attacks on alleged subversion in the nation's colleges and universities. The first wave was an attack on faculty who were Communist party members. By 1951 the student Left had largely vanished and overtly Communist professors had been purged or silenced. In 1949 the California board of regents fired a Berkeley physics professor after he refused to answer HUAC questions. In a more celebrated case that same year, three tenured University of Washington professors were dismissed and apparently blacklisted by the university after a finding by a state legislative committee that they were Communist party members. A national media debate among academic leaders followed. The dismissed professors had been afforded the hearings prescribed under AAUP guidelines, but they had been fired even though membership in the Communist party was not illegal. Those who upheld the firings, as George Hand would later do, argued that Communists disqualified themselves as faculty members by surrendering their intellectual freedom to Communist party thought-control and by engaging in the international Communist conspiracy. They argued pragmatically that to save academic freedom for the majority from the assaults of outside forces (such as those Mundel would confront) higher education must police its own ranks.[11]

In 1951 the HUAC was too busy with other investigations to look at academe. But academic bodies were already feeling well-publicized pressure from a variety of sources, including state legislatures. One imagines that the West Virginia board of education wished to keep such pressures to a minimum, by nipping in the bud any possible embarrassment over the loyalty-security issue.

Under oath in 1952, board members repeatedly denied that the "security risk" charge was involved in Mundel's firing. However, given the concerns of the moment, even to question her suitability was implicitly to raise the issue of her loyalty. Injustice to workers at the highest level of government justified and encouraged injustice at the state and local levels. By attacking Mundel, the board responded to the nationwide loyalty mania and found a new and useful tool to define and extend its authority over college presidents.

After the "security risk" exchange between Loudin and Hand, the discussion moved swiftly to Mundel's teaching performance. Hand reported no criticism of Mundel's teaching, but incautiously volunteered that he did not like her personally and even elaborated that she had at times used poor judgment. He defended his decision to hire her for another year as a way to find out whether her judgment was so poor as to justify her dismissal.

Thus, Hand sent an ambiguous signal to the board. Did he really want to keep Mundel another year or was he asking the board to assume the responsibility for her removal? The issue remained unresolved as the meeting moved to the next item of business.[12]

When they ran into each other that evening in the lobby of Charleston's

Daniel Boone Hotel, Hand learned from Loudin that she would not vote for the school's budget request if Luella Mundel's name was on it. The next morning through a third party Hand asked the board's permission to formally investigate the Mundel issue. A short time later board secretary H. K. Baer conveyed to Hand the board's permission to conduct an inquiry. In what later proved to be a costly misunderstanding, the president assumed he had carte blanche to investigate, while Baer, as he later testified, believed he had told Hand that because the board did not want a "witch hunt" there should be no investigation of the "security risk" issue. In July 1952 Baer testified that he had told Hand: "George, in the investigation of Dr. Mundel you are not in any way to consider or to give thought to the subject of Communism nor to give attention to subversive activities. George, you leave that out."[13]

If this is an accurate recounting of what he said, it suggests a colossal miscommunication. Baer, doing the board's bidding, thought he was telling Hand not to raise the Communist issue. Hand, quite understandably, thought Baer was telling him not to try to investigate Mundel's alleged subversive ties himself, but to take the matter to the FBI!

So ended the board's consideration of Luella Mundel at its May meeting. The minutes maintain a discreet but eloquent silence about her. In effect they declare her a nonperson. The only reference to the dispute is at position 17 on the approved salary list. Where Mundel's name should be there is only a blank.[14]

Hand and Loudin and the rest of the board were now entangled in a complicated struggle for prestige and power. Loudin believed that the president was leading the college astray and surely remembered the embarrassing gym incident. Hand openly challenged her before her board colleagues, even after she told him privately on the evening of May 7 that Mundel had to go. For his part, Hand opposed what he thought was Loudin's unsound educational philosophy, her interference in the affairs of the college, and her penchant for dealing with his staff behind his back. He believed she had fallen under the sway of the narrow conservative interests of the town professional-mercantile establishment and a few faculty members hostile to him. He knew that Loudin had the upper hand with the board. Her eruption over Mundel had caught other board members off guard, but his own spirited response and refusal to yield to her aroused in them feelings of group solidarity against Hand and protective gentlemanly chivalry toward Loudin. And Luella Mundel was caught squarely in the middle.[15]

Upon his return to Fairmont, Dr. Hand reports, he gave Mundel a "full account of the preceding events and advised her to do nothing personally" pending his investigation and report. Hand's news must have stunned Mundel, but she assented to an investigation and to an FBI inquiry to clear her name. It must have also stunned Loudin, who had assumed that the matter would be handled without Mundel's learning the details of what had been said at the board meeting.

As Mundel's sense of outrage grew, Loudin's charge took on ever more sinister meaning. In a few weeks the malignant phrase "security risk" metastasized in Mundel's (and Jones's) retelling into the assertion that Loudin had told the board: "That woman is not fit to be on a college faculty. She is a menace to national security."[16]

On May 10, Hand went directly from lunch at Rotary to the FBI suite in the post office to initiate a security check of Dr. Mundel. It was only a gesture. Hand claims the agent on duty told him that there would be an investigation and that he would receive a report on Mundel. However, he soon learned that the FBI reported only to the Justice Department and that the agent could tell him nothing about the disposition of the matter.[17]

The next day at 11:30 A.M. an agitated Thelma Loudin appeared at Hand's campus office. It was being said that Hand had told Mundel that Loudin had called her a Communist. She denied to Hand that she had made any such statement or that the board would even think of such a thing. Dr. Mundel, she insisted, must be told the truth at once.

What happened next is in dispute. Hand says that Loudin asked him to pass her denial on to Mundel. Loudin later testified that she asked to speak to Dr. Mundel but was told by Hand that Mundel was in class and unavailable. Whatever the truth, the two women did not meet. Later Hand called Mundel to his office. He told her of his visit to the FBI and received her assurance that she was not a Communist. He then conveyed Loudin's message, advising Mundel to let pass the "poor security risk" issue in her own best interest because the board members wanted to put it behind them. But, her reputation and career in jeopardy, she could not forget it.[18]

In the next two months, singly and in groups, various members of the faculty called upon Loudin in behalf of Dr. Mundel. Loudin remained adamant, so Hand proceeded with his investigation. He had to begin from scratch. He had not previously checked up on her teaching because it was "not polite," and his only knowledge of her classroom performance came from the "usual catty remarks" that reached him through the faculty grapevine. But he learned what he could and assembled a 2,200-word report, which he presented to the board at its July 9–10 meeting and later offered in evidence at Mundel's trial and included in his 1952 "Report" to the AAUP and AACTE.[19]

In his probe of Mundel's performance, Hand summarized interviews with eighteen students and ten college employees. Students were asked "if they liked Dr. Mundel as a teacher," to which the nine art majors replied unanimously that they did. Nine nonmajors liked her class by a margin of five to three with one abstention. But five of eight administrators and teachers reported that they had heard criticism of Mundel as a teacher. In a short paragraph headed "Dr. Mundel as a person," Hand related that all art majors liked her except one who "felt he was not qualified to say." Of nine nonmajors five liked her. The seven college staff members who ventured opinions "said they had heard some criticism" of her as a person. To this damning with faint praise Hand added a student evaluation carried out by Mundel herself which showed that eleven students rated the class "very good", thirteen "satisfactory," and five "unsatisfactory."[20]

The report seems an honest effort to evaluate Mundel and it offered no grounds for her dismissal. At the same time it was not particularly helpful in supporting her retention. Evaluation of teaching performance has always been a devilishly complicated and emotionally charged issue. To be believed, surveys must protect the anonymity of respondents. They must ask useful and unbiased questions. The Hand survey is seriously flawed by either criterion. The number of persons interviewed and the manner of their interrogation compromised the anonymity of the respondents and the questions may have been unfairly nuanced and weighted. To what standard was Mundel being compared? What valid conclusions could one draw from the fact that some students "liked" her and some did not? What did "like" mean? Could one really credit the statements of art majors who may have feared to speak their feelings in the presence of so intimidating a figure as the college president? How should one weigh the opinions of the seven faculty members who said they had heard criticism of Mundel against the silence of the rest who did not? Criticism of what? Her paintings? Her vocabulary? Her lectures? Her dress? Her ideas? Her demeanor toward other faculty members in the cafeteria? At best the report was superficial and failed to address directly some of the questions raised at the May board meeting.

The portion of the report relating directly to Dr. Mundel comprised only about 10 percent of the document. Most of the rest was a lengthy indictment of the actions of Fridtjof Schroder and Dr. Robert Carroll. Hand had gathered information from thirteen members of the college faculty who had "independently and individually" volunteered to tell what they knew. Part of what they knew the board would soon know and the reader already knows: before the May 7 board meeting Schroder had sent a denunciatory set of notes via Dr. Carroll to Loudin attacking Dr. Mundel's competence. The alliance between artist Schroder and physicist Carroll was, Hand charged, based on Carroll's desire to succeed him as college president and on Schroder's wish to get rid of Mundel and Hand. Since Carroll wanted to become president and Schroder wished to head the art department, Hand surmised that in attacking Mundel the dissidents were only using her to get at him. To show the board that the plotters did not speak for the college community, Hand had put two questions to the entire faculty. When he asked "Is George Hand fit to be a college president?" forty-nine instructors replied "yes," none "no," and two abstained. The follow-up "Should George Hand continue as president of Fairmont State College?" brought forty-seven yeas, one nay, and three not voting.[21]

The president concluded the written report with a scheme to end the dispute. The board, he recommended, should agree to retain Mundel for another year. Despite some reservations about her, Hand lacked enough adverse evidence to warrant her dismissal. Schroder, proposed Hand, should be fired, because of his passionate hostility to Mundel and his disruptive behavior. Carroll could remain because this was his "first offense" and because he was an original thinker.[22]

Hand's proposal had a nice balance and symmetry. It kept the two Ph.D. department heads who symbolized the poles of the pro- and anti-Hand axis while it eliminated the disgruntled Schroder. That the art teacher deserved tenure under the 1940 AAUP guidelines because of his four years' continuous employment at Fairmont State College gave the president no pause. By keeping Dr. Carroll, who was connected by marriage to a prominent local family, Hand must have hoped to avoid further alienating the Fairmont elite. But it really did not matter. The board ignored the report.

After Hand finished his presentation, board members fired questions at him. What exactly was Mundel's "poor judgment" that Hand had mentioned in May? The president gave them three examples: her use of "crude language in improper places"; the rumor that she admitted to being an atheist; and her remark at a meeting that she was a socialist. The mention of atheism drew the most comments from the board. According to Hand, Loudin said an atheist should not be permitted on a college faculty and one other board member agreed.[23]

Next Loudin read aloud the Schroder notes critical of Mundel, Hand, and Mundel's predecessor, Freed. Members of the board of education later testified that the Schroder letter did not influence their decision about Dr. Mundel's job. It is difficult to see how this could be, but the board maintained that it was Hand's testimony that tipped the scales. Loudin abstained from the final vote, but it is obvious that her colleagues' awareness of her strong convictions in this affair, which was after all her area of special responsibility, carried much weight. Whatever the concatenation of factors, for the first time since Hand became president in 1945 the board ignored his personnel recommendations. It rehired Schroder and Carroll and reaffirmed its decision not to rehire Luella Mundel.[24]

At 4:00 P.M. on July 10, Dr. Hand told Dr. Mundel in Jones's presence that the board had fired her and showed them a copy of the report he had made to the board urging her retention. He recollected informing them "that I had done my duty as executive officer of Fairmont State College, that I could do no more, and that Dr. Mundel would do herself harm if she fought for redress even though she might do some good for higher education."[25]

What did Hand mean by this? Did he intend that she should accept the board's decision and move on? Did Hand, resentful of the board's actions, seek to encourage her to fight for higher education in order to gain revenge against Loudin? And why did he let Mundel and Jones see his report to the board? Was it to give them ammunition to battle Loudin and the board? Was it to prove to them that he had really tried to save Mundel's job? While hardly flattering to Mundel, it did show that Hand had supported her retention and that he had found no justifiable cause to do otherwise: no immorality, incompetency, cruelty, insubordination, or willful neglect of duty—grounds for the dismissal of public employees according to the *West Virginia Code*.

Having notified Mundel, Hand washed his hands of the matter by refusing Jones's urgent request for a general faculty meeting, declining to appear before the local AAUP, and rejecting a public statement drafted by Jones supporting Mundel's position. Then he went on vacation for a full month, leaving the college and the community to toss in the wake of the board's action.[26]

In the three days that passed before the board's public announcement of its decision, local rumor mills ground out scenarios about Mundel's status. At the college, faculty members debated what to do.

On July 12 a hastily convened meeting of the college AAUP chapter that was thrown open to the whole faculty drew thirty of the forty-six summer instructors. However, Mundel's friends were unable to win passage of the two petitions offered on her behalf. At a time when normally insecure and vulnerable teachers were made more so by the public war against subversive influences, most Fairmont faculty members feared for their jobs. Therefore they used the excuse of Mundel's eccentricity and unpopularity to sidestep the constitutional and academic freedom issues raised by her dismissal. The potential for guilt by association was not lost on them. Some townsfolk were calling Mundel a proven Communist and her little band of friends a Communist cell, probably headed by her "boyfriend" Jones. The chilling effect of the rumors was apparent when the next week's AAUP meeting drew only about a dozen brave souls.

It should be made clear that Fairmont State faculty members deserve no special condemnation for their failure to rally behind Mundel. Their reaction was typical of faculties across the country during the McCarthy era.[27]

Friday the thirteenth of July proved unlucky for Mundel; on that day the board formally announced its decision. That afternoon the *West Virginian* ran the story, highlighting board spokesman H. K. Baer's declaration that Mundel had been let go "for the good of the college." The next day, Saturday, July 14, Mundel fired off letters to board president Garland Dunn and ex-officio board member state school superintendent W. W. Trent. To Dunn she protested that she had been "dismissed contrary to the recommendations of Dr. Hand" and asked to be told of the charges against her and be given a chance to answer them before the board.[28]

That same day, Mundel's ally, psychologist Dr. Spaulding Rogers went to Loudin's home in the "spirit of friendship," his wife and two toddlers in tow. He hoped to help Loudin to have a change of heart. But the interview went badly. Loudin interrogated Rogers to find out the names of faculty members who were opposing the board and, according to Rogers, suggested that dissidents should subside or move on. The subject of religion came up and Loudin allowed that she was a "theist," but would later deny Rogers's assertion that she had said that no atheist should teach at the college. The interview ended on a suitably petty and acrimonious note, when Loudin, fearing that Rogers would publicly "interpret" her remarks, confiscated the notes he had taken.[29]

Even before the board's decision, historian H. Norman Taylor, chapter president of the American Association of University Professors, contacted the organization's Washington headquarters. The AAUP seemed a logical source for help because of its familiarity with the academic world and long advocacy of academic freedom, tenure, and legal due process for college teachers. In the more flagrant cases it might also investigate and publicly censure violators. The leadership of the local chapter was firmly in Mundel's corner. She had recently joined, and Jones was chapter vice president.

However, the AAUP was a weak reed upon which to lean for vindication, retribution, or a quick fix. Since its founding in 1915 by a group of progressive luminaries of academe including John Dewey, the organization had labored for uniform standards and dignity in academic employment through the persuasion and education of trustees, regents, and boards of higher education. In the words of Richard Hofstadter and Robert Metzger, the AAUP "neither would be nor could be a police department for ferreting out, a grand jury for sifting, or a trial court for testing all reports of academic injustice." It did not attempt frontal attacks on administrators, but sought to change underlying conditions "rather than to avenge the crimes which arose from them." The authors added, in an understatement, that the AAUP's support for high principle often aroused unrealistic expectations on the part of faculty members.

Surely this was the case with Mundel. For the admirable AAUP statement on academic freedom and tenure dating from 1925 and amended in 1940 said nothing that specifically applied to probationary faculty members. And the general principles of formal tenure and academic freedom had yet to reach the inner chambers of the West Virginia state board of education.[30]

Even if such principles had been adhered to, they would have offered Mundel only partial support. The AAUP statement advocated "full freedom in research and in the publication of the results, subject to adequate performance of other academic duties." Free to discuss his subject in the classroom so long as he was "careful not to introduce into his teaching controversial matter which has no relation to his subject," outside the classroom a teacher must keep his roles as citizen, member of a learned profession, and representative of his institution. "When he speaks as a citizen he should be free from institutional censorship or discipline, but his special position in the community imposes special obligations. . . . Hence he should at all times be accurate, should exercise appropriate restraint, should show respect for the opinions of others, [and] should make every effort to indicate that he is not an institutional spokesman."[31] The AAUP had agreed in 1940 that if "the administration of a college . . . feels that . . . the extra-mural utterances of the teacher have been such as to raise grave doubts concerning his fitness for his position," it might consider charges to terminate the teacher.[32]

Although the board could thus make a case that Mundel's public utterances made her unfit for her job, to do so would be risky. AAUP guidelines clearly required that tenured employees should be informed in writing of the grounds for dismissal and be granted a hearing with an advisor present of which a full stenographic record was to be made. Even if dismissed, the teacher should receive a year's salary from the date of the termination notice.[33] On balance, Mundel's best line of defense was to claim that procedural rights should extend to probationary instructors and to attack the board for its failure to honor those rights.

On July 17, the national AAUP entered the Fairmont controversy when Secretary Ralph E. Himstead wired the West Virginia board of education urging it to clarify the facts of the case and to grant Dr. Mundel a hearing. To do otherwise, Himstead warned, would not accord "with good academic practice generally observed in *accredited* institutions" (italics added).[34]

But the AAUP wire changed no minds in Charleston. On July 19 Board President Dunn answered Mundel, stressing the technically correct but ethically evasive point that "you were not dismissed ... you were merely not reemployed." The board, he continued, did not customarily prefer charges in such cases or grant hearings to probationary employees. Leaving the door ever so slightly ajar to future compromise, he promised to place Mundel's request for a hearing before the board in September.[35]

Superintendent W. W. Trent's answer to Mundel and the AAUP took a hard line. He rejected the contention that the board was required to accept Hand's recommendation that Mundel be reemployed. A college president, he argued, was legally in the same relationship to the board as the governor was to the state senate. Like the former, a president could make personnel proposals, but like the latter, the board could reject them. The board's decision was final. Its deliberations were private and privileged. If it chose to reveal its reasons for not retaining Mundel it would do so through its public minutes. Because she did not have tenure, Mundel had no legal right to a hearing, although the board could, at its pleasure, grant one. However, Trent made it clear that he considered (or at least wished) the matter closed and the request for a hearing groundless. Mundel had, he claimed, received effective notice of nonretention. The board's refusal to accept her reemployment in May was notice that she should look for another job. Her dismissal had not become final until the July board meeting, effectively giving her more than sixty days' notice. During those two months Mundel failed to present her case to the board or look for another job. She should have. Even had she misunderstood the true nature of her probationary status, the responsibility for her ignorance lay not with the board but with the college president.

If one assumes that Mundel's status was the same as a public school teacher, Trent was on solid ground. West Virginia law established a three-year probationary period and then a continuing contract (tenure) between teachers and "their boards of education." Having served less than three years, Mundel had no protection. But did public school employees' tenure apply to college teachers? One cannot tell from reading the state school laws then in force. And if tenure did apply to college instructors, why had the board allowed Hand to fire Medora Mason in 1947?[36]

To reinforce the board's position Trent appealed to legal precedent—

Hartigan v. *West Virginia Board of Regents.* This was a 1901 case sufficiently well known nationally to be cited by Tulane sociologist Logan Wilson in his 1941 study of the professoriate as the basis for understanding the legal rights of teachers.

The case arose when a West Virginia University anatomy professor with thirteen years seniority was fired by a divided and politicized board of regents without formal charges or notice at a meeting held 125 miles from its accustomed location, the university seat. The majority of the court upheld Dr. Hartigan's firing in such a way as to support nearly absolute power over state institutions by appointive superintending bodies. It held that teachers and university professors were not holders of public office and could not claim due-process protection from arbitrary actions. A professor was "but a mere employee of the Board of Regents in legal point of view, and cannot as a matter of right" demand a hearing or the right of defense. The professor "simply accepts an offer of the Regents for compensation for no fixed term" which the regents may end at their pleasure. Regardless of teachers' ability and competence, they just might not fit in. Sufficient cause to dismiss a teacher might be "mere temperament or manner of intercourse with students, [or] there might be disharmony between . . . [teacher and students] hurtful to the institution." The legislature, the court contended, never intended to allow disgruntled public employees to clog court dockets with actions to save their jobs. Personnel decisions of the board of regents, and presumably those of the board of education, were beyond court jurisdiction.[37]

Even a half century later the Hartigan case paralleled federal court doctrine by its support of the principle that public employment was a limited privilege. But it was a questionable precedent. The half-century-old case took no account of changing realities in employer-employee relations or the growth of acceptance of academic freedom. And even in 1901 the decision had sparked controversy.

One of the supreme court of appeals judges, Marmaduke H. Dent, left a vitriolic dissent of almost thirty pages piled high with citations, starting with *Dartmouth* v. *Woodward* in 1819. In that famous case Daniel Webster argued that a professor's job or "college living" was a "freehold," the "most sacred" form of private property. Scholars were "the most deserving class of men . . . who have consented to forego the advantages of public and professional employments, and to devote themselves to science and to literature and the instruction of youth in the quiet retreats of academic life." Building on that, Dent found that teachers and professors were "quasi-public officials" with the same protections during good behavior as other public officials. As long as teachers performed competently and faithfully they could keep their jobs. Should they be dismissed, the state must furnish them with written charges and grant hearings to answer them.[38]

In coming months the board implicitly used the reasoning of the Hartigan case to justify its action, contending that Mundel was, pure and simple, an employee whose tenure was subject to the pleasure of the board. She could not claim the protections of a public official. But, pressed to explain, the board tried to have it both ways. It insinuated that she was incompetent and disloyal, grounds enough to fire her even under Daniel Webster's interpretation of a teacher's rights.

From July to September the board stood fast and tried to isolate Mundel from sources of support. With its greater financial and institutional resources it hoped to outlast her and force her to give up. It was a proven technique. But Mundel refused to quit. Replying to Dunn on July 21 she admitted she lacked legal expertise to argue the merits of the board's action. But she demanded that the board hear her case for the good of all concerned—"for the sake of rapprochement between the administrative officials, the faculty, and the students . . . , on the one hand, and the state board of education on the other." She claimed her plight had aroused "trepidation" on the campus. To deny her due process now would "seem un[-]American and sinister to most people." This was especially true because a "colleague's spiteful act of jealousy and the machinations of special interest groups" had caused her termination.

In a thinly veiled threat she warned the board that public opinion could have far-reaching reactions and good teachers might refuse employment in West Virginia. "Political repercussions" might ensue. "Acts of political injustice do not 'blow over.' "[39] The letter was more than bravado. She had a strategy—to keep the pot boiling and to seek help from outside the West Virginia public education hierarchy.

In late July Mundel and her friends broadened their appeal for national support. Besides the AAUP, they wrote to the American Civil Liberties Union, the West Virginia Education Association, and the American Association of Colleges of Teacher Education (AACTE). All seemed interested except the WVEA.[40]

Legal spadework undertaken by Mundel's allies Jones, Rogers, and sociologist Eric Barnitz showed she would need all the outside help she could get. Laws that protected some public school employees from arbitrary dismissal did not cover state college professors. Worse, in its published minutes in 1947, the board was on record as having "urged" state college presidents to "give careful consideration to . . . the three year (3) probationary period" and recommended the termination of "unsatisfactory employees" before the end of the probationary period. In other words,

Superintendent Trent could back his assertion that Mundel should have understood her employment situation. In addition, although Mundel and her friends may not have known it, the 1951 *Annual Report* of the WVEA had noted without distinguishing between public school and college teachers the establishment of the probationary period and added that in 1949 copies of it had been sent to "all members of the profession and all boards of education."[41]

Developments in the local newspapers only deepened Dr. Mundel's sense of melancholy isolation. Petty feuds, provincialism, party politics, conservative ideology, and Protestant fundamentalism soon turned the afternoon *West Virginian* against her. Early in the controversy Jones sent a letter to the paper's reporter and columnist Lawrence Boggs. On July 29 Boggs published it along with an invitation to Jones and Mundel to explain the trouble at the college. On August 1 he published their responses on page 1 in his "Ticks and Tocks" column with the sarcastic comment, "No other persons on the campus appear interested enough to write." Boggs wrote that "among the rumors going around is one that Dr. Mundel has openly stated that she is an atheist. I requested Dr. Mundel to confirm or deny this"; he then added piously that he thought no atheist should "have a part in the education of the youth of this nation."[42]

Mundel's reply, August 2, was swift, eloquent, and tactically foolish. Boggs again put it on page 1. She invoked the Supreme Court's affirmation of individual rights to privacy of belief and its prohibition of forced religious orthodoxy. She had never, she said, espoused political or religious views in classes or public forums. She had taught successfully in Presbyterian and Catholic schools where her religious views had been respected as private and inviolate. Had she publicly stated that she was an atheist? Absolutely not. Was she a covert atheist? No, not if that term meant one who held to a rigid denial of the existence of God. Rather, she wrote, "I hope I can be counted as an educated person; that is, one who withholds judgement in the absence of evidence."[43]

Such an articulate statement of intellectually fashionable agnosticism would have earned polite applause in more cosmopolitan circles, but Fairmont, if not exactly the buckle, was surely a part of the Bible Belt. Here anything less than a ringing if ritualistic affirmation of biblical inerrancy and the divinity of Jesus by a public figure was impolitic. Mundel's public stand must have hardened many hearts against her in Fairmont and caused others to grow faint at the prospect of supporting her. Whimsically, Boggs published her letter under the headline "Dr. Mundel Does Literary Rhumba" and then attacked it line by line, dismissing her arguments as "dousey-maroney," a term appropriated from Rosey Rosewell, radio voice of the Pittsburgh Pirates.

The next day Mundel's final letter to the *West Virginian* appeared in print. A foolish ad hominem attack addressed to Boggs, it reads in full:

> I am sure that your brilliant and riotous article August 2, has convinced all the people of Fairmont of the importance of being righteous Christians like their editor, L. G. Boggs.
>
> Sincerely,
> Luella Raab Mundel[44]

Distraught by the turn of events, Mundel appealed privately to the AAUP. Typically concise but uncharacteristically emotional, she wrote that she feared a witch hunt stirred up by the newspaper and was afraid to leave her apartment.[45]

Nothing suggests that Mundel was in physical danger because of her letters, but her public stance on religion devastated her cause locally, particularly among conservative evangelical and fundamentalist Protestants. The religious Right was poised for resurgence after decades of defeat and derision. Its rigid, essentially nineteenth-century commitment to dogmas such as biblical inerrancy, spiritualism, supernaturalism, and refusal to compromise with the dominant modernist and secular scientific worldview had destroyed its influence in the nation's universities and severely undercut its role in the mainline Protestant denominations. Faced with such rejection many prominent leaders of the Protestant Right had separated from the mainstream churches to build their own versions of the true church, but many more fundamentalists and evangelicals had remained to carry on the fight to restore God's kingdom, especially in the Baptist, Presbyterian, Methodist, and numerous smaller churches. After World War II many Americans reared as fundamentalists had become more affluent, better educated, and therefore more politically powerful. Apparently Mundel had run afoul of such a group.[46]

George Marsden explains in an illuminating study that post–World War II fundamentalism or evangelicalism was a complicated, confusing, and often confused movement. But it had a natural affinity for conservative politics, the Republican party, and a broad interdenominational upper-lower and lower-middle-class white Protestant constituency. Anticommunism was not the primary aim of this group. Its goal was to create a Bible-based civilization and to save America from modernism and secularism in all of their guises—be it the higher criticism, evolution, communism, or the false religion of Roman Catholicism. For many of its adherents seemingly trivial practices such as smoking, drinking, and "permissive" sexual mores probably assumed more cosmic significance than advocacy of the workers' utopia, but the two categories of evil were easily enough connected. And, Marsden suggests, the anticommunist link joined the religious Right to other conservative groups with different agendas, with American folk piety as the bridge to carry it toward the center of American culture.[47]

In this context then the fact that Loudin (although a Baptist), Carroll, Legion official L. O. Bickel, botany instructor Moore Roberts, and journalism teacher C. R. House, Jr., were all enemies of Hand and Mundel and were all affiliated with the same Methodist church is of more than passing interest. That church, Central Methodist, had been until 1939 Fairmont's Southern Methodist Church. The historic healing of the nearly century-old Methodist schism was permanent but not without friction. Since Stanley High's 1950 *Reader's Digest* article attacking the church-affiliated Federation of Social Action as "Methodism's Pink Fringe," a major internal battle had raged between those espousing liberalism, ecumenism, and centralized church administration against conservatives or fundamentalists who generally favored a decentralized church structure and traditional social and ethical values. In 1951 and 1952 the anticommunist conservatives were gaining greater influence, in part from a gusher of Texas oil money but mostly through the activism of conservative women church members. In conformity to the fundamentalist pattern noted above, such conservatives tended to link communism with a range of perversities from progressive education to violations of the rigid moral code that banned smoking by ministers. At the spring 1952 General Conference at San Francisco, the Methodists altered their official social creed from belief in "subordination of the profit motive to the ... cooperative spirit" to affirmation of the "principles of the acquisition of property ... the right to private ownership." Mundel could have alienated elements of no Protestant denomination more internally polarized about social and political deviation from traditional Americanism.[48]

· The newspaper fiasco presented Mundel with a dilemma. Her opponents clearly dominated the local newspapers and public opinion. Fairmont area liberals were ominously silent. The Fairmont establishment was set against her. To solicit outside help would surely inflame local xenophobia and undercut whatever moderate sentiment remained. But without such support she would have to surrender. If she intended to fight, Mundel really had no choice. She must seek the influence and support of the national media and of professional and civil rights organizations. The first step, a written appeal to state governor Okey Patteson, fell flat. The chief executive declared himself unequivocally uninvolved. "I am indeed sorry," he wrote, "but I have no jurisdiction whatsoever over the State Board of Education."[49]

In mid-August Mundel and Jones took her case to the state and national newspapers by sending a detailed narrative of events to Paul Allen, state correspondent for the Associated Press. Allen put the story on the AP wire with a Mundel slant. He blamed her troubles on a jealous colleague and played up the secret charges that she was a Communist and an atheist, ignoring the issue of her teaching competence. It made the "security risk" question central. This was understandable at a time when college professors lived in fear of being labeled Red.[50]

A few days later Loudin answered the AP story in an interview given to the *West Virginian.* Denying responsibility for the firing, she blamed Dr. Mundel's downfall on Hand's answers to the board's questions. Evidently to buttress her case, she gave Boggs Schroder's written complaints about Mundel, which he published without identifying their author.[51] By releasing the letter Loudin reemphasized her contention that teaching competence was the real issue. At the same time she handed Mundel apparent proof that there had been a plot against her.

Mundel's side fired the next shots in the rapidly escalating exchange of broadsides. On August 20, Himstead of the AAUP again wrote to the board asking for a hearing for Mundel, which, he noted, the AAUP's 1940 academic freedom and tenure statement mandated. This was a minimum requirement for accreditation by the American Association of Colleges of Teacher Education, to which the college belonged. On August 24 three instructors resigned. The most illustrious was Spaulding Rogers, who exited with a flourish, papering the in-baskets of journalists and politicians with copies of a letter that praised Hand, denounced the "Carroll-Schroder-Lowdin [*sic*] conspiracy," and lamented the board's "discouraging failure to grasp the principles of professional ethics." Some believed that the fact that Rogers had already obtained a better job and would have left the college with or without Mundel's firing dimmed the luster of his gesture. Nevertheless, the publicity attendant upon the resignation of Rogers and the others angered Loudin sufficiently to cause her to cancel a scheduled meeting with Hand and his staff, complaining that the "mass resignations" had been calculated for her embarrassment.[52]

Schroder launched a counterattack in a long letter to AAUP General Secretary Himstead on August 20. He admitted authorship of the published complaints against Mundel. He explained that he had signed the original letter, which had been hurriedly composed before the May board meeting, and which had not been meant for publication. He stipulated that he never impugned Mundel's loyalty, only her competence.

And he did so only as a last resort to save his endangered job, worried that Hand would dismiss him simply by omitting his name from the salary list. He had heard before the May board meeting that Hand had decided to rehire both him and Mundel, but the president had never told him so directly. The letter to Loudin was intended to be job insurance.[53]

Schroder added that Mundel had once told him that she was a poor teacher, unprepared to teach art. She had come to Fairmont desperately in need of a job. Her statement in a faculty meeting "I guess that makes me a socialist" was occasioned by her fear that she would get less pay if she were judged on her teaching ability instead of her doctorate. She was not, Schroder claimed, underestimating her teaching ability. He vowed that he had never spoken against Mundel in his classes. He asserted to AAUP officials that the college chapter did not speak for the majority of the faculty. It was controlled by a childish minority led by Spaulding Rogers, who, Schroder charged, had burst into his classroom and shouted at him in front of his students after Mundel's firing.[54]

On August 30, Schroder visited AAUP headquarters in Washington to present his side of the controversy. His strongest point during his seventy-five-minute meeting with AAUP official George Pope Shannon was to detail Hand's arbitrary personnel decisions and past disinclinations to honor tenure. After all, Hand had been about to let him go despite four years' experience.[55] Indulging a distaste for "pseudo-liberals" at the college, Schroder predicted, accurately as it turned out, that the prime example of that mentality, Hand, would not last another year at Fairmont State. He defended his breach of the academic chain of command by claiming that Hand's policies left him no choice but to go directly to Loudin. The board, he believed, had acted correctly in the Mundel affair, except that it should have acted sooner against Hand.[56]

Shannon listened, then told Schroder that even if Mundel were incompetent, she deserved a hearing to answer secret charges made against her. Furthermore, the board should not have meddled in Hand's management of routine college business.[57] But Schroder left Shannon favorably impressed with his sincerity and some of his arguments. The AAUP would continue to support Mundel but with perceptibly less enthusiasm. More and more it fixed blame for the crisis on George Hand.

Back in Fairmont, four days before the pivotal September state board of education meeting, George Hand met with Loudin at her home in the presence of a local clergyman. Hand's account of the meeting is the most complete available and was partly verified later by the clergyman. As Hand recounted it, Loudin did most of the talking. She told him that a possible AAUP sanction against the college was a minor matter. More serious, she said, was that Hand had betrayed the confidentiality of board meetings when he divulged details of the discussion to Mundel. Loudin explained that her reference to Mundel as a "security risk" meant that the art department head was undesirable as a long-term faculty member. Hand had wondered what was really bothering Loudin and she told him. She believed that academic freedom should be more limited at a state college than at a university, that maintaining public faith in the board required that employees should not criticize or oppose the board's actions—in short, that Hand should get on the team. He should "reprimand" college employees who were supporting Mundel and in the future hire more West Virginians. The meeting adjourned inconclusively after Loudin rejected Hand's proposal for a hearing for Mundel. Now all hinged on the September board meeting.[58]

In a September 5 meeting at Charleston, the board refused Mundel a hearing or a statement of charges. But its minutes, the only public record of its deliberations, do contain a sort of statement of charges against her and a rationale for the board's action. First, the minutes assert that Mundel was a probationary employee whose performance did not live up to principles "widely recognized in educational circles." As a teacher she had been found wanting when the board considered "various factors" —among them the "allegation, reported . . . by President George H. Hand, that Dr. Mundel had on occasion declared herself an atheist." Board members rejected Hand's recommendation to reemploy her because they doubted her "satisfactory adaptability to the various demands of the position and the soundness of her judgement in her public expressions." Unanimously (two members were absent) they reaffirmed Mundel's dismissal in "the best interest of Fairmont College."[59]

One wonders if the board realized the implications of its statement. Pressed for a public explanation of its action, it said too much when it acknowledged that whatever Mundel's faults might be as an instructor, they had little to do with her firing. Her fault lay in not being sufficiently adaptable to the position—a vague and imprecise charge at best—which presumably meant that she "did not fit in" at the college. Her "incompetence" had nothing to do with the way she handled classes but with what the board deemed poor judgment "in her public expressions." Of course this referred to her remarks at the Legion antisubversive rally and her general outspokenness. The board did not seem to care whether she was or was not an atheist, as long as she did not publicly express her convictions. Neither did it seem interested in the truth or falsehood of the allegations against her. It was enough that they became public and controversial. Even though the evidence against her was hearsay, the embarrassment it had caused the college and the board was good and sufficient cause to let her go. Not one board member had ever spoken with her. Not one knew her, not even Loudin. By normal standards of fairness, their investigation was shoddy and incomplete and their action arbitrary and capricious.

Why did the board insist on making an issue of Luella Mundel? Other faculty members at Fairmont State had criticized and had even argued with the Legion's anticommunist traveling circus. More than a few faculty members throughout the state system were agnostics or atheists. And, as in any educational system, a number must have been certifiably incompetent. It is obvious that the board wanted to make an example of Mundel.[60]

We have no record of the board's closed-door deliberations and board members were understandably tight-lipped, even much later on the witness stand. Dr. Hand kept notes on his part in the board meeting on September 5 which, allowing for his biases, offer interesting clues. The questions put to Hand by board members Garland Dunn, Thelma Loudin, Raymond Brewster, and Lawrence R. Lynch hint at their concern.

First, they worried about control—that Hand had lost control of the college and they of him. Why, they asked, had he not quashed the publicity surrounding the Mundel issue? Why had he allowed the "atheist debate" to reach the press? Why had he told Mundel (and even Jones) about what happened at the board meetings in May and July? Did he plan to bail out by seeking the presidency of Rutgers? Lafayette? Rollins? What of rumors that two of his faculty members were living together? Why had he not fired the faculty member who spent a night in jail? Had he checked Mundel's references? Had he reprimanded Harold Jones for his part in the Mundel affair? Above all, why had Hand not followed the board's lead? Was he ignorant of the probationary policy? Did he not know of the board's legal right to fire Mundel? Did he know that support for the college in the Fairmont business establishment was at a low ebb? At one point in the questioning when Hand replied to board member Brewster's criticism of his administration by saying he was sure that "educators" would not agree, Brewster exploded: "Educators! Educators!"[61]

In their questions the board members wrestled to discover the implications of their own educational policies. Evidently they did not understand what George Hand was trying to accomplish at Fairmont State or what its practical results might be. They continued to view the college as a normal school, an intermediate step between public school and the university whose limited mission was to turn out rough-hewn country schoolteachers and to prepare the sons (and, because it was cheap and near home, particularly the daughters) of the local area for a modest climb up the social ladder.

The faculty assembled by Hand caused the board to react as if alien life forms had invaded the "college in the clouds" to inhabit the bodies and steal the souls of the young. Their chagrin was poignantly clear when Loudin asked Hand why instead of Mundel he had not hired a local public school art supervisor who understood the problems of the school and the area.[62] Led emotionally by Loudin, the board members chose to make a public stand on their prerogatives whatever the cost. They had to get rid of Mundel to regain control of the Fairmont State College and its president.

The board's decision must have disappointed Luella Mundel, but it could not have surprised her. She was left jobless. Her reputation and character were besmirched by the board's action. A long shadow darkened her professional future. It must have seemed ironic that the shadow had been cast because she had tried to bring light to the community. She had acted as scholars and free individuals should. She had spoken her mind.

CHAPTER 4

Both Sides Will Fight: Slander or Privilege?

> For myself, when I feel the hand of power lie heavy on my brow,
> I care but little to who oppresses me; I am not the more dis-
> posed to pass beneath the yoke because it is held out to me by
> the arms of a million men.
>
> —Alexis de Tocqueville (1840)
>
> In the United States we have the right to be different.
>
> —George H. Hand (1951)

After the board's September decision, Luella Mundel and her small band of supporters (principally her friend Harold Jones and casual acquaintances drawn to her by her plight, Eric and Jeanne Barnitz) continued the battle on several fronts. One was to give her cause statewide publicity. Jones's letters were the basis for pro-Mundel editorials in the *Charleston Daily Mail*. Under the headline "TENURE OR TYRANNY" the *Daily Mail* attacked the board for hiring and firing "without reference to the express recommendations of our college presidents" and for acting upon "unidentified allegations of atheism when it chooses to go its own way, leaving the public to conclude that some religious beliefs are now required for public employment."[1]

Second, the Mundel forces prodded the local AAUP chapter (sympathetic historian H. Norman Taylor and Jones were president and vice president respectively) into formally supporting her request to the national office for a full investigation. Such an inquiry was needed, Mundel wrote to the AAUP national office, because "my colleagues and a good share of the public would like to know on what basis West Virginia teachers can expect to retain their positions and professional reputations."[2]

Third and most important, on September 26 Mundel sued Thelma Loudin for slander. Since August, Louis Joughin, research director of the American Civil Liberties Union, had been keeping tabs on the case from his New York office through correspondence with Mundel, Jones, and Barnitz. Joughin was seeking to establish a legal doctrine of academic due process for teachers who had been fired. The ACLU had no office in rural, sparsely populated West Virginia, but soon after the September board meeting he put Mundel in touch with ACLU legal correspondent,

Charleston attorney Horace Spencer Meldahl, who was to advise Mundel in her quest for justice.[3]

Fairmonters knew little about the sixty-year-old soft-spoken Meldahl, but he had long defended radical and unpopular causes in the state. He fought for Jehovah's Witnesses in 1940 when they were roughed up and dosed with castor oil by American Legionnaires in full view of the police chief and sheriff at Richwood. In August 1942 it was Meldahl who filed the preliminary complaint in federal district court for a family of Witnesses who on grounds of conscience refused to comply with the state's compulsory flag-salute law. Argued by other attorneys before the U.S. Supreme Court as *West Virginia State Board* v. *Barnette* the case was a landmark. Symbolically announcing its verdict on Flag Day, the court held six to three that the state could not force public school pupils to perform the rituals of the Pledge of Allegiance and the salute to the flag under the guise of education.[4] So state school superintendent W. W. Trent and the board of education had met Meldahl before in the legal arena and Meldahl had won.

Meldahl could be described as a fuzzy-minded armchair radical. In 1934 he had written and privately published *Maximum Welfare,* a book proposing the abolition of private property and the establishment of state socialism in the United States. He prophesied that the ideal nation fulfilling what Meldahl believed was the goal of all religions, the establishment of heaven on earth, would come to pass peacefully by means of the "cultural conversion" of the masses. This idiosyncratic book, drawing for its gritty and romantic thesis on Marx, Jesus, Thomas Edison, and Josiah Royce among others, was more than a tract for the time of the Great Depression. For in 1951 and 1952 Meldahl was still trying to attract members to join him in the "Maximum Welfare Society." According to a sample invitation to join, the society endeavored "to discover and make known how human activities may be conducted to bring about a best possible state of affairs, and make God's kingdom on earth 'as it is in heaven,' a paradise for all."[5]

Since the depression Meldahl had lost the assurance that the United States government would willingly embrace socialism or allow the American people to reap its benefits. More and more he seemed convinced that the Soviet and Chinese examples of successful socialist states and the Communist Party U.S.A. offered the best hope of progressive change. He did not, as far as can be determined, join the Communist party. However, he did attend a New York party rally in 1951. In 1949 he had protested bitterly in several letters to sympathetic West Virginia senator Harley M. Kilgore against the passage of the Nixon-Mundt Bill, which would have required registration of Communist front organizations.

He called the bill "the most atrocious proposal imaginable." Yet he remained a member of the American Legion and considered himself a Christian.[6]

In September 1951 the immediate problem for Meldahl was to find a legal remedy for Luella Mundel's plight. His first advice turned out to be impractical—to recruit support among prominent local businessmen. She was an outsider attached to no local organizations and unknown personally to Fairmont's business community or to the powerful if less visible old families. His suggestion that she seek support from the local clergy faded with the rise to prominence of the "atheism" issue. The notion that public school teachers might offer organized assistance also proved illusory. In November, after several months of correspondence, the West Virginia Education Association's Tenure and Ethics Committee declined involvement in her case. Among its reasons, the WVEA listed the fact that Mundel was not a dues-paying member, that the AAUP should handle the case, and that there was no specific law of tenure for college faculty members. But perhaps the main reason was revealed when the committee noted that it "did frown upon, from the point of view of professional ethics, the airing of the case in the newspapers prior to any attempt to work through professional organizations either on a state or national level." Although it was not stated explicitly, it was not difficult to infer from the actions of the Association for Higher Education (the higher education appendage of the WVEA) at Fairmont State that the teachers' organization was politically tied too closely to the board of education and the state public education establishment to risk supporting Mundel, even had it wished to do so. There is no evidence that it so wished, for to do so might have jeopardized its political relationship with Democratic party leader Matthew Neely. Since the WVEA claimed as members over 90 percent of the state's public school teachers and almost 30 percent of college faculty, its rebuff was a very serious setback for Mundel.[7]

Thus legal action seemed to be her only hope. But what sort of legal action? The board had the legal right to refuse to reemploy Dr. Mundel and no remedy existed within normal grievance procedures. At first glance the most promising course of action seemed to be to seek a writ of mandamus or injunctive action from the state supreme court of appeals to force the board to give her a hearing. That was Meldahl's first thought, but its success hinged upon a nonexistent ground swell of public support for his client, especially from public school employees. So the Charleston lawyer proposed a far more risky plan. He advised Mundel to hire a Fairmont attorney to join him as co-counsel to represent her in a $100,000 slander suit against board member Thelma Brand Loudin.[8]

Engaging a lawyer in Fairmont proved no easy task for Dr. Mundel. As she told the ACLU, members of the local bar shied away. After a week of consultations she found that some feared they would be ruined; others thought she could not win the case. Still others shrank from any connection with the American Civil Liberties Union, which was known as a Red group. One feared being labeled Red for defending a person who had been called a Red before the board of education. Another refused to take a subordinate role to Meldahl, a Charleston attorney. No doubt most feared the potential loss of business from town interests arrayed behind Loudin.[9]

Eventually a local attorney did take Mundel as a client. He was the veteran Tusca Morris, whose legal career spanned four decades. In 1909 the young prosecuting attorney had won nineteen convictions against members of the sinister Black Hand organization. From its hideout in remote Killarm Hollow, this criminal conspiracy related to the Mafia had been strong-arming and extorting funds from Italian-Americans. Years later Morris rose to become local chief counsel for Consolidation Coal, a leviathan interest in the region. In 1942 he won a libel suit against a local radio station on behalf of Fairmont's most famous citizen, U.S. senator Matthew Mansfield Neely.[10] Now, in 1951, the seventy-eight-year-old Morris was in the late twilight of his career and relatively impervious to the pressures that beset his younger, less established colleagues. Still, it took strong persuasion by a delegation of Mundel's friends, a retainer of $1,000 that cut deeply into Mundel's savings, and the promise of 25 percent of damages recovered to bring him on board.[11]

The decision to sue for slander brooked the advice of ACLU national staff lawyers. New York counsel Herbert Monte Levy warned Meldahl of the dangers. As Levy made clear, the ACLU would not back the suit with money or a brief. Slander was a personal matter, and the ACLU limited its direct involvement to broad academic freedom or civil liberties issues. The union was interested in the case, but it would participate only by offering advice and encouragement.

Slander suits, Levy reminded Meldahl, were hard to win and this one would be especially so. To lose might damage Mundel's reputation more than if she gave in to the board. And defeat was made likely by several formidable obstacles. One, thought Levy, was the moot question of whether calling a person a bad security risk was libel, particularly in an academic setting. No body of law supported this reading of the slander statute in West Virginia, and precedents from other states were daunting. Up to that time, courts had not generally held it to be libelous to call a person a Communist. To have a hope of winning, Mundel's lawyers would have to prove that Loudin had spoken with malicious intent. That would be difficult enough, but even if it could be established, Loudin's statements in board meetings would probably be protected by the "gift of qualified privilege" that she enjoyed as a public official.

What about the jury? Would a local, all-male jury (women had not yet gained the right to serve on juries in West Virginia) convict a staunch pillar of the community such as Loudin? In the improbable event that Mundel won, what good would it do her? She was not likely to receive a substantial settlement, and Levy speculated that losing the case would only make Loudin and the board more antagonistic. He predicted that an excuse would be found within a year to fire her before she became tenured. In summary, Levy thought Mundel's prospects were grim.[12]

Although he was less gloomy, Joughin, too, warned Mundel to think twice before going ahead with the suit. On September 13 he confided his private opinion, founded on long residence in a conservative town, that she would eventually have to decide whether protest to bring about change was more important than leaving Fairmont for her own good.[13] He worried that even informal participation by the ACLU in the case would hurt Mundel's chances in light of the opinion of many Fairmonters that the union was Red.[14]

Meldahl brushed all of this aside, insisting that he and Morris were optimistic that they would win the case and with it a victory for teachers everywhere. Apparently, Mundel believed him. So on September 26, 1951, in a thirteen-page, four-count declaration to the Marion County Court, Mundel alleged that Loudin had given false, unsubstantiated information to the board causing her to be fired—all notwithstanding Mundel's two years of acceptable performance, the recommendation by President Hand, and a petition of support signed by 125 Fairmont State students.[15]

Quite possibly Meldahl never expected the case to come to trial. The ACLU, AAUP, and Meldahl were all in their separate ways seeking an out-of-court settlement. As he boasted to Joughin, Loudin would soon probably want to persuade the board to retain Dr. Mundel more fervently than she had tried to get her dismissed. He predicted that the board might agree in order to save Loudin from having to pay damages.[16]

Such optimism was not justified. Before September 26, town gossip had it that Dr. Mundel might sue. But sue whom? The board? The American Legion? When it became known that the ACLU, an old adversary of the Legion, was interested in the case, speculation made Post 17 the likely target. When finally the suit named Loudin as defendant, officers of Post 17 agreed to donate $2,500 to her defense. Given her choice of counsel, Loudin picked U.S. senator Matthew Mansfield Neely, who was to become perhaps the central character in the Mundel affair.[17]

The seventy-seven-year-old Neely was a living legend in Fairmont.

Born in 1874 in a rural Doddridge County, West Virginia, log cabin of pre-Revolutionary Scotch-Irish and Welsh stock, he rose to the pinnacle of state Democratic politics and to national prominence. Little Salem College and then West Virginia University Law School had educated him. This, combined with marrying into the Fairmont elite and winning the support of the United Mine Workers, paved the way for a political career that took him eventually from city mayor to state legislative clerk, the U.S. House of Representatives, the state governorship, and five terms in the U.S. Senate. He was a tireless worker who was said never to take a true vacation and a voracious reader who was often seen at his Senate desk poring over a book.[18]

But it was the spoken not the written word that made Matt Neely's fame. He claimed the poet Robert Burns as an ancestor and legend has it that he memorized a bit of poetry, Shakespeare, the Bible, or McGuffey every morning while shaving. Neely rated among the Senate's most adept members when it came to finding a biblical passage with which to flay an opponent in debate.

His style was a potent weapon in West Virginia politics. Much of his home-state constituency had been scarcely touched by formal schooling. To reach them Neely used anecdote, allusion, and quotation to present issues as exciting, melodramatic battles between good and evil. If his speeches had a common theme it was that the forces of darkness and light were locked in never-ending and perilous combat, with Neely, of course, on the side of the angels.[19] He described his political path as beset by assorted enemies and evil forces. One doubts that any other twentieth-century politician jousted with more "liars more infamous than Ananias," "personifications of malicious mendacity," "hypocritical slackers," and Judas Iscariots. That is not to mention the occasional "pusillanimous political tramp," "unprincipled, hissing, snarling, snapping monstrosity," or "foul blot upon the escutcheon of human propriety and decency."[20]

To listen (and to watch) Neely was to experience not great art but diverting theater with a church-meeting flavor that had resonance for many West Virginians. However captivating for certain audiences, it was a style that could convey few subtleties and one that often grossly oversimplified complex issues by entangling them deep in a mare's nest of poetical snippets, rhetorical devices, and bathos. But one imagines that even his rhetorical excesses worked politically with many of the home folks. For it made them proud that one of their own could take the national stage and use bigger words and longer sentences than representatives of more exalted regions.

For all his intelligence, energy, and love of books, Neely was neither an idealist nor an intellectual. He was an intense, practical political boss whose attitudes grew out of factionalized Democratic politics in early twentieth-century West Virginia. He was rigidly identified with no single interest, but, insofar as he could manage it, equally with all. "Matt Neely is all things to all men," wrote political scientist John H. Fenton in 1957. His rise to power had begun in Fairmont, where early in the century he had established a clean mayoral administration energized by moral fervor against alcohol and vice. He later boasted that he had purged the city (at least temporarily) of seventeen saloons, gambling dens, and bawdy houses. He had long stood against corruption and, according to supporters, for character and honesty based on Christian values. By the 1950s he was closely tied to Roosevelt-Truman, New Deal–Fair Deal liberalism. As a senator he made several liberal causes his own — especially home rule for the District of Columbia, the cause of the United Mine Workers and other industrial unions, and federal aid to education. He deserves credit for battling against the Hollywood film moguls' monopolistic practice of forcing local theater owners to accept bloc bookings and for supporting access for television cameras to Senate hearings. At his death in 1958 the *New York Times* eulogized him as a populist, one who "seldom forsook the role of common man's David seeking out the Goliath of special interests."

That was certainly the role Neely played (or overplayed to the point of chewing the scenery) on the national stage. Yet among his rhetorical excesses one finds little Red-baiting. In May 1950, he had denounced Sen. Joseph R. McCarthy as a liar greater than Ananias after the Wisconsin Republican's famous Wheeling speech alleging the presence of Communists in the State Department. A year later he stood with Truman against Republican wrath over MacArthur's firing. The *Congressional Record* for 1951 shows Neely speaking only on legislation pertaining to his pet issues such as cancer research and the District of Columbia or plugging insubstantial matters dear to his constituency such as Mother's Day and the Moose Lodge. As a matter of fact, other than his very public stance against MacArthur, Neely had little to contribute to Senate debates of great issues of the moment. Nothing that he said resembled the rantings of the extreme Right that he would unleash in the courtroom against Mundel. There he would follow a line that appealed most to conservative Republicans. It is all rather puzzling.[21]

The key to the puzzle must be found in the rugged West Virginia political terrain that produced and nurtured the politician Neely. Away from Washington he lived in the semifeudal world of Mountain State Democratic politics where party and personal loyalty counted for everything. There he had long headed the so-called Statehouse faction with his former campaign manager, federal court clerk Homer Hanna. Historian John Alexander Williams describes Neely's role in West Virginia politics as that of a manager who served the interests of organized labor, blacks, and schoolteachers' groups. During Neely's political reign (1940–56), each of these interests attained sufficient power to block political programs which they opposed. But neither they nor any other group within the state, business or labor, was strong enough to initiate and carry out its own political agenda. Instead, argues Williams, the Neely machine flourished because it balanced in-state interests in response to the initiatives of outside forces that controlled the Mountain State's destiny — big labor, corporations, and the federal government. Thus, West Virginia was managed by its native politicians defensively in accordance with policies established beyond the state's boundaries. Its political elite was necessarily ideologically noncommittal and cynical.[22]

The machine, if it may be called that, depended on interest-group support and patronage. The state board of education and even to a degree the school system itself was a part of the patronage structure.

Beyond that Neely claimed a deep personal interest in the state's public schools. As a youth he had taught briefly in rural, one-room schools, the first year for $35 a month. He had been deeply impressed by the content and philosophy of William Holmes McGuffey's famous eclectic readers. As he told the McGuffey Society in 1954, the readers had started millions of nineteenth-century boys and girls "on their memorable joyous journeys from the lowlands of indifference, illiteracy, and ignorance to the lofty heights of education, knowledge, and glorious achievement." In 1951 he remained convinced that McGuffey's Presbyterian moralism, entertaining fables, and literary samplings remained the essence of public school education. So Neely brought to the Fairmont State College dispute a personal educational bias against "modern" educators such as George Hand and Luella Mundel who, perhaps unwittingly, had challenged values he cared about.[23]

To Neely and those who shared his views the public schools were in part to be projections of what has been called American domestic ideology.[24] This was the nineteenth-century belief that consigned to the mother-centered Christian home the responsibility for the formation of individual moral character and by extension the good citizenship that would preserve the Republic. He stood foursquare for popular symbols at the center of that value cluster — Jesus, home, and mother (that "tranquilizing trinity of wondrous words"). When he spoke of "mother" he became quite sentimental. In northern West Virginia particularly, supporting motherhood was good politics, for West Virginians claim that Mother's Day began there. Neely's Mother's Day messages were sometimes broadcast on the radio in Fairmont and his annual remarks in the Senate were noteworthy. In his 1952 Senate speech he was careful to include in his paean to mother's virtues something about her roles as educator, moral guide, and religious teacher to reassure his conservative supporters. But, with an eye to his ethnic labor constituency, he managed to weave in a denunciation of sweated labor and praise for the rising Italian-American element in West Virginia politics in his story of an Italian mother dying of consumption who worked in a sweatshop "to get grub for the little kids." Considering the man and his region one cannot easily dismiss such remarks as mere rhetoric.[25]

When Neely agreed to take Thelma Loudin's case, it meant much more than collecting a substantial fee to supplement his senatorial salary. In 1941 as governor, Neely had first appointed Loudin, Democratic party worker and Fairmonter, to the state board of education. In 1941, when Neely left the Senate for the West Virginia governor's mansion, he had named his long-time friend and associate, Fairmont State Teachers College president Joseph Rosier, to serve his unexpired Senate term.

Rosier's forced retirement in 1945 had evidently caused Neely personal discomfort. Thelma Loudin had come to him for advice. Other board members were pressing for her vote to enforce the new state law and retire Rosier, who was a decade past the mandatory age of 65. What should she do? Neely remembered that he told her that "if Mr. Rosier were 100 years old I would still vote for him." But Rosier later came to believe that Neely had helped to get rid of him. And Joseph Rosier died from a stroke on October 8, 1951, apparently still believing that Neely had acquiesced in his ouster and subsequent repudiation.[26]

The changes that accompanied the Hand administration seemed a palpable rebuke to the Rosier legacy and to the faculty members and townspeople who had worked together so long to fashion an educational institution that mirrored their aspirations. Mundel had first offended the town and now she attacked Loudin, one of the finest women in Fairmont. It was Neely's duty to defend Thelma Loudin and the reputation of the fair sex, the authority of the board of education, the Rosier legacy at the college, and the moral imperatives of Old Fairmont.

Concurrent with *Mundel* v. *Loudin* in West Virginia was much Democratic maneuvering, in-fighting, and posturing relating to the April 1952 primary election. State labor leaders who were normally Neely's allies were backing their own endorsed slate of candidates, apparently out of pique because outgoing governor and Neely ally Okey Patteson had supported legislation they deemed antilabor. The schism in the state's labor-liberal leadership, which was not mended until March 1952, opened up a variety of unpleasant political possibilities for Neely. The most immediate was that other Democratic factions would rush in to exploit the situation. And soon they did, claiming to be reformers and promising to replace incumbents with "men and women who believed in the old-time religion, the old-time honesty, and the old-time economy." Lying in wait beyond the primary were two of Neely's most despised Republican foes, Chapman Revercomb and Rush Holt, poised to win their party's nomination for U.S. senator and governor respectively.

Since the 1950 elections Democrats had feared a Republican resurgence. Even though they held a large margin in voter registration, West Virginia Democratic leaders worried that in 1952 a rising GOP tide might sweep them from power. Harley Kilgore was the likely target of a Red-baiting smear campaign similar to the one used to defeat Millard Tydings in 1950. To counter this, some state Democrats considered pushing conservative ex–American Legion national commander and ex-secretary of defense Louis Johnson's candidacy to replace Kilgore. Informed speculation had it that for the first time in memory Republicans had a chance to capture two of the Mountain State's six congressional seats. Even more disturbing, from some of Neely's backers came the startling prediction that the Democrats might be the minority party by 1954.

From November 1951 to April 1952 Neely sought to neutralize dissident labor leaders by attempting to show that the party and the unions needed him more than he needed them. He did so in several ways. Friendly newspapers proclaimed it on their editorial pages and hinted that unless he had his way Neely might quit the Senate and run for governor himself, as he had in 1942. They understood that unionized labor could hardly afford to lose such a Senate ally as Neely, especially if it meant his replacement might be a conservative Democrat or a Republican. In addition by his public actions Neely tried to demonstrate what he had long maintained—that he was West Virginia's most popular politician.

In this political context, one might speculate that a well-publicized court case such as *Mundel* v. *Loudin,* highlighted by the patented Neely oratorical pyrotechnics in defense of Jehovah, the fair sex, moral education, and small-town values with some popular anticommunism thrown in, had immediate political value. It could help to blunt conservative criticism of his recent attacks on MacArthur. It might cement the support of public school teachers, to whom Mundel seemed an outsider and a threat to the status quo and who had almost unanimously shied away from her. It might help win rank-and-file support in the southern Bible Belt region of the state where the corruption issue had the greatest potential. It could help Neely's protégé Bob Mollohan, who faced an uphill nomination fight especially in Wheeling, the population center of the First Congressional District, where he was scarcely known. By volunteering his legal expertise and political clout for an American Legion cause, Neely might make it more difficult, at least in the short term, for conservative Democrats to oppose him openly. Moreover, the exposure offered by the trial might increase Neely's popularity among labor's rank and file and thus add to his leverage against rebellious labor leaders and his image as a populist defender of the little guy against outsiders and intellectuals.[27]

Technically Neely would simply defend Thelma Loudin against the charge of slander. But so many tensions and disputes and scores to be settled lay just below the surface of the case and Neely was so pugnacious that it was likely that the defense would go beyond the obvious legal issues such as Loudin's qualified privilege of expression as a board member. The senator's vehemence against opponents was well known. Clarence "Ned" Smith, a shrewd local newsman and longtime observer of the political scene, said it best. He wrote in the 1940s that Neely was most successful when "he has something to put between his teeth and shake" and that it was "necessary for him to have a pet devil to flail with the club of righteousness."[28] Given Neely's prominence and reputation as an entertainer, as well as Mundel's need to enlist outside support, the case was as sure to attract national attention as was Luella Mundel to suffer verbal blows from Neely's club of righteousness.

In mid-October the legal skirmishing between Neely and the ACLU began. The ACLU's Joughin and Neely had several contacts in October and November. Joughin was the initiator, seeking an out-of-court settlement based on the board's willingness to give Mundel a hearing. He wrote to Neely that the ACLU accepted the premise that the suit was a private action, not really the business of civil liberties defenders. But surely, he argued, there were broad areas of the dispute that were open to settlement. Did not all agree that Mundel was entitled to her own religious views and that she should be fired only if she used the classroom to indoctrinate students with those views? Did not serious charges against a professional person require a hearing and fair trial on the merits of the case? Not to utilize due process in such a case, the ACLU lawyer continued, would be disastrous for Mundel and might label the board of education as illiberal and authoritarian. Appealing to Neely's sophistication and deferring to him as a visionary elder statesman, Joughin pleaded with him to halt the progress of events toward ever deepening controversy by using his influence with the board to secure a hearing for Dr. Mundel.[29]

Joughin got nowhere. In early November Neely reported that the board would not reconsider. More to the point, the senator would not concede any connection between the slander suit and academic freedom.

Avowing that he would always protect anyone against impingement upon his or her constitutional rights, he claimed that the issue of academic freedom could not arise for legal consideration in *Mundel v. Loudin.*[30] So much for an out-of-court settlement.

The negotiations with Neely, Joughin later said, ended acrimoniously. He found Neely liberal and gentlemanly—until the slander suit was filed. Then he became a terrifying adversary.[31]

Besides the prospect of a large legal fee if the suit went to trial, the fact that the day after Neely's participation in the case became public the ACLU issued a strong pro-Mundel memorandum must have chilled the negotiations. Although the ACLU document was primarily an internal background paper, copies circulated to almost everyone interested in the case. It covered events from Mundel's firing, her dispute with Schroder, the involvement of Dr. Carroll, and the role of the American Legion, to the charges made against her at the various board meetings. It made several points critical of the board. Principal among them was the assertion that questions asked before the board about Mundel's religious beliefs had violated both her academic freedom and her civil rights, both by the manner in which they were raised and in denying her a chance to answer them. By refusing a hearing "where accusations of incompetence, atheism, subversiveness and personal unfitness are considered" after these charges had become public knowledge, the board threatened to ruin Mundel's professional career. The memo ended with a plea for justice and a claim that the board had "subverted the established principles of academic freedom."[32]

The lawsuit further agitated affairs at the college. The Post 17 patriots rallied to the support of Loudin. On October 17 the *West Virginian* featured a front-page photo of Loudin with a Legion guest speaker, the post commander, and other dignitaries at a meeting to promote Americanism in the schools. The speaker warned the audience not to allow teachers to use their classes to promote any foreign "isms," particularly communism, fascism, and socialism.

It was at about this time that the Legionnaires discovered one of communism's disgusting hydra-heads writhing obscenely among the stacks of the college library. Complaints reached them from an ex-GI student that the library (headed by Harold Jones) was blatantly displaying subversive items on the HUAC list without warning of their dangers. Most notable among them evidently was the *Worker,* the Sunday version of the official organ of the CPUSA.

In early October, responding to the danger, a delegation of six local citizens denominated the Marion County Anti-Subversive Committee paid a visit to George Hand's office. They were a cross-section of the white-collar middle class, including a lawyer, a teacher from a small county high school, the treasurer of a local manufacturing firm, the secretary-treasurer of the Businessmen's Association, and a deputy-collector of Internal Revenue, who was also Legion post commander. Led by the latter two, the committee proposed that "subversive materials" should be "labeled," i.e., conspicuously tagged to warn away the innocent and, one supposes, to call attention to those guilty of perusing them. Hand reacted to the visit as meddling in college affairs by outsiders. Jones saw it as an assault on free speech.[33]

That the Legion was involved and that its local commander was close to Loudin and belonged to the Central Methodist Church did not go unnoticed by Hand and Jones. Both resisted the antisubversives' request. Hand gave them no encouragement. He simply passed their request to a faculty committee, assuring the visitors that the faculty's decision was final and that he would not overrule it. Jones, meanwhile, fired off letters to a number of publications and organizations to enlist their support in behalf of freedom of information.[34]

As it turned out, the antisubversive attack fizzled. The faculty committee voted six to two against the labeling. Subsequently the faculty committee's position was backed by the American Library Association and other professional and accrediting organizations. When a delegation of faculty members with the support of an educational "solid front" met with the antisubversives, the latter backed down.[35]

These recurrent disputes pressured faculty members to choose sides. On October 18, a majority voted to ask college delegates to the West Virginia Association for Higher Education (AHE, a branch of the state National Educational Association affiliate) to push for legislation to establish tenure for university and college teachers. The measure, backed by the college AAUP leaders allied with Mundel and approved by Hand, irked Mundel's opponents and evidently frightened many teachers who did not want to become involved. Although the resolution passed at a general faculty meeting with but a single dissent, many refused to vote.[36]

After the *Pittsburgh Post-Gazette* reported that the passage of the tenure resolution was evidence that Mundel had the support of the faculty, opposition to it grew. On October 22 when the college chapter of the AHE met to consider whether or not to carry the resolution to an upcoming state meeting, the atmosphere was electric. Under the watchful eye of mathematics department head H. A. Shutts, no one was admitted without proof of current membership in the organization. This effectively barred Mundel's AAUP friends except for Hand and English instructor Dr. Dorothy Lucker, who found themselves outvoted. Hand protested extravagantly that he had "never seen such a horrible exhibition of dictatorship in a meeting sparked by mass fear of not doing the right thing to be on the right side," but he could not change the result. The AHE rejected the October 18 faculty resolution and, over Hand's objections, by a 28-2 majority passed a resolution protesting "the unethical conduct of certain members and groups of members of the faculty in dragging the name of the college and its employer into controversial issues now pending."[37]

The AHE action emboldened the anti-Hand forces. One result was that two Fairmont State faculty members wrote scathing letters to AAUP Secretary Himstead critical of AAUP Chapter President Taylor, Jones, Mundel, Hand, and all who supported them. On November 5, C. R. House, Jr., the college journalism teacher, public relations director, and successor to Medora Mason, warned the national headquarters that the Fairmont AAUP chapter was under the control of a group in open rebellion against the state board of education. He expressed his belief that Mundel had no case whatsoever, deserved dismissal, and lacked the support of the majority of the faculty. He warned that he would not pay dues to the AAUP until its leadership at the college changed. A sociology professor forcibly retired by Hand's regime wrote to tell Himstead that both town and gown were turning against the AAUP because of its support of Mundel. Making explicit the issue that always lay just beneath the surface of the attacks on Mundel, he reported that some Fairmont State AAUP chapter members were being called Reds. He added that some linked the term "Red" with the AAUP and that he thought this linkage was unfair because there were many good Americans and sound educators on the faculty.[38]

Much potential pro-Mundel sentiment lay beyond the college and the town. By late November elements of the national liberal press had picked up the scent of the controversial issues brewing at Fairmont. Dedicated letter-writing, particularly on the part of Harold Jones, paid off for Mundel's forces when several periodicals took notice of her case.

Most important of these was the thoroughly anti-McCarthy, liberal Catholic *Commonweal*. In the December 7 issue under the arresting title, "Jefferson in West Virginia," John C. Cort recounted the details of Mundel's ordeal. Based on a thorough briefing from Jones and Mundel (he reported that Loudin had not answered his inquiries), the article crackled with Cort's indignation against the state board of education, his sympathy for Mundel, and his impatience with authorities who refused to protect her civil rights. He castigated the board's apparent intolerance of an agnostic or even atheist teacher in a college "that is not . . . a Catholic or even . . . Christian college." He argued for Mundel's religious freedom by quoting from the West Virginia Constitution, which stipulates that "no religious or political test oath shall be required as a prerequisite or qualification to . . . pursue any profession or employment," and the eloquent article 2 of Jefferson's Virginia Statute of Religious Liberty (1786).[39]

As a Catholic familiar with discrimination, Cort was sincerely interested in the religious issues of the Mundel case. He was at least equally concerned about the attack on Mundel's Democratic liberalism. *Commonweal* was perhaps American Catholicism's most committed voice against conservative Republicanism and, above all, McCarthyism. To Cort, the involvement of the American Legion in the case made it still another attack by professional anticommunists on liberals. And behind this kind of attack lay "the machinations of Senator McCarthy and his admirers [who] have poisoned the minds and morals of our people." "Let us hope," he concluded, "that the people as represented by the Marion County Court in Fairmont will start drawing the line in the case of Dr. Mundel and Mrs. Loudin."

Cort scolded the AAUP for its inaction in the Mundel case. The professors' group, he wrote, is "a little too dignified to behave like a trade union. Otherwise it would have raised several kinds of hell by this time."[40] This brought letters to AAUP General Secretary Himstead from concerned members around the country asking why the AAUP had not acted.[41] Cort's piece was probably the most effective national publicity Mundel's cause had yet received and it was the first to openly link her trouble to McCarthyism. This was important because *Commonweal*'s circulation was small but influential.

The religious controversy presented by Cort was intriguing, for its roots went back not only to Jefferson's ringing defense of the idea that God had created the mind free, but to Dayton, Tennessee, in 1925. There at the Scopes trial, Tennessee's fundamentalist-sponsored antievolution law had been tested in a courtroom drama that had pitted the once great William Jennings Bryan against the eloquent ACLU trial lawyer Clarence Darrow. Of course the trial had been immortalized by H. L. Mencken, the premier journalist and social critic of the 1920s. The Mundel trial, in 1951, offered the possibility of a similar confrontation—a stem-winding political orator of the old school to defend the old-time religion, a fearless civil-liberties lawyer, and a community vaguely like Dayton. Perhaps that was why the only East Coast journalist who bothered to come to Fairmont for the trial was William Manchester, who wrote for Mencken's own *Baltimore Sun Papers* and was his recent biographer.[42]

In preparing for the trial Meldahl exuded the confidence of a cheerleader but displayed little sensitivity to Luella Mundel's scruples and little understanding of the Fairmont community. He urged her to go to church a few times in Fairmont, preferably to different churches to gain public support and sympathy. He suggested that she should interrogate faculty wives to find out what their husbands knew of Loudin's actions. He assured his client that their case grew stronger by the day and in court they would overwhelm the opposition.[43]

As the mid-December trial date approached, Meldahl clung to the hope and Mundel and Jones to the belief that the ACLU would actively support their case. Despite Herbert Monte Levy's advice that the organization should not enter a libel case, Louis Joughin continued to urge formal participation. In late November Joughin approached ACLU director Roger N. Baldwin about the matter. Baldwin defined the criterion for ACLU official entry into the case as the organization's belief that it involved the public interest. Citing the ACLU's involvement in the White Plains Roger Smith Hotel libel case, Joughin held a staff meeting on the Mundel case on Friday afternoon, November 30.

Joughin proposed to staffers that the ACLU should (1) make a public statement supporting Mundel, (2) officially designate Meldahl as attorney acting on behalf of the ACLU, and (3) pay Mundel's court costs. The surviving details of the meeting are very sketchy, but Joughin's proposal lost on every count. The executives decided that the ACLU could not justify involvement in the slander suit strictly on grounds of protecting academic freedom. But Joughin promised vigorous public support of Mundel once the suit was out of the way. The difficulty, he explained, was a paucity of law to support academic freedom. And since academic freedom was the main concern of the ACLU, it would have to avoid legal action or even support while the slander suit was being tried.[44]

With less than two weeks until the beginning of the trial Mundel had been unable to obtain the active support of any legal, professional, or religious group. The faculty, state board of education, state government, and local community were against her or indifferent. So were two of the state's most popular Democratic liberal political figures, Matthew Neely and W. W. Trent. It was not an encouraging prospect.

CHAPTER 5

The First Trial: *Mundel* v. *Loudin*
or *The People* v. *Mundel?*

Modern art is Communistic because it is distorted and ugly, because it does not glorify our beautiful country, our cheerful and smiling people, and our material progress. Art which does not glorify our country in plain, simple terms that everyone can understand breeds dissatisfaction. It is therefore opposed to our government, and those who create it and promote it are our enemies.
—Congressman George A. Dondero (R), Michigan (1949)

[The trial of Luella Mundel has become a] farce [that] smacks loudly of all the bad traits of the Inquisition and of the Crucifixion.
— F. Graham Luckenbill, Rector, Christ Episcopal Church,
Fairmont (1951)

On a cold, blustery Monday morning, December 17, 1951, began two weeks of humiliation and frustration for Luella Mundel. That morning both sides filed preliminary arguments in *Mundel* v. *Loudin* in a grand, if somewhat seedy, 500-seat courtroom. Presiding was common pleas judge J. Harper Meredith, a major political force among the Democrats. In 1944 Meredith's photo had shared a campaign poster with that of Matt Neely. In 1958 he would be Neely's pallbearer. But now the judge's reputation for fairness would be tested by the challenge of controlling the powerful and unpredictable Neely in the courtroom.

Although they promised to provide full, unbiased coverage, the fairness of both local newspapers was open to question. The conservative Republican *West Virginian* had long supported Loudin, and its editor assigned trial coverage to legal reporter Logan Carroll, the brother of Hand's and Mundel's accuser Robert L. Carroll. The moderate morning Democratic paper, the *Fairmont Times,* was less ostensibly anti-Mundel but it would never dare to openly oppose Neely. It was not that either paper lacked professionalism. Rather, it was that their staffers' roots were local, their perspectives those of townspeople, and after the trial they would have to live in Fairmont, Matt Neely's town. As a result, both papers used the tactic of printing long, almost verbatim accounts of the daily progress of the trial, accounts devoid of a discernible point of view.

Presumably because of the ACLU's and Neely's involvement and the letter-writing of Jones and Mundel, the national press showed interest. The *New York Times* used a Fairmont stringer and the wire services for its daily inside-page coverage. So did the Pittsburgh and Charleston (W.Va.) papers and the *Washington Post.* This led to gaffes, one of which produced guffaws among Mundel supporters. The *New York Times* published a photo of the handsome Loudin and identified her as the plain Luella Mundel. (Journalists' sketches and Fairmonters' recollections made much of the contrasting physical appearances of the two women. Loudin was tall, dark-haired, and attractive. Mundel was just five feet tall, blonde, and frail-looking, and was perceived as plain-looking by comparison.) Of the major East Coast papers only the the *Baltimore Sun Papers* sent a reporter, William Manchester, and he was on hand for only part of the trial. In contrast to the local journalists, he portrayed the proceedings as a sort of second Scopes trial pitting the Enlightenment against religious bigotry.[1]

The first two days' proceedings, December 17 and 18, were taken up with preliminary motions and written arguments. These focused on what Loudin had said or not said to the board of education, whether she had intended harm to Dr. Mundel, and whether her remarks were made in the line of duty. Mundel's attorneys, Meldahl and Morris, charged in their bill of particulars that at the May board meeting Loudin had said Mundel was not fit to be on a college faculty and was a bad security risk "implying, insinuating, and meaning" that she was a "fellow traveler or sympathizer of the Communist Party, or some other organization or movement." They added that she had called Mundel an atheist, incompetent, and a person of "bad personal traits" before the board, and had stated that "she did not think that an atheist should be on a college faculty." The fragility of Mundel's case was obvious in the bill of particulars. The essential witnesses to Loudin's statements (there was no written evidence) were Hand and the board members. Her case depended on hearsay.[2]

The written defense argument for Loudin filed by Matthew Neely relied on Loudin's special privilege as a school board member and upon a denial that she had uttered the statements alleged by Mundel's side. It claimed that she had only made a "few inquiries" at the board meeting in exercising the statutory powers of board of education members to oversee teacher training and the education departments of colleges such as Fairmont State. She interpreted her duty under these statutes as to "help" to determine the "ability, education, character and loyalty to the United States and its form of government and . . . freedom from atheistic, communistic or any antireligious or unamerican taints or infirmities" of all professors and teachers. She claimed that Hand himself had told the board that Mundel "had on occasion said she was an atheist." Loudin deposed that she had simply passed on the remarks of Carroll and Roberts (she neglected to mention the letter from Fridtjof Schroder). She had not personally investigated the allegations against Mundel because she trusted "the good reputation for truth and veracity of her informants."[3]

So Loudin's case was also flawed, depending in part as it did on hearsay evidence from informants who held grudges against Hand and Mundel. It drew no strength from her equation of the board's fiat to oversee teacher training with her right to fire professors whose views did not coincide with her own.[4] Still, pretrial odds strongly favored Loudin. She undoubtedly possessed special privilege as a board member to discuss personnel in a closed board meeting. More to the point, she was an insider in the closed system that Mundel had attacked. It was hard to imagine that a Fairmont jury would find against her, especially after it had been harangued by Senator Neely.

The jury of twelve old-stock white men was selected without dispute or incident when the trial began on Wednesday, December 19. The panel seems to have reflected a fair cross-section of the mostly blue-collar community, made up as it was principally of employees of local industrial plants and retail establishments. It included no representatives of the region's newer arrivals—notably Italian-Americans. Mundel's counsel did not try to exclude jurors who were familiar with the publicity surrounding the case. At least one member of Loudin's church was impaneled. Whether the American Legion packed the jury, as Mundel's allies suspected, is unclear. What is certain is that it was a jury unlikely to be sympathetic to Mundel. Its members owed their livelihoods to the established merchants and corporations, not to the college. None had gone beyond high school and most seemed underqualified to judge the aesthetic and pedagogical technicalities of the case. They would surely understand Loudin's defense of Jehovah, home, and womanhood more easily than Dr. Mundel's advocacy of agnosticism, abstract art, and arcane psychological theory.[5]

After the jury was seated the crowd in the courtroom heard Meldahl and Neely square off for the first time. In a conservative suit that belied his intellectual radicalism, the graying Meldahl quietly and logically laid out Mundel's case. After summarizing his written arguments he described the damage Loudin had done to Mundel. Former friends would not associate with her because of her alleged atheism and communism. The assault by Loudin and her associates, Meldahl continued, had left Dr. Mundel "poor in health," "nervous, sleepless," and with "difficulty in digesting her food." Apparently hoping to strengthen the resolve of his key witness, Meldahl painted George Hand as a victim who had risked his job doing "the right thing in seeing truth and justice prevail."[6]

Meldahl dismissed Loudin's proposed defense by qualified privilege as mere "confession and avoidance." He promised to prove that Mundel had been properly qualified, properly hired, and had performed well at the college. He charged that Loudin had conspired with the local American Legion to persuade the board to reverse Hand's recommendation and fire Dr. Mundel, despite student petitions and the wishes of the ACLU and AAUP. Finally, he claimed, Dr. Mundel would deny that she ever made the statements attributed to her, notably that she was an atheist, Communist, or socialist. In the end, claimed Meldahl, the jury would learn that Luella Mundel was a truer Christian than Thelma Loudin.[7]

The opening statement for the defense was vintage Neely. Captured by Manchester in the flamboyance that belied his teetotaling cultural conservatism, the senator was "a chunky jut-jawed figure in a double-breasted suit and blue suede shoes, crouching over the jury box." Holding forth for more than an hour before a jury characterized by the reporter as the "awestruck twelve," the senator began by establishing that Fairmont, the court, and the college were his domain. He reminisced about his part in the first case ever argued in the courtroom, "51 years and 21 days ago yesterday." He reminded the court that as governor *he* had named Loudin to the state board of education. She was a native of the area, "born and reared just over the hill." He described telephoning Hand the previous spring to warn him that "unless peace is restored on the hill [i.e., at the college] and you get rid of your annual clean-up, you are going to wake up one of these days and find that the Legislature has . . . adjourned without appropriating a single dollar for Fairmont State college."[8]

This was a very simple case, he proclaimed. The board of education indubitably possessed the "right to purge its schools of teachers it believes incompetent, atheists, Communists, horse thieves, murderers, or just too ignorant to teach children." Mundel's case was about as strong as his own would be to sue all of those who did not vote for him when he lost a bid for the Senate in 1942. In getting rid of Dr. Mundel, Loudin and all decent citizens were only trying in a "God fearing, civilized educated American way to educate their children and grandchildren." If the jury wanted a situation where one could not complain about a fellow employee with Communistic or atheistic views working by his side, it should find for Dr. Mundel. He spoke of his warm regard for schoolteachers and support of legislation on their behalf "from A to Z." He stood solidly for "qualified teachers who believe in God and subscribe to no 'isms' but good old fashioned Americanism." West Virginia needed no teachers with "high-falutin ideas about not being able to prove there is a God." They would corrupt the minds of students "in the sunny morning of life" and make "kindling wood out of their little hopes." Waxing ever more bombastic, he pledged not to serve as a "stalking horse to make Communists look like liberals," but would "help tear the mask from them and expose them in their hideous, naked ugliness just like they are."

Everyone at the college knew, Neely claimed, that Mundel was an atheist and had said she was a socialist or Communist. The American Legion (" 'those boys in the first world war' who 'left their last best hope on the altar of their country' ") and patriotic teachers ("who believe in the old-fashioned American way our forefathers handed down from the time the barefooted soldiers of Washington stained the snows of Valley Forge with their precious blood") were the antithesis of Luella Mundel. She was a woman who would "tear down the man of Galilee from the Cross," and who "boasted of painting pictures which arouse sexual desires in men." Rambling on through a denunciation of "godless Russia," he appealed to West Virginians to drive "tainted persons" from their midst.[9]

Building to a climax worthy of a parodist, Neely used the courtroom American flag as a prop, embracing it while proclaiming himself against any school that tolerated communism, atheism, "or other godless philosophy in its halls." The jurors, he urged, should "burn incense on the altar of almighty God, asserting the right of every American to sing such songs of gladness as 'Jesus, Lover of My Soul' and 'My Country, 'Tis of Thee,' " which, according to Manchester, he recited in a quavering voice. "If that's reactionary," he concluded, standing Patrick Henry on his head, "make the most of it!" As Neely's tirade grew more polemical and neither the judge nor her lawyers intervened, Dr. Mundel retired to the ladies' lounge, where it was said she wept.[10]

From the vantage point of more than three decades, Neely's performance seems merely outrageous and cruel buffoonery. But it was hardly that. Samuel Stouffer's 1954 polling data suggest that Neely clearly understood what Americans feared when they thought of the Communist threat of internal subversion. It was not sabotage. Those polled most often cited the antireligious or unreligious tendencies of Communists as the greatest threat. Only 3 percent of the sample had ever met a Communist. In imagining who might be Communists, most thought it likely Reds would be educated white-collar workers, persons who were against religion and/or "crack pots," "queer people," or "warped personalities." This, from the perspective of many Fairmonters, might have been a group portrait of Hand's liberal new faculty (with Luella Mundel's likeness on every face) as Neely would characterize them at the trial.[11]

The first witness (and the key witness) for the plaintiff was George Hand, and it was with Hand's testimony that Mundel's case began to falter. Possibly because his own job as college president was in jeopardy and because he personally disliked Dr. Mundel, Hand proved an ineffective witness. Under ninety-six minutes of Meldahl's friendly questioning Hand recounted his difficulties with the board and Loudin over Mundel. The gist of it was his July report to the board on his investigation of Mundel (see chapter 3), which, over defense objections, he was permitted to read to the jury. Then under Mundel's own lawyer's questions he made several damaging admissions. First, Loudin had told him the day after her "security risk" remark that she had not meant to imply that Mundel was a subversive. Second, he had learned from special agent Ed Fleming in May 1951 that the FBI could report only to the Justice Department on Mundel (or anyone else). This last undercut his assertion in his report to the board of education that the FBI had cleared her of subversive taint, for it had not reported any information at all to Hand. Neither could he deny describing Mundel to the board as "personally obnoxious to me." Instead, he acknowledged that he might have said something like that. He admitted that he had mentioned to the board her "poor judgment." He explained that he had been referring to her use of crude language and alleged statements that she was an atheist and socialist.[12]

Matthew Neely then cross-examined Hand, concentrating on Mundel's use of crude language. Pressed by the senator, Hand told the story of a small private dinner party attended by three couples where Mundel had repeated a psychologist's joke. She had painted a very abstract and asexual nude and given it to her friend Harold Jones. Learning of this, Spaulding Rogers remarked to her as one psychologist to another that she must be trying to make Jones masturbate. Manchester reports that when the word "masturbate" was uttered, ladies in the courtroom reacted with shock, one of them running in tears from the chamber, her galoshes clutched in her hand.[13] That word damaged Mundel's case. In it all the rumors and questions about the college came to life. Fears and fantasies leaped forward from the darker recesses of people's minds to be projected onto Mundel and the evil crew of outsiders around her.

The irony was that probably the audience and the jury missed the point of the joke. Psychologist Rogers had hurled a barb at the unintelligibility and asexuality of nonrepresentational art. Both Rogers and Mundel had been amused by the antieroticism of the "nude." It was one of several instances in Fairmont when Luella Mundel found herself in trouble for speaking over the heads of her audience, or at least to a different audience than the one available to her. In 1983 one of the jurors remained convinced that faculty members would take "pictures" to parties to arouse themselves for orgies. To provide material for the underdeveloped fantasy life of some in the Fairmont community was a heavy price for Mundel to pay for repeating a colleague's arguably tasteless remark to a small gathering at a private dinner party.[14]

As Neely's interrogation continued, Hand's believability visibly tarnished, and with it, Mundel's case. The president admitted that he might have told the board that Mundel had said she was an atheist. "If I said that at the time I was crazy because I didn't have the information then, but if the board says I said it, I did." Neely pried from Hand the admission that he did not care for Mundel personally or socialize with her or approve of her lapses of judgment and crude language.[15]

The strength Hand showed was in sticking to his contention that none of what had occurred justified Mundel's removal. But even in this, he opened the door to Neely's later demolition of Mundel's reputation by avowing that he would not knowingly hire an atheist to teach at the college. In effect, this invited the senator to try to convince the jury that Mundel was exactly that.[16]

The day ended in acrimony. The courtroom was filled for Hand's testimony. College students in the crowd responded to Neely with laughs and rude noises during Hand's cross-examination, causing the senator to protest that the president had dismissed classes in order to pack the courtroom.[17]

On Thursday, December 20, the hard, wooden courtroom seats were filled with citizens awaiting Luella Mundel's appearance on the stand. After an interlude of three minor witnesses, at about 11:00 A.M., they had their wish. Frail, bespectacled, wearing a dark coat and a yellow hat, she spoke in a clear but quiet voice. Led gently by Meldahl, she detailed her academic qualifications and told of her coming to Fairmont State, her subsequent dismissal, and her efforts through the ACLU, AAUP, and other organizations to retain her position. She denied categorically that she used her classes to indoctrinate students with her political or moral views. She avowed that she was no Communist or atheist. She recounted her exchange with Victor Lasky at the 1951 Legion seminar (see chapter 2) and pointed to Thelma Loudin as having been there. Next, she described the now notorious dinner party at the home of Mr. and Mrs. Robert Layer of the college economics department for their guests, Dr. and Mrs. Hand, Harold Jones, and Mundel. She reminded the court that it had been a private party and that she had only repeated someone else's "clever remark." She described her job-hunting difficulties since her dismissal. She held up for more than two hours of direct examination by Meldahl, but then had to endure a harrowing hour and forty-four minutes of Neely's questions.[18]

Neely had hinted at the main defense tactic in his opening statement when he attacked the character and beliefs of Dr. Mundel. Now he would paint her as the defendant instead of Loudin. He would uphold his client the same way a clever lawyer would defend an accused rapist against his victim. He would blacken Mundel's reputation and separate her in the jurors' minds from the "good women" of the town who needed and deserved protection. Under his assault perhaps Mundel would break, and if she could not testify, her suit would collapse.

Neely began by quizzing Mundel about her background—her Iowa upbringing, marriage, separation, and subsequent divorce. Then he pressed on her teaching record, disputing her claim that her first teaching job had been at Dubuque, Iowa (1935–36), and disagreeing with her over whether she had taught at Michigan State University or Michigan State Normal at Ypsilanti for twenty-four weeks in 1939. He asked her why she had left Phoenix College (Arizona) and forced her to admit to personal difficulties with the former head of the art department there. He asked why in 1949 she had not submitted to Fairmont State a letter of recommendation from Park College, Missouri, where she had taught in 1946–47. She replied that she had left Park in the middle of her second year for the better-paying Phoenix job because she thought her contract had expired. She claimed that she could get a recommendation from the Park president now. Neely pounced on this. "Not if he feels the same way he did when he wrote this letter on November 2." Accusing the senator of masterminding the board's actions against her, Mundel flared, "You've been investigating me? . . . You fired me without it and then made an investigation after the newspapers put the heat on you!" Neely (both were shouting) fired back: "Yes, after you and some of your friends dragged this case through every newspaper in the United States that you could get to print something about it. . . . You and Jones and that clique . . . got this case into the newspapers and the radical papers all over the country."[19]

Now Neely had planted the idea with the jury that Mundel had a history of trouble with colleagues. He had cast doubt on her integrity, memory, and ability to hold a job. He had visibly shaken her self-confidence. He had exposed her apparent ignorance of the technicalities of academic tenure when he showed that she seemed to think that adding up the time she taught at other schools would count toward her tenure at Fairmont State. He had also aroused her to visible anger.

Next he turned to her art, seeking to portray her as a lascivious woman and to tie her knowledge of psychology to the manipulation and demoralization of youth. What color, he wondered, would produce sexual passion? She answered that she had not done any research on that point. Then why had she made the remark about her picture? "I was repeating a joke," she responded. "My pictures . . . have no subject matter. They are patterns in color and design." Neely then thrust an example of her work, a cubist study, at the jury box and asked if she taught pupils to draw pictures "like THIS thing?" She was silent while the jurors examined the painting, turning the frame this way and that, some giggling with incomprehension. In *Harper's* Manchester noted the irony of the scene: before they were allowed to view the painting it was veiled with a page from an old *New York Herald-Tribune* bearing a photo of nine Long Island drum majorettes, "white legs rampant."[20]

Next came what everyone remembered most about the cross-examination, the atheism debate. Neely began by quoting Mundel from John Cort's December 7 *Commonweal* article: "I avoid doctrinaire and dogmatic theories such as 'atheism.' I have no proof of the non-existence of a supreme being. On the other hand, I have no proof of the existence of a deity and I wish to withhold an opinion on the matter."[21]

Mundel acknowledged that the passage reflected her beliefs. There followed a dramatic twenty-minute exchange between plaintiff and defense lawyer: she arguing that she had never *denied* God's existence; he trying to get her to admit she had never *affirmed* it and was in fact an atheist. She relied on a dictionary definition, admitting to her belief in God as "something man worships. I worship truth. I worship Christian ethics and the teachings of Christ." After a series of questions designed to show that she belonged to no organized religion (not Christianity or Buddhism or the polytheism of ancient Greece), he led her to elaborate on her materialistic belief in an infinite and orderly cosmos. She said: "I live in a universe in which there are thousands and thousands and millions of suns. And thousands and millions of super-galaxies, and we are told space is curved. The scientists say in 600 million years we will be looking at the backs of our heads, only our heads won't be there. I know that somewhere in all this there is order, but these things are too difficult for me, an art teacher, to understand. If you can explain them, I'd be glad to listen to you."[22] Under further questioning she retreated to a relativistic definition of deity—what a man worships and deifies is God to him.[23]

The day ended with Mundel's cross-examination by Neely unfinished. Observers seemed to agree that she had done well on the stand. Whether or not she had convinced the jury was another matter. She showed spunk, wit, and erudition, but she had not made her peace with the local culture. Neely had led her to reveal to Fairmonters just how unlike most of them she was and how full of strange ideas. To earn community acceptance she would have to renounce the ordered chaos of the Einsteinian cosmos and affirm their anthropomorphic Christian deity and their Newtonian universe. As late as 1983, a Fairmonter commented on television that he could not accept Mundel's religious arguments: "I believe in God. The Supreme Being can be anything; I believe in God. If she believed in God, she should have said that. Now, there's no other Supreme Being but God, and if you don't believe in Him, then you're an atheist in my opinion."[24]

The following day, Friday, December 21, the courtroom filled early with those eager to hear the Neely-Mundel debate to its conclusion. According to Manchester, Denis Loudin, husband of the defendant, "toiled" into the courtroom carrying an armload of biblical reference books. But there would be no more debate. Mundel, after a sleepless night tormented by the prospect of further public grilling, pleaded illness and was excused from the trial, leaving her lawyers to hastily improvise a parade of mostly ineffective witnesses.[25]

Virtually every ploy Meldahl attempted that day failed. Judge Meredith denied his motion to enter into evidence religious freedom clauses from the United States and West Virginia constitutions after Neely objected that only the judge himself could read the law to jurors. Psychologist Spaulding Rogers was able to testify that in July Loudin had told him she was a "theist and would have to stand judgment" if she condoned atheism and that anyone at the college who questioned the board of education or protested to the AAUP should "move along while the moving is good." But he could not swear that he had heard Loudin call Dr. Mundel a Communist, atheist, incompetent, or unfit to serve on a college faculty. Nor was he able to corroborate his wife's claim that Loudin had called Mundel a Communist and "not the sort of person we want." This despite the fact that he had been speaking directly to Loudin while his wife had been busy tending to two small children and had heard only snatches of what was said. He believed that Loudin had by innuendo imputed atheism to Mundel. But the word of an eccentric professor was unlikely to prevail against a school board member and pillar of the community. Anyway, Neely could argue that Loudin had been speaking in private conversation about a professional matter in which she had a legitimate interest.[26]

Three of Meldahl's potentially most important witnesses failed to advance his case. The first, J. Clair Jarvis, pastor of Fairmont's First United Methodist Church, had been present at a September 1 meeting about Mundel between one of his flock, George Hand, and Loudin. To everyone's surprise Jarvis would not discuss the meeting because, even though the conversation had not been concerned with confession or forgiveness of sin, he believed to speak would compromise his role as a religious counselor. In an unusual and controversial ruling Judge Meredith refused to direct Jarvis to testify because of the judge's personal acquaintance with him — "If he tells me he received this in his ministerial capacity, the Court will not require him to answer."[27]

A second recalcitrant witness was botany professor C. Moore Roberts. Meldahl had hoped that the obviously unfriendly Roberts would say under oath that: (1) he had been ill and away from the college in 1950–51 and had not attended the faculty meeting where Mundel made her "socialist" statement against merit pay; (2) he had heard about Mundel's statement second-hand and had thought it sounded Communistic; and (3) he had then told Loudin that Mundel had admitted to being a Communist before the entire faculty. But Moore proved so hostile on the stand that Meldahl was forced to dismiss him without eliciting any useful testimony.[28]

The last disappointing witness of the day was Madelaine Hand, wife of the college president. Not having been there, she could not confirm the details of any discussions between her husband and Loudin or other board members at Charleston. Alas, she did recall the details of Mundel's famous "masturbate" remark. Before she told the story there was a pause for chivalrous discussion at the bench to decide if the search for truth justified forcing Hand — a lady of delicacy and breeding (and a Randolph!) — to use crude language.[29]

Truth prevailed and so did Neely's ploy. Madelaine Hand then repeated Dr. Mundel's remark. Without objection from Meldahl, Neely asked the witness her opinion: "As an outstanding cultured lady of this community, do you think it was appropriate for a college professor to make that remark in the presence of the college president and others who were there?"

> *Hand:* I would not have made it.
>
> *Neely:* I know you would not have, Mrs. Hand, but that is not answering my question. Do you think that remark was appropriate?
>
> *Hand:* I do not think so in our presence.[30]

The jury could hardly miss the striking contrast between the obvious gentility and refinement of Madelaine Hand and what must have seemed the shockingly crude and unfeminine behavior of Luella Mundel.

More than a half dozen students, former students, and colleagues testified to Mundel's teaching and subject-matter competence, but none had heard Loudin slander her. Her ally, sociologist Eric Barnitz, stated that she was not a Communist, atheist, or fellow traveler. In the cross-examination, even with the help of a dictionary, attorney and witness could not agree on a definition of atheism.[31]

The day's best witness for Mundel proved to be B. Katherine Roberts. She had taken classes from Dr. Mundel and had taught part-time at the college while her husband, the hostile Moore Roberts, had been ill and without salary. Angered by Mundel's dismissal, she had protested to the college dean and signed a student-circulated petition in behalf of Dr. Mundel. She had defended her action to Loudin as the democratic and Christian thing to do and had obviously startled her by asserting that as teachers (Loudin gave private music lessons) the two were in many ways alike. She thought both were primarily artists, who taught "from the inside out, did not force their impressions upon the pupil, and drew out the student." Loudin demurred, saying that Dr. Mundel was not a good teacher and that she belonged to a clique at the college that was "dangerous because of certain opinions they held." When Roberts defended Dr. Mundel as "less dangerous" than others, Loudin had asked who the others were, but then said it did not matter; "we have them already." Katherine Roberts finished by characterizing Loudin's mind as closed when it came to Luella Mundel.[32]

The best news of the day for the plaintiff was surely that Judge Meredith recessed the trial until after Christmas. Mundel would have almost a week to recover her health and courage.[33]

Neither the yuletide season nor the usual holiday fires, car wrecks, and assorted disasters kept the trial out of the papers during the recess. Logan Carroll of the *West Virginian* reported that Fairmonters were trying the case via the party lines and that the wire services wanted full coverage. Everyone was asking if Dr. Mundel would be able to continue. Unless she returned to the witness stand so that Senator Neely could finish his cross-examination, the judge would dismiss the case for nonsuit. It also appeared that with the plaintiff scheduled to call fifteen more witnesses and the defense yet to present its case, the trial would run into the new year.[34]

While Neely slipped off to Marietta, Ohio, on December 22 to a secret meeting of state Democratic politicians and labor leaders to squabble over a candidate slate for the May 1952 primary, Mundel remained in Fairmont awaiting future purgatory in the witness box. She must have wondered why she seemed to be on trial instead of the defendant. Through it all Meldahl managed to appear optimistic. Writing to the ACLU's Joughin on Christmas Eve, he omitted mention of Mundel's trepidation about further cross-examination or Hand's weak testimony. Instead he reported the case in "good shape." Although the judge had refused his motion to enter the West Virginia Constitution into evidence, Meldahl told Joughin that its prohibition of religious tests overrode Loudin's special privilege as a board of education member. He added that state newspapers were on Mundel's side and that barring the unforeseen, he felt confident of a favorable verdict and a large settlement. His assessment of Neely was fanciful. He compared the senator to the month of March—coming in like a lion, but going out like a lamb. Even if Mundel lost, Meldahl believed this case was an excellent one to appeal to the state or even the federal Supreme Court. This letter leads one to doubt Meldahl's grasp of the true situation. Was he simply self-deluded and overconfident or for some reason was he consciously trying to present a ridiculously rosy picture of the trial's progress?[35]

The plaintiff's first order of business when the trial resumed on Thursday, December 27, was to establish that Loudin and the board of education had violated the tenure guidelines of the North Central Association of Colleges and Secondary Schools and American Association of Colleges of Teacher Education, and that Fairmont State College belonged to both organizations. But when Neely objected that tenure rules were irrelevant to a slander suit, the judge sustained him. Another arrow from Meldahl's quiver fell harmlessly to earth.[36]

During the Christmas recess Mundel had felt better. Despite a sleepless Wednesday night (the twenty-sixth) she was in court when the trial resumed Thursday morning. But her emotions were barely under control. As she entered the courthouse, the pop of a photographer's flashbulb reduced her to tears. She seemed calm enough when she took her place in the courtroom. However, apparently sensing her vulnerability and a way to end the trial without ever having to call Loudin to the stand, Neely sought to rattle her. He announced that he planned to question her for at least two and a half hours. Then he began what even the Democratic *Times* called a "gruelling" cross-examination. It pried into her most private beliefs and was calculated to confuse and upset her.[37]

After the court stenographer read back the last question from her testimony of the twenty-second, Neely asked Mundel what she meant by the truth she said she worshipped. She replied that it was the "truth governing the cosmos, the order that either can be seen or is yet to be determined." Dissatisfied, Neely pressed her to define truth more precisely.

Mundel: I can't define truth, Mr. Neely, I suppose it is a relative matter. At one time people accepted it as a truth that the earth is flat. Now we know that the earth is round. Truth is relative to the information we have at a certain time.

Neely: You say that is what you worship. Does that answer indicate a being or substance or an imagination or whatever it may be that you worship?

Mundel: I suppose I am a relativist.

Neely: I do not care what you suppose you are. I want to know if your answer indicates what you worship.

Mundel: Yes, it indicates a principle that I worship.

Neely: Then it's a principle you worship instead of truth. Unless they are synonymous. . . . I ask you, not as an illiterate person but as a Doctor of Philosophy, as a highly educated woman, if you will not clarify what you do mean. You have said you worship truth and you have said you worship principle and that they do not mean the same thing. Does that mean you have two gods, truth and principle?[38]

Visibly rattled, Mundel could not answer a "compound question." If Neely would ask a single question, then she could answer it. Neely persisted in demanding that she distinguish between truth and principle and she mumbled that she could not. Her answers were becoming progressively less audible, prompting the judge to urge her several times to speak up. Now there was no answer. The questions and answers were read back by the clerk. While Mundel shrank as far away as she could get from Neely in the corner of the witness box, with her chin in her hand, her own lawyers said nothing. Finally she turned to the judge saying: "Your Honor, I can't handle such a question. They [*sic*] seem absurd and ridiculous to me. I don't know what answer to make to such a ridiculous question." Neely would not let up:

> *Mundel:* I don't worship two gods, truth and principle. Where did you ever get that notion?
>
> *Neely:* You testified under oath that you worship truth, is that correct?
>
> *Mundel:* I worship truth as it appears to me at any particular time.
>
> *Neely:* You have testified that you worship principle, is that correct?
>
> *Mundel:* I don't believe I said I worshipped principle.[39]

Again the record was read back and Judge Meredith asked: "Do you understand the answers that have just been read out to you?" Mundel replied, "Your Honor I don't understand what we have been talking about." The judge again, "Those were your answers weren't they?" Mundel said nothing. The judge yet again: "Do you understand what the senator is trying to get at?" Mundel, barely audible, "Not very well." Neely again, "Did you say, 'It's a principle that I worship?'" Mundel then turned to the bench and said quietly, "You must excuse me, I am ill." Sobbing loudly, she fled from the courtroom by a rear door.[40]

Now, belatedly, Meldahl, who had kept mum through Mundel's ordeal, jumped to his feet to complain of Neely's "browbeating" the witness. Realizing that Mundel could not stand much more, he announced that he would rest Mundel's case without calling additional witnesses if Neely would proceed with the defense. Neely refused, saying that he intended to question Mundel "at great length."[41]

When Meldahl blamed Neely's "ridiculous" questions for her illness, the senator brushed him aside. He was not responsible, he said, for her condition or "for her inability to answer questions which could be answered by anyone in this vast audience." His questions were only difficult for one intent upon hiding the truth. What had Mundel expected when she brought suit? He vowed "to be as pitiless and as thorough as I am capable of as my duty to my client and my country." It was just past 11:00 A.M., when Judge Meredith adjourned the trial until the next morning.[42]

At this point everyone involved in the suit was unhappy. Mundel's allies feared that she would be unable to face Neely again. Bullying Mundel had certainly worked as a courtroom tactic from Neely's point of view. But it appeared to be winning some community support for Mundel. The audience at court each day seemed to include more and more women. Some were surely pious Bible-thumpers come to see Neely smite an agent of Satan, but many watched thoughtfully and possibly critically. Even Judge Meredith must have worried. This difficult and much publicized case was embarrassing to the town. Perhaps the spectacle had gone on long enough.[43]

That night at her sparsely furnished apartment Luella Mundel became distraught. According to witnesses, lamenting that she was broke, jobless, with nothing to live for, she talked of suicide and requested of a physician who was called that she be committed to the state mental hospital. Jeanne Barnitz reported that Mundel tried to bar her bedroom door in order to jump from the second-floor window. Later she threatened to slash her wrists with a kitchen knife until Jeanne Barnitz wrested it from her. Eventually she calmed down and declined a sedative injection offered by her doctor.[44]

The next morning Mundel did not appear for court. After the jury was excused from the courtroom, Eric Barnitz gave a detailed account of the events of the night before and a physician testified that he did not believe she was competent to undergo cross-examination.[45]

Tusca Morris asked Neely to proceed with his defense and allow the plaintiff to rest her case. Neely refused. He was close to a dismissal for nonsuit. Then Morris proposed that Mundel be examined at her home. In reply Neely launched into a long monologue blaming Dr. Mundel for her predicament. It was she and her friends who were to blame "for the disgraceful publicity about Fairmont State College that has probably wrecked it." It was they who had used "radical publications" to attack the board of education for only "trying to protect the people and children of this state against godless and unamerican philosophies and teachings." He taunted Mundel's lawyers for calling witness after witness who failed to support her case. He denied again that he had browbeaten Dr. Mundel. "All I did," he said, "was to be insistent" and to bring out that she was not qualified to teach. Winding down somewhat, he asked God's mercy for Mundel and agreed to examine her at her home.[46]

The day ended with an angry exchange between Meldahl and Neely. Meldahl began it by chastising Neely for his "crazy" questions that unnecessarily invaded Mundel's private life and raised "matters that have broken her heart." Then Neely interrupted to call Meldahl a "barefaced" liar and challenged him to "go outside."[47]

Court officers without the jury met in Dr. Mundel's living room the next morning, Friday, December 28. In this setting she gave her deposition, surrounded by her books and watched over by what a reporter called a "huge surrealistic" painting by Fridtjof Schroder.[48]

Away from the prying eyes in the courtroom and free to smoke while she talked, the shy and nervous Mundel endured more than an hour of Neely's questions. Although she tripped over some of the details of the Christian religion, she more than held her own intellectually and remained calm and coherent throughout.[49]

Neely began where he left off, probing Dr. Mundel's religious beliefs. Asked to define the Christian ethics that she had testified to worshipping, she cited the New Testament ethics of Jesus and selected portions of the Old Testament, mainly the Ten Commandments. Her answers showed and she admitted that she did not have the "commandments straight" by number and that Neely's knowledge of the Bible was superior to hers. But she did not become confused or flustered.[50]

When Neely characterized her abstract paintings as graven images that violated the Second Commandment, Mundel replied dryly that their resemblance to what Neely characterized as "anything in Heaven above, on the earth beneath, or the waters under the earth," was very remote. When he tried to get her to admit that she worshipped three gods—truth, undefined principle, and Christian ethics—she calmly pointed out that

Catholics believed in a Trinity, three gods in one, and that the number three held no significance for her. Anyway, what she worshipped was "a spirit of benevolence and order." "The universe," she said, "is arranged so that it is benevolent toward life, life on this planet. It has order." Perhaps inspired by the cigarette she was smoking, she characterized this benevolence as being "in the arrangements of the stars and conditions of the planets so that we can live and it manifests itself in such a minute form as the tobacco mosaic, which is simply an atom as far as I know."[51]

To silence Neely's incessant demands to know what she worshipped, she explained, like the patient teacher she was, that she used "worship" to mean "admire," while he used it to mean observance of "ritual." She invoked cultural relativism and comparative religion to justify her belief in a benevolent order, which she modestly said was a belief shared by many twentieth-century Americans. Then she made explicit what she had been saying implicitly: she was an agnostic, but not an atheist. Because she kept an open mind, she could not deny the existence of the Christian God, nor could she affirm it. The evidence was inconclusive.[52]

Answering questions about her teaching contract, she acknowledged that she had been fully paid for the term of her contract. Therefore, technically the board of education did not fire her, it simply did not rehire her. She insisted, however, that in letting her go without notice at the end of the school year "for the good of the college," the board had to all intents and purposes ruined her. Then Neely accused her and her friends of writing to national magazines and papers to get publicity. Had they not done that, he asserted, no one outside West Virginia would have known that she was not rehired and her reputation would still be unsullied. She disagreed. The wire services had broadcast the story and it ruined her job prospects. College presidents, she said, "don't like trouble with the community and they'll not touch anyone who has been accused of being a poor security risk and atheist, or being incompetent."[53]

Neely then asked her if she believed the board could refuse to employ "notorious" Communists. Despite Neely's effort to get her to say that she would hire prominent CPUSA leader Earl Browder to teach at Fairmont State College, she remained steadfast. She thought a "good Communist" might be an asset to a large university, where there would be many other professors to refute him. But the board of education had no right even to inquire into the political views of job candidates or faculty as long as those views were not illegal. Since communism was not illegal, the board had no jurisdiction. As to Browder, she did not know what his academic qualifications were and academic qualifications and job performance should be the only criteria for employment. When Neely asked if the board must then hire qualified "atheists" and "infidels," Mundel reiterated that private religious beliefs were none of the board's business.[54]

Neely then explored Mundel's political activity and learned that Mundel had not registered to vote in West Virginia until a few weeks before the trial and had not voted at all since 1944. However, her delinquency in voting and apparent apathy toward political activity did little to abet Neely's portrayal of her as a dangerous activist radical. Neither did her subsequent testimony in redirect that she had always registered as a Democrat and "always voted for Roosevelt."[55]

Mundel seemed to gain confidence and eloquence as the examination continued. The senator's sarcastic inquiries about when she had decided to become a West Virginian did not faze her. She came for the job and had stayed for the job, she said. As the court could see, she had bought books and paintings which would be difficult to move. Was that not evidence of her permanence?[56]

She was most effective when Neely turned to her grievance against Loudin. She acknowledged that she had never met Loudin and had not heard her utter the alleged slanders. But, Mundel insisted, Loudin had slandered her when she accepted and acted upon gossip from "two or three people who had axes to grind" against her and/or the college president. What motive could Loudin have to attack Mundel, a perfect stranger? Political aggrandizement, answered Mundel. "I think this is a period in which you kill dragons: That is so-called communists, to raise yourself in public esteem, and if you can root out some so-called communists, you become a great hero or heroine to the public."[57]

At this Neely ended his examination. Then the trial adjourned until Monday morning, the thirty-first, when, if she failed to appear for court, Mundel's testimony would be read to the jury.[58]

On Sunday, December 30, during services at Fairmont's recently dedicated Christ Episcopal Church, Rector F. Graham Luckenbill paused in his announcements to extemporize about the Mundel-Loudin suit. He had recently offered the invocation at the college commencement and had judged its M. M. Neely oratorical prize competition, so he was interested in the institution. Up to that moment, like his more prudent fellow clergymen, he had kept silent about the trial. Now he spoke. He had a local reputation as a master of exegesis and most of what he said had to do with theological teachings. He expressed the opinion that neither Neely nor Meldahl understood the correct Christian meaning of the words "truth," "prove," and "God." Mundel had made her point when she testified that she believed in truth, for truth was synonymous with God and righteousness. Mundel had exhibited tactlessness and poor judgment, but she was no atheist. And because everyone seemed to be against her, the church must protect her. The trial, he said, had become a "farce" that "smacks loudly of all the bad traits of the Inquisition and the Crucifixion." State college teachers should not be chosen for their religious views and Luckenbill's own parishioners should think and behave like true Christians.[59]

A local newspaperman in Luckenbill's congregation heard it all, and on Monday morning the *Times* reported the priest's remarks under the banner headline " 'DAYS OF INQUISITION NOT OVER.' " After an hour-and-forty-five-minute meeting with counsel in chambers Judge Meredith declared a mistrial. He said that Father Luckenbill's "ill-advised" remarks "from the pulpit" made it impossible for the jury to give a fair verdict. The obviously pained Meredith strenuously denied that the trial had become a farce. He said he had at all times conducted it in the American tradition of allowing both sides to say what they wanted to say. As the spectators filed from the courtroom, stunned, no one could say who had won or lost or what the next step would be.[60]

CHAPTER 6

Between the Trials:
Surviving a War of Attrition

> Like men with sore eyes: they find the light painful, while the
> darkness, which permits them to see nothing, is restful and
> agreeable.
>
> — Dio Chrysostom (A.D. 40–120)

After the mistrial more than six months were to pass before *Mundel* v.
Loudin resumed in court. The period January to July 1952 was consumed
with maneuvering and posturing by both sides. The apparent Neely-
Loudin strategy was to wage a war of attrition designed to delay resump-
tion of the suit, minimize the influence of outside forces (such as the
national liberal press, ACLU, and AAUP), drain Luella Mundel's emotions and pocketbook, and drive her allies from the college. It aimed to
kill the suit without a retrial while Mundel's story faded from public
consciousness and the media turned elsewhere. Naturally, Mundel sought
the opposite. Her lawyers and allies tried to schedule an early retrial,
raise money to keep the suit alive, keep the issue before the public, and
pressure the ACLU and AAUP toward more active support.

The mistrial created a sensation. The opposing lawyers claimed they
would have won if the trial had proceeded. Following a southern Protestant church tradition of keeping silent on controversial political or social
issues, the Fairmont Ministerial Association quickly moved to censure
Luckenbill. Noting that the Episcopal priest had never been a member of
their association, a spokesman made clear that members did not "feel
they had the right to try any pending case . . . in the pulpits of our
churches."[1] The sanctimonious pose of neutrality ignored the part played
by prominent church members (particularly some from the Central
Methodist Church) in causing Mundel's dismissal and the central role of
religion at the trial.[2]

Liberal journalists rushed in where Fairmont clergy feared to tread.
They charged that Dr. Mundel had neither received a fair hearing nor
been treated with common decency and that the state had applied an
unconstitutional religious test to her employment. The most scathing
editorial appeared in the *Louisville Courier-Journal* on January 3, 1952.

Describing the trial as a scene of unreality echoing the Scopes trial and the Salem witchcraft hysteria, the editorial pictured Mundel as a "nervous, harassed young woman," whom Neely had pilloried.[3]

The *Courier-Journal* also blasted the Fairmont papers and the judge for timidity and inaction. Neither local newspaper criticized Neely or responded to the out-of-town critics.[4]

Three days after the mistrial a CBS sound and camera crew headed by a young reporter, Joseph Wershba, arrived at Neely's Fairmont office to film a television segment for the network's infant public affairs show, "See It Now." Finished in a half day, the three-minute segment aired the next Sunday, January 6, giving Fairmont its first national television exposure. It did not mention the Mundel case. So CBS joined the major national weeklies, including *Time, Life, Newsweek,* and the *Saturday Evening Post,* in ignoring the Mundel affair.[5]

Sunday, January 6, Neely left Fairmont for Washington, admitting to reporters that the Mundel-Loudin case had worn him out. During its run he had managed no more than five or six hours of sleep a night. But now despite his age he felt fine, was undecided about running for reelection, and was ready to begin a series of important Senate hearings. One might read his statement several ways. In the light of the ongoing liberal Democratic schism Neely might have been reminding dissident union leaders that he was their best friend in Washington. In the same context the indecision about running again could be perceived as a threat to enter the race for governor unless dissidents accepted his slate of candidates, which he called the "First Team." With regard to *Mundel* v. *Loudin* it supported the informed rumor around the county courthouse that Neely would use his Senate business as an excuse to delay a new trial, some thought until November. And no one thought Mundel's health and savings could stretch that far.[6]

Mundel's forces were reassessing their position. Meldahl left Fairmont to try other cases and to consult with ACLU officials in New York. On January 4 he met with Herbert Monte Levy. Meldahl related the details of the trial and complained that the mistrial decision was unfair because the judge required no proof that any juror had read or knew about the Luckenbill comments. He told Levy that Neely had insinuated that the ACLU was a Communist group. Again, to no avail, he asked the ACLU to support the slander action. He then made the extraordinary claim that Loudin was scared, and was willing to agree to a large out-of-court settlement and reinstatement for Mundel. When Levy urged him to take the settlement, Meldahl declined. He believed that Mundel could win and to prevent future abuses to teachers' rights he must go ahead with the trial. But Meldahl did promise that once the slander case was settled he would bring suits against the board of education to get Mundel a hearing to win damages for religious discrimination. Levy then intimated that the ACLU might pay the expenses of the former suit and would file an *amicus* brief in the latter. But Meldahl would not drop the slander trial in favor of the suits recommended by the ACLU, even after Louis Joughin of the ACLU wrote to Meldahl seconding Levy's advice.[7]

Meldahl ignored the ACLU and, having failed to win its financial support, wrote to Jones forwarding bills for more than $200 in expenses and proposing to spend a larger sum for a trial transcript. He encouraged Jones and Barnitz to raise a war chest by soliciting state schoolteachers.[8]

There was now confusion among Mundel's supporters. Her other lawyer, Tusca Morris, was telling the newspapers that Mundel might sue the board instead of Loudin. Jones and Barnitz wrote earnest letters of inquiry to the ACLU to find out what its position actually was, and a sympathetic faculty member, Norbert Zeimes, visited ACLU headquarters. Joughin advised Zeimes to get the support of prominent Fairmonters and leave the legal strategy to the lawyers. Barnitz thought that approach was useless. If Luckenbill, whom he judged to be Fairmont's greatest liberal, would not even talk to Mundel's supporters, what was to be expected of the rest of the community?

The only way to continue the case, Jones and Barnitz concluded by late January, was to set up a national defense fund. This, even though they now knew that they were likely to lose their jobs at the college.[9]

Despite her receiving more than forty letters of support, her friends reported that Luella Mundel suffered a big emotional letdown after the mistrial. Both Jones and Barnitz feared for her health and stamina. In February a pall descended on them when a belated, unofficial poll of the jurors showed that most had thought that she was linked to radicals and Communists and that when the mistrial had been declared all would have voted to acquit Loudin. It now became clear that Mundel was likely to lose the retrial. For the first time Barnitz realized that the sympathy for Mundel was largely in reaction to her being bullied in the courtroom, not to what seemed to him the transparent justice of her case.

Mundel herself evidently had second thoughts about suing Loudin. The art teacher was not vindictive; she only wanted her job back. Would it not be better to sue the entire school board to win a hearing? Wily old Tusca Morris favored that approach. So doubtful of the wisdom of the slander suit strategy was Barnitz that bypassing Meldahl and Joughin, he wrote to ACLU general counsel Morris L. Ernst.[10]

Although he knew his client was wavering and that funds were in short supply, Meldahl stuck to his strategy. The slander suit remained the best hope, he insisted. The important thing, he cautioned Tusca Morris, was to get the trial over with as soon as possible. National anticommunist hysteria was reaching a fever pitch. To wait until the June term would risk retrial in an even more hostile political climate. He urged Morris to press hard for a March date, made urgent appeals to Jones and Barnitz for payment of his expense money, and even advised Luella Mundel to appease local taste by painting a picture for the next jury that it would regard favorably as wholesome, uplifting art. When she tried, Jones called the result "pretty grim."[11]

Jones and Barnitz then began a campaign to raise money. On February 6, they petitioned the Fairmont State College AAUP chapter to sponsor a Mundel support committee. Local AAUP members shied away, for by then they had become her enemies or were too intimidated to associate with her. It was therefore no surprise when the vote went against the Jones-Barnitz motion 22-3. According to Barnitz the argument that killed it was that by supporting her the AAUP would be entering a dangerous, private matter. Fear of the power of the board and of Neely had cowed the majority.

Undeterred, Jones and Barnitz went ahead with the "Mundel Support Fund," of which they were the sole sponsors. At first they tried to follow the lawyers' injunction to raise money locally by publishing ads in the two Fairmont papers as well as "four or five others, at least" in the state. The results were dismaying. By March 6, the fund had received three contributions, all from Fairmont, that totaled $5.00.[12]

Just as their failure to win support from town or gown the previous spring had persuaded them to take their case to the national press, the pitiful response to their local fund-raising caused Jones and Barnitz to launch a national direct-mail appeal aimed at scholarly organizations and influential liberals. Their canvass eventually encompassed two large mailings of 4,000 and 7,000 letters that included American Sociological Association, American Psychological Association, and American Political Science Association members, "900 unitarians," AAUP local chapters, and dozens of publications. Seed money to begin the fund came from Jones ($100), Barnitz ($50), and Rogers ($50). The Barnitzes, Jones, and two part-time employees got out the mailings. By the time the fund closed its books in August, Barnitz calculated that $2,014 had been raised at a cost of $1,200. The more than $800 net went mainly to pay Meldahl's expenses.[13]

Mundel heard from liberal religious organizations. Some Episcopal nuns invited her to their convent. Unitarian officials in Yellow Springs, Ohio; Pittsburgh, Pennsylvania; and Huntington, West Virginia, sent letters reflecting their view that Mundel was fighting for everyone's religious freedom. A Long Island Methodist minister took up her cause and scolded the ACLU for its halfhearted support of her. A Boston Unitarian group, the Church of the Larger Fellowship, saluted Mundel and Jones as "liberal pioneers of the new social age," made a large contribution, and offered her a "free trial membership."[14]

Jones wrote tirelessly, the typewriter in his apartment clacking away late into the night. Letters went to all sorts of publications, political and religious organizations, the ACLU, the AAUP, Meldahl and Morris, "all Republican senators except Joseph McCarthy," the governor, legislators, the board of education, educational officials and organizations—to anyone who conceivably might pay heed. Some letters included the Mundel Support Fund two-page description of the case. Others asked for mailing lists to extend the appeal. Still others offered information and proposed campaign strategy.

If hard work had been enough to win, Mundel and company would have carried the day. Their efforts brought widespread national interest in her cause, but at a high price. The publicity angered and embarrassed opponents, but it could not defeat them on their own territory. Giving members of the local community a feeling of being under siege by outsiders encouraged them to close ranks and made it impolitic for any of them to speak up in Mundel's defense.[15]

The Neely-Loudin campaign against Mundel made use of local newspaper publicity. It fed on gossip, sought to ostracize the art teacher and her allies, and portrayed Christianity and patriotism as one and inseparable. It received help from the conservative Republican *West Virginian,* whose staff seemed more than willing to oppose Mundel, her lawyer, and her cause. Although it promoted a far-right line through its featured columnists, George Sokolsky and Fulton Lewis, Jr., the paper refrained in January and February from direct comment on the Mundel-Loudin suit. But when March brought irresistible opportunities to score against Mundel and Hand, the paper twice broke its silence.

On March 10, the newspaper editorialized on Brendan Gill's *New Yorker* review of Mary McCarthy's just-published *The Groves of Academe.* It found that the novel perfectly paralleled the situation at Fairmont State. The plot of the powerful and complex satire centers on an eastern progressive liberal arts college circa 1950 and the dilemma confronting its young president, who out of a sense of moral duty gives a temporary contract to a professor whose radical reputation makes it difficult for him to find a job elsewhere. At the end of the academic year the president wants to fire this victim of persecution who, it turns out, is a mediocre teacher. If he does not, the professor will almost surely be granted tenure. Desperate to retain his job, the professor invents a life-threatening illness for his wife to win sympathy and alleges that the Red smear against him is the real cause of his firing. Eventually the internal politics of the college and liberal pressure compel the president to rehire the professor. In the climactic irony of ironies, while the professor stays on at the college the president is forced to resign after it is discovered he has violated his own principles of academic freedom by surreptitiously investigating the radical professor's political affiliations.[16]

The *West Virginian* savored the *New Yorker* piece at length. Particularly delicious was the description of the fictional college president as about equally famous for "his rampant good looks and a no less rampant liberalism." Hand was no Adonis and Fairmont State was no fancy eastern liberal arts school, but the surface fit was close enough to inspire editorial winks and smirks. In the gloss upon a complex and chilling story, the parallels to the Mundel-Loudin controversy must have seemed striking. Certainly they fed the recurrent rumors that Hand had nurtured Mundel and her clique of Reds and incompetents.[17]

On March 17, 19, and 20 the *West Virginian* gave major play to a *Pittsburgh Press* story about an interview with Horace Meldahl published March 16 in the official voice of the CPUSA, the *Worker*. The article stemmed from Meldahl's participation in the Pittsburgh show trial of Steve Nelson and other minor Communist party officials. That Meldahl was acting as counsel for defendant Irving Weissman, reputedly the head of the West Virginia CP, was shocking to conservative Fairmonters.

Even more shocking was what he told the *Worker*. Asked to explain why he was defending a Communist, the Charleston lawyer offered among his reasons: his belief in his client's innocence and constitutionally guaranteed right to a fair trial; his wish to test the constitutionality of the Smith Act, which in effect outlawed the Communist party; and a desire to air all sides of the debate about communism. Readers who persevered through the fine print of the *West Virginian* coverage would doubtless remember most of what Meldahl said as being about as subversive as a high-school civics text. The trouble was, most readers probably saw only what the paper stressed.[18]

Under the banner "MELDAHL ARTICLE HOLDS RED SEEKS TO BETTER WORLD," and just above a reminder to readers that Mundel and Weissman had the same attorney, the *West Virginian* led its reprint of the interview by quoting Meldahl: "I represent a communist because I believe that he is trying to bring about a best possible state of affairs in America and our world."[19]

The *West Virginian*'s revelations brought confusion and consternation to Mundel's camp. Meldahl was outraged. In a letter to Joughin he blamed Neely, probably unfairly, for the article and charged the senator with "pole cat methods, trying to stink Dr. Mundel and me out of court." Somewhat belatedly, it would seem, he worried that it would be impossible for Mundel to have a fair trial in Fairmont.[20]

Jones, Barnitz, and Tusca Morris apparently had not known of Meldahl's part in the Pittsburgh trial. Mundel may or may not have known; the documents are inconclusive. Asked by Mundel's associates to clarify his position, Meldahl categorically denied that he was a Communist. He acknowledged to Morris that he had attended a CP legal defense fund rally in New York. He explained that ever since his political science courses in college he had been interested in ways of improving the material conditions of life and in finding an alternative to competition and survival of the fittest. Alluding to his book *Maximum Welfare* (see chapter 3 above), he proposed that a good way to clear the air in Fairmont and to raise money for Mundel would be for him to give a benefit lecture on "Maximum Welfare." He calculated that Mundel's allies could probably sell 1,000 tickets at one dollar each.

Jones took this absurd proposal seriously enough to criticize Meldahl's view that communism was an idealistic political philosophy. Skirting the all-too-obvious point that "Maximum Welfare" would be anathema to the generality of Fairmonters, he tactfully reminded Meldahl that a free local appearance by popular war correspondent and liberal writer William L. Shirer a few months earlier had drawn only about 200 souls. The strain of battle showed when Jones irritably added that in Fairmont only "evangelists passing the plate" or "hill-billy singers" seemed to do well. The normally articulate Barnitz could find no words to describe the *Worker* interview and Meldahl's response to it except "merely amusing."[21]

"Bizarre" is the only way to describe the campus doings throughout March and early April. Classes continued to meet and, presumably, students to learn as a new library building neared completion. But partisans of Mundel and Loudin studiously avoided each other except to spy and plot. Conservative political messages appeared and liberal materials disappeared from the bulletin board in the library. Student workers, particularly a telephone switchboard operator, became Hand's eyes and ears to monitor the phone traffic of Schroder, Carroll, and others. Jones filled letters to Morris and Meldahl with largely unverifiable gossip from all over town, especially from Hartley's, Fairmont's principal department store and social crossroads. In his "Report," President Hand even cites as evidence of Loudin's collusion with Schroder a student's tally of the number of used teacups at the Schroder house after a "council of war" there. Some of this overdramatic activity stemmed from the climate of the times, some from the insecurity and defensiveness of nearly all the principals, and some, no doubt, from the freshness of the war experience of many of the younger faculty.[22]

Surely the strangest incident of March was the Rosier portrait caper. On March 3, public relations director and Schroder-Carroll ally C. R.

House, Jr., asked Hand for permission to dust off and touch up a five-year-old unfinished portrait of the late president Rosier by former art department head Ernest Freed. Although House said he wanted to hang the portrait to publicize the new Rosier memorial scholarship for teacher training, he certainly knew that it would embarrass Hand by invoking the late former president as a symbol of the opposition. Hand, suspicious of House's motives, took the request under advisement. After a week without a reply from the president, House proceeded to hang the portrait, which Schroder had retouched, on the first floor of the administration building and had it photographed for the *West Virginian.*[23]

The next day, prodded by House's action, Hand took the portrait issue to a committee of three senior administrators. He proposed that they should select the best of several existing paintings of Rosier and decide where to hang it permanently. On March 18, the committee had still not made its decision when the *West Virginian* printed a front-page story on the Rosier scholarship featuring a photo of the controversial Freed painting. Hand was furious. At noon the next day after the three-by-five-foot canvas had vanished, House appeared at the president's office to ask, "Did you take the picture?"[24]

Hand then called the city police. The next day, searches of campus buildings by both administrators and police turned up nothing. The whereabouts of the purloined painting remained a mystery until April Fools' Day when the head of the speech and drama department found it, minus its frame, behind a radiator in a storage room wrapped in a March 19 copy of the *Pittsburgh Press.* The police were able to lift fingerprints from cellophane tape on the wrappings and spent much of April 2 fingerprinting the faculty and staff. The affair ended puzzlingly on April 3 when political scientist Alton Lawrence, like Mundel and Schroder a graduate of Iowa and the last of the faculty to be fingerprinted, told police the fingerprints were probably his. He said he had found the portrait earlier, but had been afraid to report it.[25] At last the brouhaha ended.

As setback piled upon setback, March vied with April for the cruelest month yet for Mundel's beleaguered faction. Early in the month Meldahl petitioned the court to reschedule the slander suit for the March term. Judge Meredith tentatively docketed it for March 24 but a few days later yielded to Alfred Neely's claim that "matters of momentous importance, both to West Virginia and the Nation" would keep his father in Washington except on weekends for the next several months. So the case was put off until the June or November term.[26]

In late March Hand went to Charleston to meet with the board of education on the Fairmont situation. The board wanted to end the continuing unfavorable publicity and apparent dissension at the college. From Hand's point of view the trial's postponement until at least June, the unresolved legal situation regarding Mundel, and the need to have a budget for the next fiscal year made consultation urgent. More to the immediate point, Hand must have wondered if he was about to be fired. His relationship with the board had become so strained that to secure a hearing he had had to approach a fellow Methodist, board member Judge Lawrence R. Lynch.

This time Hand could not complain of the secrecy of board meetings. A Charleston newspaper's protests that the board had withheld the details of Mundel's nonretention in July 1951 had forced the board to open its sessions to a newspaper reporter.[27]

Hand entered the board's chambers late in the afternoon of March 27 and remained for an hour. He told the board members that he had not met with any of them since the lawsuit began or with Mundel so he could remain an impartial witness at the trial. But the trial had not ended and so he must discuss personnel matters for the next academic year. Board members sat silently as the Fairmont State president delivered a monologue about whom to fire next at the college. He discussed five faculty members: Mundel's brain trusters Jones and Barnitz and the three active Loudinites Schroder, Carroll, and House, who was Medora Mason's successor in public relations and who attended the Central Methodist Church.

Hand listed the sins of each for the board members. He blamed Jones for starting the slander suit, condemned his "tabloid" letter writing and use of his job title on letters designed for publication. He thought that Jones had crossed the boundary from freedom of speech to license. Still, Hand was not sure Jones should be dismissed. Barnitz's crimes were mere peccadilloes. He was an employee of the board who was collecting money (the Mundel Support Fund) for a private suit against a board member. Also Barnitz had written a letter to the *Fairmont Times* in September 1951. Hand recommended that Barnitz should be retained.[28]

The president reiterated his July 1951 charges against Schroder and Carroll, adding that Schroder was a major actor in the Rosier portrait imbroglio. Concerning Carroll (see chapter 3 above), Hand claimed the physicist was using his classes to indoctrinate students "in his theory and against Einstein's" and that he had written the paper one of his students presented at a state Academy of Science meeting.

Medora Mason's successor in the journalism and public relations department, House was new to Hand's enemies list. Whether Hand was aware that in November 1951 House had written to the AAUP against his administration is not known. But he did know that House was a central figure in the Rosier portrait business. He also knew that as a member of the college policy committee House had proposed labeling library books, arguing that the HUAC was a better judge than educators to determine what belonged in the library. Hand claimed that House had even opposed soliciting community contributions to buy library books lest they include gifts of Communist propaganda. In conclusion, Hand proposed, although he did not formally recommend, the firing of all three Loudin allies.

The board minutes, newspaper and wire service accounts, and individual board members all reported that Hand recommended firing all five faculty members. Why else would he bother to bring up their names? Later, however, Hand strenuously maintained that it was not so. His only aim, he wrote, was to open for the board a preliminary discussion of the five men as sources of controversy to consider the merits of their cases. He was not making recommendations.[29]

His explanation is not convincing. True, he suggested rather than recommended dismissals. But a plausible reading of his action, which Hand would probably deny, would be that he wanted to regain control of the college by ridding it of his opponents Schroder, Carroll, and House. That tactic had worked in 1947 when he had gotten rid of Medora Mason and Blanche Price (and nineteen others). Now he appeared willing, if the board insisted, to fire Jones and Barnitz. It is worthy of note that in discussing their termination, Hand made no mention of the probationary period or AAUP tenure guidelines. All five had satisfied the time requirements for tenure.[30]

A silent board greeted the completion of Hand's presentation, excusing him without taking action on his proposal. That evening Board President Garland Dunn came to Hand's hotel room to tell him of its unanimous decision to "release" him from Fairmont State effective June 30. Publicly, the board refused to fix responsibility for the "diversity of opinion and discord" among the faculty and constituents of the college, but it concluded that the dissension had "so adversely affected institutional harmony and unity of effort as to call for a change of administration."[31] Hand played his last card to no avail when he warned Dunn that his firing would cause trouble with accrediting organizations.

He remained convinced that the board members had succumbed to the machinations of Loudin and her allies on the faculty. Much of the press sided with him. But in retrospect it is easy to follow the board's reasoning. Hand had become the center of the controversy and a public liability. To retain him would have only fueled more controversy. To have dismissed the five employees might have achieved a temporary truce at Fairmont, but it would not have quashed the Mundel lawsuit or silenced the clamor against Hand's administration. To allow the chaos to continue at Fairmont would have raised legitimate doubts about the board's ability and will to manage the other state colleges.[32]

On a related matter Hand may have been close to the mark when he claimed his firing was meant to warn other West Virginia state college presidents and faculty members to obey the board and put their campuses in order. Most of the other state colleges were comparatively isolated from newspapers and the wider world. Less publicized problems existed at several of them. In the wake of Hand's dismissal a Shepherd College professor wrote to the AAUP praising the board's summary action. He wrote that both at Fairmont and Shepherd "promiscuous" hiring practices had created much trouble and that Hand's dismissal would make the Shepherd president more conciliatory toward veteran faculty.[33]

Hand's termination at the end of the fiscal year had a predictable effect at the college. Barnitz wrote to Joughin that the old faculty and Loudin supporters were filled with glee, smiling like Cheshire cats, and planning a national publicity campaign attacking "pseudo-liberals." Liberals and Mundel's partisans were confused and dismayed. Barnitz and Jones wondered if Hand had really meant to fire them. Hand denied it to them, but they learned from Board Secretary Baer that everyone at the meeting understood that that was the intent.

Nevertheless, they rallied to Hand's support. In the many cases of dismissed campus Communists and radicals that she studied, Ellen Schrecker found few sympathetic resignations-in-protest by colleagues. Fairmont State was different. Perhaps because there was no tenure instructors had less to lose. But people did resign from Fairmont State over the Mundel affair. Barnitz nailed his resignation to a college bulletin board. Resigning with him were dean of women Olive Horton, business teacher Norbert Zeimes, social science chairman Dr. A. W. Chapline, and economist Robert Layer. All were young Hand appointees. By the end of the school year three more would be gone: Harold Jones was fired, and Dr. Dorothy Lucker and H. Norman Taylor carried out their threats to resign in protest. Protest meetings that drew an estimated 400 students voted to send a delegation to appeal to the board of education on Hand's behalf and to ask the North Central Association (the accrediting agency) to investigate. But it was all to no avail. The Loudin forces were getting what they wanted, a housecleaning. And they turned up the heat on the remaining college liberals.[34]

On Saturday April 5, Post 17 held its third annual antisubversive seminar with the Mundel case obviously in mind. More advance publicity heralded this meeting than the previous anti-Red conclaves. The list

of speakers made it clear that no quarter was to be given to local noncon-
formists and liberals. Among the dignitaries conspicuously present were
the ex-officio board member, state school superintendent, and Mundel
opponent W. W. Trent; the president of the state Council of Churches
and Christian Education; the state Legion commander; and the Legion's
national commander Don L. Wilson. Later in the month, as if to underscore the union of churchgoer and superpatriot in Fairmont, Legion
Post 17 cosponsored an all-churches parade through the downtown streets.

Among the imported anticommunist experts were some familiar faces,
including Vincent S. Hartnett, who in 1950 had allegedly told Hand
there was a Communist cell on the campus. This time Hartnett focused
exclusively on Red infiltration of entertainment and the news media.
Another speaker, Benjamin Gitlow, emphasized Communist hatred of
the Christian religion. Perhaps the most direct reference to Mundel's
cause came from Dr. Felix Wittmer. After seventeen years on the faculty
of Montclair State Teachers College in New Jersey, where he had fought
"Reds, Pinks, and Progressives," he had resigned to battle full-time
against the spread of "subversive education." He defined subversive
education as socialist education, which destroyed individual self-reliance,
and linked socialism to the NEA and progressive education in general.
The Fairmont papers reported the speeches and noted that they had
been followed by short discussion periods. They reported no controversy.
Apparently the "prominent educators" reported as being in attendance
did not include Fairmont State's liberal contingent.[35]

Despite the mobilization of sentiment by the Right and Hand's dismissal,
Mundel fought on and public controversy continued. Jones and Barnitz
continued to work for her. Students tried to help. In April three officers
of the Fairmont State student government presented a petition on behalf
of Hand to an unrelenting board of education. The *New York Times,*
Washington Post, Washington Evening Star, and the wire services continued
to report developments in the story. In what amounted to a small media
blitz, Jones and Barnitz bought time in May on a Fairmont radio station
to broadcast Mundel's side of the controversy. From March through June
they managed to get space in a number of national publications ranging
from letters to the editor in the *Nation* and *Art News* to an article in the
Nation and front-page coverage in the *Harvard Crimson*'s annual *Academic
Freedom* issue.[36]

All this publicity increased donations to the Mundel Support Fund
and assisted Jones and Hand in finding new jobs. At the end of June,
Barnitz was still job hunting. Mundel had tried without success to find a
job through several academic placement offices. Jones and Hand were
more fortunate. The former joined the library staff of Brooklyn College

and the latter became an assistant to the president of Southern Illinois University, a former coal-country college moving in the direction that Hand wanted to take Fairmont State.[37]

In April 1952 William Manchester's *Harper's* article, "The Case of Luella Mundel," inflamed the Loudin-Mundel controversy. Of all the words written about the affair his were and are the most influential. Academicians and AAUP, AACTE, and ACLU officials based their judgments in part on it. This is all the more remarkable because Manchester's direct knowledge of the case was limited to newspaper accounts, some correspondence with Hand and Mundel's supporters, and a brief visit in December to cover the trial.[38]

"The Case of Luella Mundel" is a well-crafted, insightful, highly partisan narrative of events from Hand's accession to the college presidency through the spring of 1952. Its centerpiece is the slander trial. The main heroes are Hand, the courageous defender of freedom and teachers' rights; Luckenbill, the voice of conscience in the wilderness; the graying, quiet civil liberties lawyer Meldahl; and of course Mundel, "frail, bespectacled, somewhat nervous," but with spunk and determination. The villains are Neanderthal American Legionnaires; ignorant and indifferent townsmen who tolerate "crackpots" but do not allow Communists; time-serving old faculty members; "dark and regal" Loudin; and the hypocritical, pompous, and bullying but entertaining Senator Neely.

It is a parable drawn in the starkest black and white of the travails of a truth-seeking intellectual adrift and sinking in the sea of religious bigotry and ignorance that was Joe McCarthy's America. Fairmont is a Menckenian (or Breugelian) landscape populated by strange creatures: ignorant, superstitious yokels, boobs, superpatriots, and bible-thumpers pitted against brave, sensitive, independent liberal intellectuals striving and sacrificing to bring light to a dark and sooty corner of the land. Its impact on sophisticated urban readers can be easily measured by the pro-Mundel letters to the AAUP and ACLU that it inspired and by its inclusion as must reading for AAUP and AACTE investigators.

Unfortunately for her, although it was avidly enough read, Manchester's essay did Luella Mundel no good in Fairmont. Barnitz wrote to the ACLU that the city's normal ten-to-fifteen copy monthly allotment of upper-middlebrow *Harper's* multiplied to 208 copies and then another 150 but still fell short of demand. He and Jones found the piece interesting and welcomed it as ammunition for Mundel's cause. But most Fairmonters paid less attention to Manchester's analysis of the academic freedom issues than to his portrayal of Fairmont. Many were hurt and angry at what they took to be the author's cruel and inaccurate representation of their town. In a few pages he portrayed the "barn-like courtroom" in the courthouse, "a Corinthian mass of Cleveland sandstone"; ignorant jurors, and locals who salivated over the painting that would make them masturbate in front of the Main Street shop that displayed girly magazines. He immortalized the town for national readers for its "garish" business district that daily grew grimier, "a deeper and deeper gray," from the passage of soot-spewing coal trains within blocks of the courthouse.

Worst of all was Manchester's portrayal of Locust Avenue, the street leading from downtown to the college. Fairmonters who paid attention thought of it as tree-shaded and lined with large and spacious houses, a potpourri of frame, brick, and native stone, some elegant and well sited, and several dating to the early nineteenth century. Yet Manchester saw this street as "a mile of sore-eyed frame houses pitched awkwardly on steep sloping hills." It was a street that led to the college gridiron, well-kept Rosier Field, whose future was to be "covered with soot."[39]

In an editorial, "Inside Manchester," the *West Virginian* castigated the Baltimore journalist. Cleverly, the editor defended Fairmont's appearance, listed numerous alleged distortions and omissions in Manchester's piece, and deftly sidestepped every one of his substantive arguments. Apparently in answer to Manchester, the paper ran a three-part series (May 7, 8, 9) by Fridtjof Schroder that characterized the pro-Mundel crowd as intolerant, privileged, "pseudo-liberals," an intellectual oligarchy that considered itself "elect." Its aim was to make the discredited radical "isms" of the early twentieth century into the stale orthodoxy of the present. Its method was to use championship of academic freedom as a cover for criticizing the American political system and parroting faddist theories and social concepts. Less inclined to philosophize, the Fairmont board of realtors sputtered and fumed over a motion "deploring" Manchester's article. A newspaper columnist from neighboring Morgantown defended the town. Fairmont, he said, was a place like any other. People there had made a lot of money, lost a lot of money, and had lots of fun and sorrow. It was a liberal community without institutionalized bigotry. Its citizens might well worry about subversion because it had been the "happy hunting-ground" and "nerve center" of coalfield communism.[40]

Its defenders to the contrary, Fairmont was an easy target for a liberal journalist. To an outsider, it can be difficult to adjust to life and common attitudes in the bosom of Fairmont's steep dark hills that seem to shrink the sky and to press in on one. Houses perched precariously on hillsides were and are a common sight not just in Fairmont but in the narrow valleys of the entire region. But what could anyone do about geography? Typical of industrial areas, there was much to offend the eye. In winter, when Manchester visited, the desolate hills against the gray sky could be depressing. And there was no denying that the attitudes of some of the locals were as narrow as the hollows between the snaggletooth hills. Granting all of this, Manchester's description was unfair and incomplete. More important to the freedoms at risk—academic, cultural, and religious— what did it matter if the houses in town were sore-eyed and ugly or sloe-eyed and beautiful? Manchester may have assumed correctly that the Fairmont majority could not be persuaded to see Mundel's side, but by picking on the town, he obscured his message and provided the townspeople with yet another excuse for ignoring the plight of Luella Mundel.

In the outside world, Mundel still had strong supporters—none of them more ardent than ACLU research director Louis Joughin. In late March he circulated an office memo calling hers the most important academic freedom case of the last nine months and declaring himself frustrated by the union's inability to help her.[41]

Early in April, alerted to the latest turmoil at Fairmont State by letters from her supporters, Joughin and executive director Patrick Murphy Malin tried to persuade AAUP general secretary Ralph Himstead to join with the ACLU and the National Education Association to pressure the board to grant Mundel a hearing. Himstead was uncooperative, advising them that the AAUP and AACTE were already talking with the board and expected to win a hearing for Mundel. Himstead warned that public ACLU intervention could ruin Mundel's chances with the board. On April 2 the ACLU officials agreed to take no action temporarily to allow time for the board's reply. Privately the ACLU officials believed that Himstead was giving them "a run around" motivated by "organizational jealousy." Still, the possibility of a hearing for Mundel caused the union to await the result of the AAUP–AACTE negotiations. This, despite awareness that the months of delay that might ensue might make it difficult for the ACLU to provide any real assistance to the beleaguered art teacher.[42]

It was probably just as well for Mundel that the ACLU withheld its formal, public support. Such intervention would have reinforced local rumors that she was associated with communism. Much of the political Right had long charged that the ACLU was dangerous and un-American. As a defender of unpopular causes, it had given legal aid to all sorts of radicals, including Communists. The California Un-American Activities Committee had for years called the ACLU a "communist front or 'transmission belt' organization." Paid FBI informer and ex-Communist Herbert Philbrick charged there had been Communist infiltration of the Massachusetts CLU. Senator McCarthy's researchers told him that ACLU Director Baldwin and General Counsel Ernst had a penchant for supporting liberal and Communist front causes and organizations. In the spring of 1952, McCarthy was orchestrating an attack on the Americans for Democratic Action by stressing its connections to the ACLU. Joining the hunt against the ACLU were its long-time enemies, the American Legion and HUAC.[43]

For whatever reason, the cautious approach prevailed through April and May and was confirmed and extended after Director Baldwin read Manchester's article in *Harper's*. In a memo to Joughin, Baldwin reaffirmed his opposition to ACLU intervention in the slander suit. He believed that the suit was about personal opinions given outside a board of education meeting. He recommended that the ACLU should try to get the AAUP and other organizations to act, and if the board would not give in, to black-list Fairmont State. In what seems an incongruous statement from the leader of an organization dedicated to defending individuals against tyranny, Baldwin continued that Mundel should not have gone to court in a place where she would be sure to challenge the local mores. He called the courtroom procedures disgraceful, adding that the only bright spot in the whole affair was Father Luckenbill's well-justified blast at the proceedings.[44]

With formal, direct ACLU support out of the question, Joughin did what he could. In mid-April he wrote to George Hand to reassure him that the ACLU was following the case with great interest and to inquire after the details of his dismissal. He asked about the status of Jones, Barnitz, Schroder, Carroll, and House. He asked Hand to report on board of education–AAUP negotiations, obviously as a check on Himstead. He even tried to help Barnitz and Mundel find new teaching jobs and authorized the Mundel Support Fund to quote the ACLU in its appeals.

In June, with Joughin's blessing, liberal members of the National Council of Jewish Women and Young Women's Christian Association conceived a plan to launch a national campaign for freedom. It would be designed to remind the public that it should support the right of Americans to advocate and express freely their political and social opinions without fear.

The focal point of the campaign would be "a drama, based on the Luella Mundel case" to be staged in nearly 250 cities. In June 1952 Bernice Solomon of the NCJW produced a draft, "The Case of Gertrude Young: A Mock Trial in Two Acts." It was a political drama set in "Lovely, West Virginia," a town where the people were friendly and set in their ways. It told of art teacher Gertrude Young, brainy, aloof, shy, and tart-tongued, who lost her job because of wild rumors and the accusations against her by school board member Thelma Corey, "a do-gooder gone awry." Through the character of the school board member's husband, Willy Corey, Solomon portrayed the hypocrisy of the town. Weak, henpecked, and cynical, Willy Corey relished trashy novels while his wife suppressed liberal publications in the college library. Another prominent character was the college president, Dr. Tobey S. Cool, a principled but self-important administrator. The play was heavy with allusion to seventeenth-century Salem witchcraft (Giles and Martha Corey played major roles in that affair) and to Harriet Beecher Stowe, who 100 years earlier had dramatically called attention to the national sin of slavery. Read thirty-five years later, the play seems contrived, heavy-handed, and preachy. It is hard to mourn the fact that it remained unfinished and apparently unperformed when the Mundel trial ended.[45]

Unlike the ACLU, the American Association of University Professors wanted to keep Mundel out of the headlines. A file bulging with newspaper clippings and letters from all over the country attests to the fact that AAUP General Secretary Himstead was well informed about the Mundel matter. Yet Mundel's allies remained frustrated by his inaction. They complained that he rarely answered their letters, almost never returned their phone calls, and seemed to be ill or on vacation much of the time. Barnitz told Joughin in April that as far as he knew the AAUP had done nothing in the Mundel case since August 1951.[46]

The inaction had many causes. Himstead had ably managed the AAUP office and edited the *Bulletin* since 1936. To many in higher education he was "Mr. Academic Freedom." Critics found him thin-skinned, weak in public relations, and a perfectionist who always liked to look after every detail himself and had great difficulty in delegating work to others, even when the work load grew too large to bear. In part because of the relative decline in pay and status of college teachers in the immediate postwar years, AAUP membership had grown from about 17,000 in 1945 to more than 37,000 by 1950. The volume of academic freedom cases grew proportionately and outstripped what he could handle at the time his physical powers were beginning to fail.[47]

But these reasons aside, Himstead's cautious approach to the Mundel case was deliberate. Information that reached him about the case was contradictory. Against the pile of pro-Mundel evidence from Meldahl, Jones, Barnitz, Norman Taylor, Norman C. Meier (Mundel's Iowa mentor and dissertation director), and the ACLU, he had to weigh letters, clippings, and opinions from Schroder, Horner, House, board member Lynch, retired professor Lively, and anonymous anti-Mundel individuals. From fall 1951 until spring 1952, despite a substantial volume of letters, mostly from campus chapters demanding to know what the AAUP was doing to help Mundel, Himstead took no visible action.[48]

More important, with Himstead at the helm, the AAUP preferred to operate quietly through peaceful negotiations with academic authorities. It aimed first to protect and extend faculty rights, not to help individuals, however deserving. The blacklist was its weapon of last resort, and the lawsuit was not even in its arsenal. It focused on administration and dealt with situations from a quasi-administrative perspective, seeking accommodation and gradual structural change. Its stated goal in the Mundel case from beginning to end was quietly to convince the West Virginia board of education to deal fairly with Luella Mundel and with other faculty members in the future.[49]

After the mistrial in December, the AAUP had to decide if it should go ahead with a formal investigation of the Mundel case or wait until after the retrial. In mid-February it decided to proceed cautiously in cooperation with the American Association of Colleges of Teacher Education. Himstead then wired AACTE associate secretary Edward C. Pomeroy to arrange a meeting because the "PRINCIPLES INVOLVED ARE OF PARAMOUNT IMPORTANCE AS REGARDS ADMINISTRATION OF INSTITUTIONS OF HIGHER EDUCATION."[50]

More than a month later, on March 21, officials from both organizations finally met and decided that one representative of the AACTE and one from the AAUP would study the case. The two would cooperatively examine the documents, talk to the parties in West Virginia, and prepare a report. It was almost another month before the team was chosen — Himstead from the AAUP and Dr. Carter V. Good, dean of Teachers College, University of Cincinnati, for the AACTE. Both organizations had extensive files on the case, to which were added Hand's "Report," a fifty-six-page brief he filed with both organizations soon after receiving his notice of release from the board. The "Report," which is cited frequently in this study, enriched the investigators' knowledge of the case by its detailed account of the whole Mundel episode and must have colored their opinions of the harried and overwrought Hand himself. By May, Manchester's article added to their working knowledge.[51]

From May 15 to 17 Good and Himstead put in three hard, busy days in West Virginia (Charleston and Fairmont) interviewing those involved in the affair. They dined with board members in Charleston and met privately with state school superintendent W. W. Trent. In Fairmont they talked to Hand, AAUP Chapter President Taylor, and Mundel, but not with Jones or Barnitz. If they met with Schroder, who requested an interview, or with Loudin privately, it was not mentioned. Although neither investigator spoke publicly about these meetings, judging from the surviving letters, they agreed in their evaluation and recommendations. But they decided to withhold a formal report until the slander suit was resolved and, in the meantime, to quietly negotiate with the board of education.

As far as the suit was concerned, then, Mundel would get no direct help from either the ACLU or the AAUP.[52]

In the negotiations carried on in May and June, Himstead tried to persuade the board of education to pay Mundel a year's salary, in return for which she was to drop the slander suit and the demand for a hearing. Himstead seems to have been unaware that the board simply could not make such an arrangement legally. On the other side, in late June the AAUP lavished $28.72 to bring Mundel to Washington, where she enjoyed a brief escape from Fairmont and a visit to the Phillips Gallery. While she was there Himstead sought to persuade her to drop the suit and may have told her of his efforts to get her a year's severance pay. Their meeting convinced him that she really did not want to continue the suit but felt compelled to by her lawyers and Jones and by the need for money from the support fund. After she went back to Fairmont, Himstead confided to Good his belief that Mundel was not mentally strong enough to withstand a second trial and was sure to lose. Mundel later denied the AAUP had ever recommended that she drop the suit, but even before the visit she had begun serious efforts to find another job.[53]

Himstead's hopes that Mundel would drop the suit were dashed at the end of May. Meldahl went before Judge Meredith seeking the earliest possible trial date in the June term. But it was still Neely's senatorial and political schedules that controlled the court's timetable. He agreed to a July 7 trial date, which happened to coincide with the congressional recess for the Republican National Convention. The date fitted perfectly into Neely's courtroom strategy. National media attention to the Eisenhower-Taft nomination struggle would bury the Mundel-Loudin case somewhere near the classified ads in the national press, and most of the college students who had heckled him in December would be away from the campus.[54]

As July neared, Mundel's key witness George Hand got cold feet. Himstead and Good had already concluded that the Fairmont situation originated from Hand's "bungling" of personnel and personal relationships with town, gown, and board of education. In early June, almost a month before the formal expiration of his contract, Hand departed Fairmont for his new job at Southern Illinois. Understandably, he wanted to put Fairmont and its problems behind him. He wrote Himstead that the Hands were happier in Carbondale than they had been since 1945 when they had lived in Vermont and made clear that the thought of returning to Fairmont was painful. He obviously wanted to disentangle himself from the slander suit. Following Himstead's counsel, he did not give copies of his report for the AAUP and AACTE to Mundel allies — the press, Joughin, or Mundel's attorneys. In mid-June he rationalized that since Mundel's advisor Himstead wanted her to drop the suit, he should refuse to be a witness. Worried that a trial would cause him to be charged with perjury and called a liar, Hand reasoned in a letter to Himstead that that would cause Mundel to lose the suit, which would vindicate the board. He wanted to do what was best for Dr. Mundel and for national and professional principles of freedom, truth, and justice.[55] Himstead's reply was swift and unambiguous. The AAUP general secretary wired Hand on June 23 that if the suit went ahead, Hand should testify for the welfare of Dr. Mundel.[56]

Until the trial began Himstead continued to try to strike a deal for Mundel. He was reconciled to the near certainty that Mundel would lose the retrial, but he did what he could to limit her pain and suffering. Just before the trial began he wrote to Board President Dunn, with copies for each board member, including Loudin, assuring them that their statements to him and Good had been held in total confidence and asking them to curb Neely's courtroom excesses: "I hope that the defense in the second trial . . . will not misrepresent the issues in the suit and/or the motivations, attitudes, and actions of the West Virginia State Board of Education in reference to Dr. Mundel. It is important as regards the welfare of the Board and of the institutions administered by the Board that the defense in the second trial not be of the nature of the first trial."[57]

Despite his assurances to the board, Himstead did one other service for Mundel. He passed on to her side the information that board members would say at the trial that Loudin's remarks had not touched on Mundel's loyalty or religion. That would be the limit of the AAUP's advice until after the trial.[58]

By May it was clear that Neely's defense of Loudin had not done political harm to the senator or his party in West Virginia. Beginning in January, Neely courted the public eye in Washington. He conducted hearings on television access to government committee meetings and on corruption in the District of Columbia. He took the lead in the passage of a watered-down federal coal mine safety bill. He supported unsuccessful bills to provide home rule for the District of Columbia and federal funding for cancer research. Despite less than resounding legislative success, Neely had reason to be optimistic about the upcoming elections in West Virginia. As he reported to the Senate on Democratic "good tidings from West Virginia," the Democratic candidates he backed—junior senator Harley Kilgore, gubernatorial candidate William Marland, and First Congressional District hopeful Bob Mollohan—had all won their primary contests handily. On account of his party's overwhelming registration majority in the state, he predicted a Democratic sweep in the general election that would put liberals in all the state's six House seats. Crowing somewhat, he projected a national Democratic victory in the fall. Had not West Virginia supported the victorious candidate in every presidential election since 1912?[59]

As July 7 approached and disappointment followed disappointment, Mundel's followers must have sensed approaching doom. But Meldahl remained sanguine. He planned to take a new and tougher courtroom posture toward Neely's excesses and, at Jones's request, to boost Mundel's confidence by having her sit between him and Morris at the lawyers' table during the trial. He touted the latest of his many surprise weapons— his discovery that Legion Post 17 had paid Loudin's lawyer fees to the tune of a $2,500 retainer for Matthew Neely. He said that he felt certain Mundel would win this time. And even if she did not, she would eventually win on appeal.[60]

Left: Joseph Rosier, Hand's predecessor as president of the college; *right:* John W. Pence, Hand's successor as president of the college. (Courtesy Fairmont State College.)

Left: Ernest Freed, Mundel's predecessor as art department head; *right:* Fridtjof Schroder, Mundel opponent and art department colleague. (Courtesy Fairmont State College.)

Group photo at ground-breaking for college library, 1949. *Front row: center,* Thelma Brand Loudin; *third from right,* Harold D. Jones; *second from right,* George H. Hand. *Back row: center,* John W. Pence; *third from right,* Eric Barnitz; *second from right,* Regis Larkin. (Courtesy Fairmont State College.)

Mundel allies. *Left:* Spaulding Rogers; *right:* Harold D. Jones. (Courtesy Fairmont State College.)

Mundel opponents. *Left:* Robert L. Carroll; *right:* C. Moore Roberts. (Courtesy Fairmont State College.)

Matthew M. Neely. *Above:* as friend, in 1954 campaign portrait; *below:* as foe, denouncing MacArthur after his firing by Truman in 1951. (Courtesy West Virginia and Regional History Collection, West Virginia University Library.)

CHAPTER 7

The Second Trial: The Ordeal Ends

> If there is any fixed star in our constitutional constellation, it is
> that no official high or petty, can prescribe what shall be ortho-
> dox in politics, nationalism, religion, or other matters of opin-
> ion or force citizens to confess by word or act their faith therein.
>
> — Mr. Justice Jackson for the majority of the Supreme Court in
> *West Virginia State Board of Education* v. *Barnette* (1943)

> I don't want, regardless of what Thomas Jefferson, the Constitu-
> tion of the United States and of West Virginia, and all the law
> books say, a tax dollar or a tax mill of mine spent to hire a
> teacher to teach my grandchildren and yours that nobody knows
> that there is a God. If I were on the board, I would vote no
> against . . . such a teacher and it wouldn't make any difference
> how many screwball newspaper editors said, "You're violating
> academic freedom."
>
> — Matthew Mansfield Neely to the jury in
> *Mundel* v. *Loudin* (1952)

The second trial of *Mundel* v. *Loudin* received less press attention than
the first. The reasons for the absence of Manchester or any other metro-
politan journalist were many. But basically the case was yesterday's news.
One could expect only stale revelations and little suspense. The outcome
seemed a foregone conclusion. The big story that week was the Republican National Convention. At mid-trial courtroom spectators were seen
scanning banner headline editions of the local papers announcing Ike's
nomination.

Still, even without the novelty and histrionics of the first, the second
trial offered its share of verbal fireworks. More important, with more
than six months to prepare, both sides presented carefully reasoned
cases. And the trial gave Thelma Loudin and the rest of the board of
education a chance to explain their side.

From beginning to end it was obvious that Judge Meredith did not
want to repeat the previous December's fiasco. He muzzled attempts by
either side to raise any but the narrowest issues in connection with the
suit. He would not permit Hand's July 1951 report to the board on
Luella Mundel to be entered as evidence even though he had allowed it
at the first trial. He denied Meldahl's efforts to put the board of educa-

tion on trial. He silenced Neely's sallies against Mundel's loyalty and rhetorical fulminations against the Soviet Union, saying those were not the issues.

For his part Neely backed away from the first trial's defense theme that Mundel was part of a subversive clique at the college. Instead he sought to paint her as one of Hand's collection of "screwball" professors who did not belong in the classroom. His method was to focus on what for Fairmont were her unorthodox ideas about religion, art, and academic freedom and her unladylike utterances about sex.

Meldahl, too, narrowed his case. Instead of trying to prove that Mundel had been called a Communist, he sought to convince the jury that Loudin's privileged remarks to the board of education had led its spokesman to slander his client. His contention that private statements could make an individual liable for slander committed by a public agency was an interesting, if untested, idea. He also concentrated on showing that Mundel was not really a screwball and on protecting her from Neely's badgering.

Monday morning, July 7, was given to a dispute over jury selection. Mundel's counsel wanted American Legionnaires barred from the jury pool. The week before, the *Times* had revealed that unbeknownst to some of its members, Fairmont's Post 17 had "loaned" $2,500 to the Marion County Anti-Subversive Committee (see chapter 4 above). The committee, largely made up of Legion officials, had passed the money on to Loudin to pay Matthew Neely's retainer. In light of this, the judge disqualified all "active" Legionnaires.[1]

In retaliation Neely moved to bar contributors to the Mundel Support Fund. It was embarrassing to Mundel's supporters that none of the seventy prospective jurors had donated to it. And, if we are to believe Jones and Barnitz, only they and three others of Fairmont's nearly 30,000 people gave to the fund.[2]

The second jury, like the first, was composed of old-stock white and mostly lower-middle-class service or industrial workers. Although Fairmont lay in the heart of coal country, not a single miner was on the panel. This jury was even less favorable to Mundel than its predecessor. Sitting as foreman of a jury that included glass and metal workers and a service station attendant was a representative of the local establishment. Edward Chauncy Griswold had belonged to the Legion since its inception but claimed he had never attended a meeting at Post 17. He was executive vice president of a local bank and manager of a furniture store. Another juror, E. B. Horner, was employed by the county board of education and thus indirectly connected with the state board, a party to the case.

Mundel's counsel did not exclude Griswold or Horner or a third juror who may have been a Legion member.[3]

Newly sworn and already sweltering, the jury heard opening statements in the afternoon. The usually humid and often fetid Monongahela Valley was suffering through a heat wave, with the temperature surpassing 90 degrees. To add to everyone's misery, the courtroom's noisy exhaust fans had to be shut off so the jury could hear. Throughout the trial the weather kept the audience below capacity when neither Mundel nor Loudin was on the stand. Observers reckoned that those present were a different sociological mix compared to the first trial. It being summertime, there were fewer college students. Housewives predominated in the mornings before radio soap operas began. The after-lunch crowd included more men in business suits.[4]

In a tactical move that played up Mundel's local ties, Fairmont lawyer, the venerable Tusca Morris, delivered the opening address for the plaintiff. In thirty-five minutes he told Mundel's story, striking the main theme that the May 1951 board meeting had become "an explosion of words" and that Loudin's words had been full of malice toward Mundel. He granted the defense contention that Loudin's board membership might legally shield her when she referred to Mundel as a security risk and an incompetent teacher. It might even protect her when she gave the Schroder letter to the *West Virginian*. But when the board's spokesman told the world that Mundel had been let go for the good of the school it had ruined the art teacher's reputation and job prospects. It had made her "untouchable" — a victim of the Second Commandment, "Thou shalt not bear false witness against thy neighbor."[5]

In what for him was subdued style, Neely outlined the defense. The senator said that Loudin had simply been doing her job as a board member, defending "your children and my grandchildren against incompetency, vulgarity, and other objections in teachers." He reminded jurors that he had originally appointed Loudin to the board of education and three later governors had reappointed her. The college, which in Joseph Rosier's day was "the pride of Fairmont," had, under Hand, become filled up with "screwballs." Under these circumstances Loudin's duty required her to speak out against Mundel. Even if she had not, Neely claimed, Hand would probably have fired Mundel anyway.[6]

Neely then turned to the issues of tenure and the power of the board of education. Board members, he claimed, had the moral and legal right to "get rid of this woman if they thought she was incompetent or for any other reason they choose." He scoffed at the idea of tenure. If a farmer hired a woman who could not milk a cow and kept her for the time they had agreed to, it "would be absurd to say that he couldn't get rid of her because she had tenure."[7]

George Hand was the only witness on the first day of the trial. While Dr. Mundel sat stiffly, the papers said looking "wan and small" between her shirtsleeved attorneys, Hand answered Morris's questions for an hour and a half before a half-empty courtroom. He recounted his version of the events that led to Mundel's firing, adding some new information. After the July board meeting he had informed Mundel that he had done all that he could for her and that now she had better "forget it." He said that on several occasions after the May meeting Loudin had denied to him that she had ever called Mundel a Communist, but had said the art teacher was "not the proper type of person to be on a college faculty."[8]

Neely's cross-questioning of Hand, which ran over into the next day's session (July 8) shook the ex-president's story. A series of questions suggesting that the senator may have had access to information from the FBI bared lapses of Hand's memory about the details of his May 1951 contacts with the bureau. For example, Hand could not remember whether he had told the FBI about Mundel's statements at the antisubversive seminar or whether he had phoned the bureau four days after his first visit to tell the agent that Loudin had not meant that Mundel was a Communist or a fellow traveler.[9]

Hand admitted that he had hired Mundel without interviewing her. But he had studied her credentials and called her previous employer, the president of Park College. That gentleman had told Hand he did not know Dr. Mundel personally, but only that she was regarded by some as a "man-hater." Since Hand did not think that disqualified her for the Fairmont State faculty, he had hired her. He admitted that before May 1951 he had known that Mundel liked to make shocking statements. When asked during a follow-up about one of her "shocking statements" if he would hire a socialist, Hand stood firm, saying that as long as there was no law against being a socialist "I insist it is not my business to inquire."[10]

The president's testimony suggested that he had not tended carefully to personnel matters. He was unable to explain why the salary list he had submitted to the board in 1951 credited Mundel with fourteen years of teaching experience when actually it was less than three. He dismissed the error cavalierly: "Why should I pay attention to those details? My secretary had all the papers, and she can count as well as I can."[11]

Asked for his view of academic tenure, he replied that he doubted that the board had any tenure policy. His own was that as long as their work was satisfactory, faculty could "stay forever." If their work became unsatisfactory they should be let go regardless of length of service. When Neely brought up his firing of veteran employees Medora Mason and Blanche Price, Hand responded, "That proves my point, sir."[12]

Hand stuck to his story that Loudin had brought up Mundel's religious views at the May board meeting, saying she did not think an atheist should be on a college faculty. He still did not recall that he had ever told the board that he found Mundel "personally obnoxious," although he might have let it be known that their personalities did not "harmonize."[13]

The rest of the July 8 session was mainly a replay of the first trial. Four of Mundel's former students appeared as witnesses to her competence. Katherine Roberts, a former faculty member and a student in one of Dr. Mundel's classes, offered her opinion that Mundel was a good teacher and reported that Loudin had said that Mundel, Dorothy Lucker, H. Norman Taylor, Harold Jones, and Spaulding Rogers constituted a dangerous clique at the college—"dangerous because of its point of view towards communism and its view of religion."[14]

Neely was waiting to discredit Roberts, who had been a strong witness for Mundel at the first trial. Apologizing as he did so, he forced her to reveal that a decade earlier, in 1941, she had spent several months in psychiatric hospitals and had later seen a psychiatrist. Meldahl objected and, indeed, one wonders how the witness's mental illness more than ten years before could compromise her testimony about events only a year old. But the information had its effect. Mundel's lawyers hurriedly excused her from the witness stand.[15]

Former psychology department head Spaulding Rogers came down from his Maine summer retreat to testify for Mundel. His wife, hampered by a difficult pregnancy, remained at home, but her testimony at the December trial was entered as evidence. Rogers again described the July 14, 1951, meeting of his wife and himself with Loudin at her home. Adding to his evidence at the first trial, he said Loudin had told him that some night-school students had complained to her about Mundel's teaching. She had said the board had dismissed the art teacher solely on Dr. Hand's recommendation, adding that anyone (i.e., any faculty member) who questioned the board's authority or actions ought to move on "while the moving was good." Rogers claimed that she had belittled the significance of an AAUP investigation. Finally, she had stated, "I am a theist and I would expect to stand judgement if I condoned its opposite." Still, Rogers could not confirm his wife's testimony that Loudin had said of Mundel "that woman is not fit to be on a college faculty." Neither could he say he had ever heard Loudin call Mundel a Communist, atheist, or an incompetent person with bad personal traits.[16]

Next, the Reverend Mr. J. Clair Jarvis was called to testify about the meeting he attended at Loudin's home between Loudin and Hand. At the first trial Judge Meredith had upheld Jarvis's refusal to speak on grounds of ministerial privilege. Jarvis again claimed to have been at the meeting as a "ministerial counselor" and considered what he heard to be privileged. Again the judge granted the minister's right to keep silent on the matter, although he admitted he might be making a legal error. Then Jarvis changed his mind and agreed to answer questions. But by now his memory had faded and he could remember little that would help Mundel's case, except that Loudin had wanted more West Virginia University graduates teaching at the college.[17]

The plaintiff scored a small victory when journalist Lawrence Boggs, a hostile witness, testified that Loudin had given him the controversial Schroder notes to publish in the *West Virginian,* and then they were read in their entirety to the jury. But at the end of the second day of the trial, Mundel's side had not built much of a case. It had not shown convincingly that Loudin had acted with malice or that she had said anything at all about Mundel outside of her official role as a member of the board of education.[18]

The courtroom was filled to overflowing when Luella Mundel took the stand on Wednesday, July 9. Dressed in a light blue suit and black hat trimmed in white that covered most of her dark blonde hair, she sat rigidly in the witness chair and through the early part of her testimony nervously twisted a pair of white gloves in her hands. But she remained composed, her voice strong, her answers sharp. For about two hours Meldahl led her through the story of how she came to Fairmont and lost her job: the American Legion meeting, the board actions of May and July, and her contacts with Hand. She testified that she was an agnostic who believed in Christian ethics, but she was not an atheist or a Communist. She denied being a member of a "dangerous clique" at the college or having said in the cafeteria that she was an atheist.[19]

It was much the same testimony that she had given at the first trial except that she now seemed more crisp, confident, and self-assured. She was less deferential to George Hand, whose weak testimony and effort to distance himself from her were apparent. She testified that when Hand told her of the board's action after the May meeting he had not mentioned that she might be fired. He had simply said that her contract would be held up until he completed an investigation. She had then asked if she should look for another job and he had explicitly told her no. To put the dinner party banter, and thus her own "masturbation" story, into context, she repeated an indelicate story she said Madelaine Hand had told that evening.[20] However, on the crucial issue when pressed, Mundel could not say from her direct knowledge that Loudin had acted with malice toward her. She could only point to the fact that she had been let go for the good of the college.[21]

Her morning testimony was only prologue to the ordeal of Neely's afternoon cross-examination, which was marked by unconcealed mutual hostility. Mundel was sharp-tongued and argumentative and Meldahl punctuated Neely's questioning with objections. Resplendent in an off-white suit, the senator larded his questions with sarcasm, always addressing the witness as "Mrs." never "Dr." Mundel, except on those occasions when he called her "Mrs. P.H.D. Mundel" or, once, "Mrs. Meldahl."[22]

So baited, Mundel exhibited the tartness that had contributed to her downfall at Fairmont State. Tweaked by Democratic political boss Neely about her recent registration as a voter, she told him that she had always voted the straight Democratic ticket, but would not do so again because of his conduct at the trial. In what the *Fairmont Times* called a "colloquy" with Neely over the relative merits of the conflicting testimony of C. Moore Roberts (pro-Loudin) and his wife B. Katherine Roberts (pro-Mundel), Mundel declared herself a victim of Neely's "character assassination and McCarthyism which you go to Washington and fight and then come to Fairmont and do what's expedient."[23]

When Neely again tried to discredit Katherine Roberts's testimony by references to her eight months of psychiatric treatment a decade before the trial, Mundel defended her friend by pointing out that she was a highly intelligent woman and that the board of education must have thought so when it hired her to teach in 1950.[24]

Neely next asked Mundel if she could say under oath that Loudin had called her a Communist. Mundel replied "No, but she said I was a poor security risk." And that information, she admitted, had come to her secondhand from Hand and Katherine Roberts. But she added that the word "Communist" was the first thing that popped into anyone's mind in connection with "security risk."[25]

Then the senator attacked Mundel's religious views. She admitted having accepted a provisional membership in a Boston Unitarian church shortly after the first trial, but denied that it was to advance the lawsuit. She explained with some heat that she had "always thought along those lines." Even so, Neely managed to cast doubt on her zeal when he forced her to acknowledge that she had never attended a Unitarian service (there was no local church) and that she did not even know if the Unitarians had communion.[26]

He then resurrected the details of the deposition taken at her home during the first trial, forcing her to explain again that she deeply believed in Christian ethics but had "no opinion" on the Creation. The judge refused to allow a series of questions requiring her opinion as to whether those who did not believe in a supreme being made the best teachers. But Mundel was forced to expound in detail on whether or not Communists should be hired as teachers. Defending the right of students to learn "everything," she said again that as long as communism was legal, then a qualified Communist should be hired. Under Neely's questioning she conceded that Fairmont State was too small to have a faculty reflecting the full spectrum of political opinion and that she would "recommend" a Communist faculty member only for a campus of about 20,000 students. When Neely suggested that if she were on the state board of education she would "see to it that at least one Communist was on every college faculty," she shouted "No!"[27]

Mundel answered questions about the Mundel Support Fund (it was Meldahl's idea and she had nothing to do with the solicitation), her relatively brief teaching experience prior to that at Fairmont (Neely was using a "lawyer's trick" to distort the truth), and whether she was absolutely sure she had seen Thelma Loudin at the American Legion meeting (she was not). Then Neely tried to establish that she had not really looked for a job since May 1951 and therefore had no proof that Loudin's statements had actually harmed her employment opportunities. Mundel answered that she was looking for a job and that being called a poor security risk was the worst slander possible. He then tried to spring a trap. How, he asked, could Mundel say being called a Communist was slander that would ruin her job prospects when she thought there ought to be a Communist on every campus?[28]

It was unbearably hot in the crowded courtroom and it was nearing the hour of adjournment when Neely baited Mundel by bringing up the seemingly unsinkable masturbation story, which led to a sharp exchange. It began when Neely claimed a teacher who told a dirty joke should be fired and ended when Mundel accused Neely of having a "filthy mind."[29]

Thursday, July 10, a break in the heat wave and the prospect of hearing the defense brought a capacity crowd to the courtroom. Meldahl completed his case in the morning. Pro-Mundel witness sociologist Eric Barnitz denied that there was a subversive clique at the college and explained that he had worked for Dr. Mundel because he "thought she had been wronged and a suit was her only method of redress." He admitted to being an agnostic and testified at considerable length about the origin and progress of the Mundel Support Fund. He said that Mundel's dismissal had damaged her health and caused her to behave strangely on occasion—he mentioned in particular her apparent suicide attempt in December.[30]

Next a genial and expansive Harold Jones took the stand to testify that

Luella Mundel was an excellent teacher. With considerable self-assurance he described her contribution to the design of the color scheme of the new college library and even urged the judge (unsuccessfully) to provide taxis so that the jury should go and see it. Jones asserted that Mundel's dismissal "violated every precept of good personnel policy" and described her as "active, happy, and congenial" until her nonretention caused her to lapse in depression. Neely made no attempt to shake this witness, except to lead him to say for the record what was obvious—that he was strongly pro-Mundel. At the end of Jones's testimony the plaintiff rested.[31]

Neely opened the defense by calling six members and the secretary of the board of education, all of whom swore that Hand's answers to their questions at the July board meeting caused them to terminate Mundel. Leading off and setting the tone was attorney Lawrence R. Lynch of neighboring Clarksburg, who said that Hand's statements to the board "completely undermined and destroyed" his recommendation to retain Mundel. Her name had never come up until May 1951 and none of the board members knew anything about the art teacher except what George Hand told them. Loudin had made no statement against Mundel at the May meeting. Lynch said that Loudin had asked if Mundel was a "good security risk for that position." When Hand had inquired if she meant a Communist, she had replied, "I did not use that word. I don't mean that word. Please bear in mind that you used that word, not I." He added that Loudin had abstained from the vote against rehiring Mundel. Her only statement at the July meeting against the art teacher had been to report the complaints of several women about the language Mundel used at a party (the masturbation remark).[32]

Perhaps the most fascinating testimony had to do with the FBI investigation of Mundel. Lynch said, and other board members echoed him, that the board wanted no witch hunts and that it had instructed board secretary H. K. Baer to tell George Hand to leave hunting Communists to the FBI.[33] Testimony from the other board members took up the rest of the day. So repetitive was it that the packed courtroom steadily emptied as the day wore on. Even the minor differences among the witnesses seemed to confirm that it was Hand who wanted to get rid of Mundel. It is difficult to judge without an official transcript, but their collective testimony sounded carefully rehearsed to some and their recollections too precise about events more than a year old. All denied that Loudin ever said that Mundel was unfit to be on a college faculty or that they had intended any malice to Luella Mundel. Board president Garland Dunn added that Hand had disapproved of Mundel's public utterances at the American Legion meeting and that Hand had said if he had it to do over he would not have recommended rehiring Mundel. J. Kelvin Holliday, a small-town newspaper publisher, complained that he had received "propaganda" from the Mundel Support Fund. Ross H. Tuckwiller added that Hand had said he had "utter confidence" in the man who had heard Mundel say she was an atheist. It was Hand's statement, the board member claimed, that had influenced him to vote for her nonretention. Board Secretary Baer explained that for the "good of the college" was his own phrase, not the board's. He had intended to make no statement about the affair, but "pressed and pressed and pressed by the press" he had given that explanation to a wire service reporter. Everything the board did, he added, was for the good of the college and he had meant no harm to Dr. Mundel.[34]

Next to the stand came college dean of men George H. Turley to say that Mundel had described herself as an atheist while sitting across from him at the college cafeteria. He added that when a "look of disbelief" came to his face, everyone at the table laughed. He did not know if she was joking, but the statement was "so unusual" that it stuck in his memory and he later passed it along to George Hand.[35]

Robert L. Carroll followed Turley. The physicist repeated his claim that Mundel had said to him in January 1950 that a belief in God was not socially acceptable. He admitted he had never thought that George Hand was the "right man" for the college presidency and that he wanted the job. He acknowledged that he had carried some "rough notes" from Schroder to Loudin complaining about Hand's procedures. He denied that he had ever said that God ordained him to be president of the college or that he had actually ever seen God. However, he added, God might appear to someone "under the influence of a strong drug." He allowed that he had undergone several surgical operations and that he might have seen God in an "ether dream." So ended the first week of the trial.[36]

On Monday morning, July 14, defendant Thelma Loudin testified. The heat was back and all sorts of fans were in evidence, including more of the old-fashioned palmleaf kind than old-timers had seen "since the last Chautauqua." A court officer tried to move three women who had preempted the seats by the only open window so that all might share what little air there was. But personal discomfort was soon forgotten as all eyes turned to Loudin's appearance on the stand. She was tall, slim, and attractive with a striking gray streak in her dark hair. At first she answered so softly that it was difficult to hear her even in the dead-still courtroom. As she gathered confidence, her nervousness disappeared and she became animated and relaxed.[37]

Her direct testimony, which lasted until the noon recess, was a denial of all charges. She had said nothing about Mundel outside her official duties as a board member; she bore no ill will toward the art teacher, whom she had never met or spoken to. She had never called her a Communist. By her "security risk" question at the May 1951 board meeting she had only wondered aloud if Mundel was a good prospect for a long-term faculty.[38]

She swore that the first complaint she had heard about Mundel had been in December 1950 from Hand himself when he had described Mundel's opposition to his proposal for faculty merit pay raises and had quoted her remark that she was probably a socialist. He had added that Mundel did not want to be rated on her teaching because she was a poor teacher who knew that she was unpopular. So she had wanted to be paid based on her degree alone. The witness then gave her version of the sequence of complaints from Roberts, Carroll, and Schroder. She acknowledged that she had gone to the May 1951 board meeting armed with this "information" about Mundel. So primed, she had asked Hand why he proposed to rehire the art teacher at a $200-a-year raise. Loudin said she asked Hand if he had any criticism of Mundel: he replied that he had heard a rumor that she had declared herself to be an atheist, but that he thought she just said such things to shock people.[39]

Loudin said that she had told Hand several times after their May meeting in his office that she was interested only in Mundel's teaching effectiveness, not in her politics. She testified that at the July board meeting Hand had said that Mundel was personally obnoxious to him, that he avoided her "on every occasion," and that she had used poor judgment in "heckling" American Legion speakers. He had told the board that to reemploy Mundel for a third year would be to give her "enough rope to hang herself."[40]

Loudin flatly contradicted the testimony of Elizabeth Rogers about what had been said at the July 14, 1951, meeting with Dr. and Mrs. Rogers at her home. She said their meeting had been held out of doors and that Elizabeth Rogers could not have known what was said because she was constantly tending to two small children while a noisy motorized lawn mower roared nearby. She said that Spaulding Rogers had told her that Luella Mundel was "extremely unhappy" and might commit suicide. He had explained that Mundel came from a background "marked by altercations over religion." As Loudin recalled it, she expressed sympathy for Mundel, saying "I am sorry she has no comfort. I am a theist and I get great comfort from that." She admitted confiscating Rogers's notes of their conversation but adamantly denied making the "arrogant" statement that anyone who disagreed with the board should move on. She denied that during her meeting with Hand and the Reverend Mr. Jarvis she had referred to Mundel as a Communist or that she had remarked to Katherine Roberts that Mundel was part of a clique at the college. Loudin ended her direct testimony by avowing: "I bear no malice in the world toward the plaintiff. I never have."[41]

After lunch Meldahl cross-examined Thelma Loudin. She explained that in April 1951 she had been undecided about whether to challenge the rehiring of Dr. Mundel. She had not spoken to Mundel about the derogatory allegations because as a board member "she never disassociated herself from the board in matters of official action." She had not consulted with Hand or advised him that she would oppose Mundel at the May meeting because she "wanted to see what he would do" about Mundel. She said she bore no enmity toward George Hand. All this was unconvincing in light of her contacts with Carroll, Moore, Schroder, and others concerning Mundel and Hand.[42]

Asked about her attitude toward communism and education, Loudin gave her opinion that public school students should seriously study communism. She had no objections to remarks Mundel made in private conversation, but "a teacher might impair her usefulness by making statements that shock people. Our schools are character building institutions, and a teacher might impair her usefulness by making certain kinds of statements." A few minutes later, after Meldahl failed again to persuade the judge to admit into evidence Hand's July 1951 report to the board on Mundel, Loudin was excused and the defense rested its case. A short time later, the plaintiff also rested. Now it remained only for the lawyers to give their summations, the judge to instruct the jury, and the jury to give its verdict.[43]

The crowd that packed the courtroom Tuesday, July 15, overflowed into the corridor, anticipating what one reporter called the "finest forensic fireworks" in years. Tusca Morris spoke first, his voice booming through the cavernous chamber. He blamed Neely, Loudin, and the board for mismanaging the college and maliciously slandering Dr. Mundel. He characterized the board as a highly politicized reflection of the desires of politicians for pliant and controllable board members. Thelma Loudin was such a member (presumably controlled by Neely). She had acted with malice when she gave the Schroder notes to the *West Virginian*. Luella Mundel was not a Communist or an atheist. The college was no hotbed of radicalism. Mundel was right to speak out at the Legion seminar, for ex-Communists were "the worst there is." When they sinned once they would sin again: once a Communist, always a Communist. Morris closed his appeal to the jurors with Shakespeare ("Who steals my purse, steals trash") and the Bible ("Thou shalt not bear false witness").[44]

Next to speak was Alfred Neely, the heretofore silent member of Neely and Neely. The senator's son said that Mundel had booby-trapped the May 1951 board meeting, Hand had lighted the fuse, and there had been an explosion. Fairmont State College, he said, belonged to the taxpayers, not to "the gang which has been prosecuting the case for Mrs. Mundel." Loudin had acted for "you" the taxpayers. The college was established to educate students, not to guarantee a job to Luella Mundel. If the jury found against Loudin, "you might as well dump the whole school system, because no board of education will then be able to inquire into the qualification or eligibility of any teacher."[45]

The elder Neely then followed with a long, overwrought, arm-flailing (and possibly prejudicial) speech. Enlisting in his client's cause such figures as Job, Ananias, Sapphira, and Barabbas, the senator worked himself into a lather imploring the jury to cast out the devil from the college. He painted Loudin as "an unpaid public servant who has done her duty as is shown by overwhelming proof." She was wresting control of the campus from "agnostics, socialists and screwballs" and returning it to "courageous, self-sacrificing, patriotic men and women." There was no place on college campuses, he said, for those who do not believe in the Bible, for colleges must stand "on the solid rock on which the cross of Jesus Christ stands in this and every other civilized country." Waving a coin at the jury, Neely noted its motto, "In God We Trust," and pronounced that no agnostics could be found "squeaking, squealing, whimpering there." Jurors should not accept the testimony of witnesses who did not take their oath in good faith and believe in God.[46]

Defending the American Legion, which had paid his retainer, Neely said he was proud that Mrs. Loudin had the support of "one of the greatest secular organizations in the country," an organization committed to fight communism, "the most vile, vicious system of government ever seen on the face of the earth since God said, 'Let there be light.' "

That is what Mrs. Loudin and the board of education are fighting against. They have started to clean out this nest of vipers which has made Fairmont State college [sic] a hissing and slander and humiliation for the last four years. . . . I don't want, regardless of what Thomas Jefferson, the Constitution of the United States and of West Virginia, and all the law books say, a tax dollar or a tax mill of mine spent to hire a teacher to teach my grandchildren and yours that nobody knows that there is a God. If I were on the board, I would vote no against . . . such a teacher and it wouldn't make any difference how many screwball newspaper editors said, "You're violating academic freedom." I want teachers who believe "in God we trust."[47]

To protect his grandchildren Fairmont State must be freed from "vulgarians." It must have no teachers such as Mundel who thought it would be a good idea to have a Communist on the faculty of a great university. She was not the "kind of a teacher wanted by those with boys in Korea or with soldiers' graves in the cemetery, or those who believe in the Declaration of Independence and the Constitution of the United States." A Communist in every university would lead progressively to a Communist in every college, then finally to the "Hammer and Sickle" flying over every schoolhouse in the land.[48]

He closed with a portrait of Loudin as the true victim of the affair, an innocent public servant pilloried for doing her duty. Loudin had not fired Luella Mundel or slandered her. Luella Mundel's own eccentricities had "disqualified" her from teaching at the college.[49]

The last speaker was Meldahl. Gray and reserved with heavy-lidded eyes, coatless and perspiring, the Charleston lawyer placed before him a stack of three-by-five-inch cards. He spoke without raising his voice or moving about for seventy minutes. He began by saying that Mundel was better qualified for her position than "anyone he ever knew." George Hand was a "wonderful man" whom Meldahl was going to invite to lecture at a project he was trying to start, "The People's University." He said that Dr. Mundel had been convicted on hearsay evidence and ostracized by many persons because of statements made about her. He pointed out that the defense had not produced a single student who said she was a poor teacher. The board made no effort to find out what she actually said at the Legion meeting and had simply relied on Loudin's opinion. A few Legionnaires (Meldahl himself was a Legion member) with a misguided notion of patriotism threatened to bring that great organization into disrepute by actions such as paying Loudin's lawyer. The board of education was really the "board of ignorance." The defense made too much of "little remarks at a private dinner." The Bible was not a complete summary of human knowledge. Some things in the Good Book, he presumed to say, were "filthier" than Rogers's psychological joke. The nation's colleges could ill afford "mental blackouts" or faculties selected from liars and hypocrites to the exclusion of the honest and truthful. The affair had cost the college the "flower" of its faculty. Many students were leaving. Justice, he concluded, required that the board give Mundel a hearing and a substantial monetary settlement.[50]

Read three decades later, Meldahl's summation establishes with little room for doubt that Luella Mundel was the victim of small-minded bigotry and inept administration. What it does not establish is that Loudin overtly slandered her. Worse, at the time, Meldahl's dry style of delivery that so contrasted with Matthew Neely's evangelical oratory seems to have left both jurors and reporters unimpressed.[51]

The rest of the day's session was taken up by Judge Meredith's controversial jury instructions. He rejected several important instructions requested by the plaintiff and accepted a number from the defense over Meldahl's strenuous objections. One, in particular, rendered Mundel's case nearly hopeless. Meredith told the jurors that if they believed that Loudin acted in the discharge of her duty then she was privileged and immune from liability. But he did not specify under what particular circumstances she might be acting for the board. Thus he allowed the jurors to define the powers of a board member without guidance or reference to enabling statutes. Meldahl thought that the instruction was "improper from every standpoint" and that West Virginia law did not sanction board of education members acting individually. Mrs. Loudin had acted on her own when she gave the Schroder notes to the press. This brought harm to Dr. Mundel and could not be protected as a privileged action.[52]

The jurors were also instructed that to convict they must find that Loudin's words were defamatory, were actuated by malice, and, echoing the law's early nineteenth-century origin as an antidote to dueling, "tended to violence and breach of the peace." Meredith refused to inform the jury that it should consider the provisions of the United States and West Virginia constitutions that prohibited religious tests for public employees and guaranteed their freedom to express political views and freedom of speech.[53]

The next morning, Wednesday, July 16, the jury deliberated for an hour and forty-three minutes before finding Thelma Loudin innocent. Afterward Dr. Mundel left the court quietly with Jones and Barnitz, leaving Loudin surrounded by a large crowd of well-wishers, some of them in tears.[54]

Spewing bits of verse in all directions, Matthew Neely held an impromptu news conference at the courthouse. He told reporters that the verdict was one of the most important ever given in the state because it guaranteed that public officials could do their duty without fear of the opinions of some private citizens. It was a victory for those who wanted Christianity to play an active role in the schools. The verdict insured "that we may sing in our colleges: 'Long may our land be bright with Freedom's holy light, protect us by Thy might, Great God our King!'" Now it would not become "'socially unacceptable' for us to continue to return thanks 'to Him who stills the raven's clamorous nest. And decks the lily fair in flow'ry pride. Would the way his wisdom sees the best for all our wants provide.'" The ending was more than a courtroom triumph for Neely. It had serendipity, for in it he must have perceived a vindication of his version of Christian ideology, a legal precedent that would buttress the politicians' control of the board of education and the colleges, and a resounding campaign statement that gave the lie to Republican claims that Democratic political leaders were not good Christian men.[55]

In the next morning's *Fairmont Times,* sharing the front page with the story of Mundel's defeat and the grand opening of the Moose Club's new Antler Room (the decor was pastel greens, dark reds, and flowered plastic wall drapes), was the announcement that Thelma Loudin had been reelected vice president of the state board of education.[56]

CHAPTER 8

The Aftermath:
Closing the Books and Moving On

Brains or no brains she was never intended to hold a position in a respectable institution. . . . Freedom of speech means reasonable things and people [who] talk too much in the wrong places need to learn a few things. At least they will surely have to account hereafter. A few so-called brains don't seem to believe in the hereafter. That is a bad influence on the youth of this country.

—Anonymous to the Mundel Support Fund (1952)

Democracy as a way of life . . . holds fast to its abiding elements: Its respect for human personality, its insistence on the fullest freedom of belief and expression for all citizens, its principle that all should participate in decisions that concern themselves, its faith in reason, its deep obligation to promote human well-being. These ideals . . . must permeate American education from the nursery school through the highest reaches of the graduate and professional schools.

—The President's Commission on Higher Education (1947)

In the days immediately following the verdict Dr. Mundel's depression grew more and more severe. Meldahl wanted her to appeal. With enough time, money, and patience, he was certain he could prove reversible error. But Mundel had no job and little money, was ill, and for the moment felt lost. She was angry at Jones, Barnitz, Meldahl—all those who had led her to disaster.

On July 21, the day Fairmont State's new library building formally opened, Eric and Jeanne Barnitz became alarmed and called the police when Mundel did not respond to their knocks at her door. The police reported that when they entered her apartment they found Dr. Mundel in the bathroom sitting on the edge of the tub wrapped in a blanket. She said she had been about to take a shower because of the heat and refused medical attention. They noted that the door from her apartment to the hall had been taped and they thought they smelled gas.

The next day the Barnitzes petitioned the authorities to take Mundel into custody for her own self-protection on a formal charge of "lunacy." Jeanne Barnitz claimed that Mundel was "highly nervous and distraught," had roamed the streets the night before in a robe, and had inflicted upon her "bruises and a slight laceration on one arm." Mundel remained in the county jail, the only available facility, for several days.

There was talk of sending her to Pittsburgh for psychiatric evaluation, but instead her sister came from Iowa. On July 24, Luella Mundel was released in her sister's custody and departed the Friendly City to rebuild her life and career.[1]

Liberal editorial writers across the nation condemned the jury's decision and sympathized with Mundel. West Virginia's best-known newspaper, the *Charleston Gazette,* conceded that Mundel had not established at the trial that she had been damaged by maliciously spoken words or innuendo. The jury had considered the evidence and her case at length. She had received due process. But the trial clearly established that she had been dismissed because she spoke up at the American Legion seminar, held unorthodox religious views, and "repeated a dirty joke in what is chastely called 'mixed company.' " The editor thought it "incredible" that a teacher in a tax-supported state institution could be dismissed for such reasons. He questioned the right of the board or M. M. Neely to prescribe what is orthodox and pointed out that Neely's own "fire and brimstone fundamentalist theology" was considered unorthodox by many Christians. And, since Neely never tired of quoting Shakespeare he must know that the Bard's ribaldry far exceeded Mundel's "dirty story."[2]

The *Denver Post* ended a fervent editorial that largely ignored the second trial except to note its decision, saying that "liberty, justice, truth, and tolerance have taken a frightful kick in the teeth from bigotry in West Virginia. Persecution of the art teacher served neither God nor country."[3]

William Manchester's report on the second trial to readers of the *Nation* invoked Ibsen's dark drama about the suppression of truth and persecution of a truth-teller in a small Norwegian town by its title, "An Enemy of the People?" He was careful this time to refer to Fairmont only as a "hillside town seventy-five miles south of Pittsburgh." The report was mainly a rehash of the earlier *Sun* and *Harper's* articles with additional commentary on the second trial and Mundel's subsequent detention. It was by no means the "witch hunt article" that the *West Virginian* called it, but it was heavily biased toward Mundel and certainly overdramatized the more pathetic aspects of her plight. It also overstated the case and overemphasized the power of outside opinion by asserting that morale at the college was "shattered," that the Legion post was in an "uproar" over paying Neely's retainer, and that the city had suffered palpable damage because of what had happened to Mundel.[4]

In a departure from standard press policy toward this case, evidently the *Christian Science Monitor* actually sent reporter Roland Sawyer to Fairmont to do a story after the trial. According to his article reprinted in the *West Virginian,* he found startling contrasts. Fairmont seemed "a pleasant county seat on a summer's Saturday afternoon." Streets were crowded with shoppers in from the country, gasoline station attendants were friendly, waitresses cheerful. Yet hanging over the idyll was a savage war within the community—the Mundel case. The jury had spoken, but the people remained divided. Its result was a parable of the times. Mundel had been "more bold than wise. . . . She was right in her public challenge at the . . . Legion's seminar. But she was vulnerable to understandable criticism and that led to suspicion. Here is the tragedy of this drama of the times in which we live."[5]

While some of the press fumed, Meldahl and the ACLU considered more legal action. Although Mundel obviously did not wish to carry on the suit, Meldahl was eager and willing to appeal the case to the state supreme court of appeals. He proposed to Barnitz that the Mundel Support Fund should send out another appeal. Barnitz was not enthusiastic. It would take several thousands of dollars just in start-up funds to launch another appeal and it was unlikely that the appeal would raise the needed amount. Barnitz had a wife and three small children. He was unemployed and without prospects. The fund would have to pay him a salary of at least $250 a month to continue fund-raising. In short, that approach was hopeless.[6]

Another possible source of funds was the ACLU itself. In mid-August Meldahl turned up in New York and convinced union officials Levy and Malin that there was a reasonable chance that the verdict would be overturned on appeal because of the judge's errors in instructing the jurors. But upon consideration the ACLU stuck to its position against entering a private slander suit. Malin thought Meldahl was overenthusiastic. Even if the verdict was overturned, it would mean only that there must be a new trial, which would have the same eventual outcome.

Malin did, however, search for funds. Meldahl told the ACLU that a million schoolteachers would surely give a dollar each to help Mundel. Starting with that doubtful premise, Malin tried without avail to prod the AACTE and AAUP. He was particularly frustrated by Himstead of the AAUP. It took several phone calls to reach Himstead's secretary on August 13, who had professed ignorance of the Mundel case. She reported that Himstead was away on vacation until after Labor Day, that he had left no address where he could be reached, and that none of his associates knew anything about the case.

In mid-September the ACLU began to close its files on the Mundel affair. Malin wrote to Meldahl that once the libel case was finished the ACLU would undertake an energetic educational program to make Fairmonters aware of the injustice they had allowed in their community. He added that in the meantime the organization would try to pressure the AAUP and AACTE to publicly condemn what had been done to Mundel. Two years later the ACLU was still waiting upon the elaborate fact-finding that it expected to be made by the NEA, AAUP, or AACTE before beginning its attempt to educate the public on the academic freedom and civil liberties issues of the case. In 1959 Joughin, who was by then working for the AAUP in Washington, reported that by and large the nation's courts still upheld the right of trustees to hire and fire faculty members at will. The law defending teachers' rights remained weak and vague and still afforded no defense whatsoever for probationary employees such as Luella Mundel.[7]

On August 11, 1952, Secretary Himstead wrote to his coinvestigator Carter Good that they must prepare a draft report on the Mundel case. They would base it in part on newspaper reports of testimony at the second trial, which had been sent to the AAUP by board of education member Judge Lynch and Secretary Baer. They would compare these with statements made to them earlier by Mundel, Hand, and the board members. But Himstead had already made up his mind. He thought Mundel's situation was pathetic. He blamed it first on poor administration at the college, then on bad advice from her colleagues and ACLU lawyer Meldahl. Himstead concluded that she had been left in a hopeless position. The next day he left for his holiday.[8]

When he returned, Good's reply awaited him. The University of Cincinnati dean proposed that Himstead should draft their report on four categories: the West Virginia board of education, George Hand, Dr. Mundel, and the future of Fairmont State College. Good believed the board was made up of well-meaning citizens. But they had the almost impossible task of overseeing all the state colleges except West Virginia University. With a proper leader at Fairmont State the board probably could have been induced to follow AAUP–AACTE tenure and academic freedom guidelines. The board was within its rights to fire Mundel. It had stood together in its testimony that Loudin had only asked questions. She had not made statements that Mundel was a security risk. Good admitted that Loudin's defense had been undignified and had strayed far from the real issue. But he dismissed that as a minor concern. Board members, Good concluded, should be told in no uncertain terms to follow professional rules of tenure and academic freedom in the future or risk the loss of AACTE accreditation and AAUP good standing.[9]

Good believed that George Hand lacked sufficient training and experience in college administration for the Fairmont State presidency. Good concluded that the former president had failed to get along with his subordinates and had botched town-gown relations. He asserted that an able administrator, given the six years Hand was at Fairmont State, could have educated the board to embrace professional principles of tenure and academic freedom.[10]

Hand must surely bear a large responsibility for the Mundel affair, but Good's conclusion seems excessively harsh and self-serving. After all, Hand had inherited a very difficult situation in 1945. When his predecessor Rosier had passed him the torch, he had passed it lighted-end first. Good's opinion seems strongly colored by the primary AAUP–AACTE goal—to retain good relations with the state board of education. In fact, none of the college presidents in the West Virginia system had sufficient access to the amateur and overworked board to "educate" its members. One or two other presidents had similar if less publicized troubles with the board's tendency to approach higher education with the same parental attitude that might be applied to elementary and secondary schools. By what logic could George Hand, the president of one of eight state colleges, be singled out for not impressing upon board members the principles of academic freedom and tenure, while his counterparts at sister institutions were held blameless? One suspects the answer is that the Fairmont case became a public matter and the others did not.

On the evidence of her behavior at the trials Good thought that Mundel was "a sad, pathetic case of a woman with fair ability and good training," driven to the edge by "conditions of stress and strain." He could see no way that either the AACTE or AAUP could help her. It should be remarked that Good chose to psychologize about Mundel's emotional state based on conservative stereotypes of single female teachers instead of concentrating on the important academic principles for which she had stood.[11]

As to the future of the college, Good and Himstead had advised the board to appoint a president who was a good administrator with extensive experience and training. The board should adopt a written code of academic freedom and tenure, and the staff of Fairmont State College should turn to the future and the main job of teaching students, and forget past bickering and fears.[12]

The public and the interested parties never had the chance to know these judgments. Possibly because of illness or his work load or because he felt it would serve no purpose, Himstead never issued a report on the Mundel case. Whatever his reasons the inaction was typical of his handling of academic freedom cases at this time, as is demonstrated by Ellen Schrecker in her *No Ivory Tower*.[13]

Officially the legal aspects of the affair concluded on October 6 when

Meldahl failed to post the $200 bond necessary to appeal the suit to the state supreme court of appeals. Meldahl wrote to Jones in Brooklyn that he wanted to go ahead with the appeal even without Mundel's cooperation, but that she wrote him such insulting letters he could not. More than a year later, Meldahl, ever the optimist, remained convinced that the verdict would have been overturned on appeal. He still hoped that Hand, Mundel, Jones, and Barnitz might receive ACLU citations of merit for their defense of civil liberties; and even that with the help of Jones and Barnitz his beloved Maximum Welfare Society could attract "millions of people!"[14]

In November 1952 Republican Dwight Eisenhower won the presidency from Democrat Adlai Stevenson by more than six million votes, broke the Democratic solid South, and made inroads among traditionally Democratic Catholic and blue-collar voters. The GOP also won narrow majorities in both houses of Congress. But in West Virginia the Neely machine stemmed the Republican tide. It was not a complete triumph to be sure, for, despite a 7 to 4.5 edge in voter registration, the Democrats lost one of the state's six House seats to the Republicans and saw their usual 100,000-vote victory margins in statewide races reduced to as little as 27,000. But they delivered the state for Stevenson and easily retained control of the governor's mansion and the legislature. In the only race where anticommunism figured as a major issue, incumbent Harley Kilgore ran well ahead of the ticket despite repeated charges by Republican challenger Chapman Revercomb that he was soft on communism.[15] Neely strongly supported Kilgore, and since Revercomb was an old political foe, the victory must have given him pleasure. So did the success of his protégé Bob Mollohan in the First Congressional District. But no doubt Neely's greatest satisfaction came from the gubernatorial race. There, in a nasty name-calling contest, Neely's standard bearer, thirty-four-year-old William Marland, defeated the man Neely loved to hate, Rush Holt, who, once the nation's youngest U.S. senator, had since his defection from the New Deal in 1936 become Neely's bête noire.[16]

It was a victory in which Neely and his supporters pulled out all the stops to win. John L. Lewis was persuaded to publicly endorse Marland, whom state labor leaders opposed. In April the *Fairmont Times,* which usually spoke for Neely on political matters, praised Marland as a candidate who could fill the state's need for "good Christian, right-thinking, morally clean men at the head of our Government." In May Neely himself described Holt as "a notorious political chameleon, political deserter, and political renegade . . . [whose] mentality and political maturity never developed from the hour of his birth." The Democratic campaign against the hated Holt culminated in a series of six October attacks first published in the *Fairmont Times* that gave no quarter. In view of Mundel's recent ordeal it cannot go unnoticed that the lead article accused Holt, a Methodist once associated with Father Charles Coughlin's National Union for Social Justice, the America First Committee, and various right-wing fringe groups, of "socialist and atheistic leanings." It quoted at length an old antichurch verse attributed to Holt's *father,* who had once led the state socialist party.[17]

One can hardly say that the Mundel-Loudin affair had an effect on the election or that Neely's vigorous courtroom defense of Jesus, home, motherhood, and loyalty and his support for Legion anticommunism took the wind out of McCarthy-style Red-baiting West Virginia Republicans (or deterred Louis Johnson from seeking Kilgore's Senate seat). But it is certainly plausible that Neely's awareness of the political climate of 1951 and 1952, concern over Democratic in-fighting, and the certainty that Republicans would use communism, religion, and corruption against them, influenced his decision to defend Loudin by wrapping her in the flag and to come to the aid of the Legion. Clever lawyer that he was, Neely surely knew that to win the case he had only to establish that Loudin's actions against Mundel had been privileged.

One can say with more assurance that Neely had successfully defended part of the patronage system that sustained his power in West Virginia. By getting rid of Hand, Mundel, and the others, Neely helped to insure that Mountaineers would get more jobs in the education system, that teachers would continue to be trained at Fairmont State (and probably like their lobby, the WVEA, support Neely), and that the board of education would retain its power and political orientation. It is perhaps belaboring the obvious to add that it was Matt Neely's town, his court, his college, and his political power that crushed Luella Mundel.

Self-evidently, the national urban liberal effort to help Mundel failed. Partly this was because of problems that might have arisen almost anywhere. The national political and religious Right was very active. Through the Republican party, the Chamber of Commerce, the American Legion, and certain church groups it was carrying its message into most communities. More important was the deep division in the national liberal community over the proper response to the Red Menace without an FDR to lead it and no Great Depression or world war to unite the country. This disarray enfeebled efforts to create a pro-Mundel consensus at the ACLU and AAUP. Liberals generally internalized a key assumption of the anticommunist Right: that communism was unlike any other ideology and Communists were unlike other zealots. Therefore the civil liberties of suspected Communists, fellow travelers, and even the merely eccentric must be curtailed. Certainly such individuals should not be allowed to teach.[18]

What Mundel represented — academic freedom and due process, privatist religion, modern art, a psychological worldview, and free thinking — was still novel and controversial outside the major university centers. Also, typical small-town ignorance, provincialism, and suspicion of big-city modernism and liberalism influenced the responses of the local small business–professional elite, distorting admirable voluntarism and community activism into a meddlesomeness that stopped just short of vigilantism. Most important, the barrage of national anticommunist rhetoric furnished the lurid setting for emotional excesses and conspiratorial thinking on both sides that obfuscated discussion of the substantive issues.

The local reaction to Mundel does not suggest a "populist" uprising against her and her kind so much as a popular feeling that what was happening to her was not a matter of public concern. Only a small group that drew its strength and inspiration from the national conservative movement, from the religious Right, and from the involvement of the FBI and HUAC in the community through the American Legion lifted its hand against her. It could have been defeated easily if only part of the community had extended its hand to help her. This seeming coldness is not easy to account for. Fairmont had its share of decent, fair-minded citizens. Local leaders thought of theirs as a tolerant and liberal community. But several givens so deeply embedded in its culture that they were rarely articulated worked against Mundel. One was what might be called the southern agrarian idealization of local government based on tradition, custom, family, and individual masculine self-reliance. Corollary to it was the belief that there were always a few wicked persons (outsiders) conspiring to destroy local autonomy and liberty and to bring unwanted change. "Vipers" was what Neely revealingly called Mundel and her kind, serpents who threatened his hill-country Eden.[19]

More important perhaps was the barrier against liberal ideas posed by the West Virginia mind-set that operated in a world of utilitarian ethics, political cynicism, and limited possibilities. The state had been born out of the political and military circumstances of the Civil War, a union of distinct and scarcely compatible geographic sections. Its population had been divided about equally between partisans of North and South. A century later the state remained divided. A combination of isolation bred by the geographical setting and the powerlessness felt in a state subjected to economic and political colonialism over four generations caused many West Virginians to fear and reject outsiders, even those from other regions of their own state or other hamlets in their own county. Moreover, wave after wave of reformers or exploiters (or those somewhere in between) had "invaded" the Mountain State, usually from the Northeast. They sang siren songs that promised a better life for the natives. But they usually turned out to be interested only in changing the state: either by ravishing its natural resources or in remaking its people through unworkably idealistic schemes. Be they exploiters or reformers, the common wisdom held that the outsiders generally left West Virginia poorer than they had found it. Among the natives the lesson to be drawn was: beware of outsiders and outsiders beware.[20]

In retrospect it is easy to see that Mundel's efforts to keep her job were doomed from the start. By the end of the summer of 1951, while national anticommunist hysteria was surging, formidable state and community powers were arrayed against her: most of the Fairmont State College faculty, including her own enemies and those of George Hand, the board of education, the state superintendent of schools, the American Legion, local female bluestockings, some Methodist lay folk, the town Republican newspaper, the state's most powerful politician, and the tradition-bound working folk of the county. Neutralized or scared off from supporting her were the town's Democratic paper, sympathetic clergy, the invisible liberal element, the governor and legislature, and the WVEA. Against the opposition, she could muster the unqualified help of only a handful of faculty members and the limited support of George Hand, a few distant urban newspapers, the ACLU, AACTE, and the AAUP.

That Luella Mundel lost her job and her suit is not surprising. What is surprising is that with little real outside help she was able to cause the stir that she did. It seems likely that had it not been for the sensitivity of liberals to McCarthyism, the existence of two local newspapers, and George Hand's quarrel with Loudin, she just would have been let go quietly and forced to move on in 1951 or 1952. For the anticommunist issue was, at least in this case, a two-edged sword. It was the rationale used to fire Luella Mundel and it was her defense against being fired. And just as the opposition to it was not enough to save her, neither, obviously, was anticommunism itself enough to get her fired. It was not McCarthyism or temporary mass hysteria that cast her out of campus and community; that was only a convenient cover. It was, sad to say, cynicism and a shallow, lip-service commitment to the principles of academic freedom and civil liberties by both town and gown.

It would be gratifying to be able to say that in the wake of the Mundel affair hysterical anticommunism waned, the West Virginia state board of education adopted the AAUP academic freedom and tenure policy, and the college became a paragon of academic excellence. The fact is that for a time little changed. Even though McCarthy was censured by the Senate in 1954 and died in disgrace in 1957, the Second Red Scare did not end until the late 1950s.

In January 1953 the HUAC held hearings on Communist infiltration of American education. A number of witnesses from the university community were called. Some, historian Daniel Boorstin and literary critic Granville Hicks, were cooperative. Others were defiantly uncooperative. The hearings failed to establish the existence of widespread Communist penetration of education. In its final report the committee admitted it had found no evidence of classroom indoctrination in Communist ideology. What little proselytizing it found was largely in the form of extracurricular "study groups." Undaunted, the committee warned that even a few Reds in the classroom placed the nation at risk.[21]

Despite AAUP recommendations, West Virginia state college faculty had to wait almost twenty years until the creation of the state board of regents for formal, written, legal tenure and academic freedom. And untenured Fairmont State College faculty continued to be "nonretained" without stated cause as late as 1971.[22]

Hand's successor was dean John W. Pence (M.A., Oberlin), a political scientist. He had all the safe, conservative qualifications the board was looking for. He had been at the college since 1926. He once had been a public school teacher. He had managed to stay in the background of the Mundel affair, even though he had sat on the tenure and ethics committee of the West Virginia Education Association when it refused to aid Mundel.[23]

Pence's inauguration on May 1, 1953, was a celebration of the triumph of anti-Hand, anti-Mundel forces. Among the dignitaries present were state board of education members, most notably the board's new vice president, Fairmont's own Thelma Brand Loudin. The ceremonial benediction was given by the pastor of the Central Methodist Church, some of whose adherents had played such a prominent role in the affair. Three hundred and thirty-five Fairmont State alumni turned out to honor both Pence and the new alumni association president, who in 1951 had been a member of the Marion County Anti-Subversive Committee, which paid Neely's retainer in *Mundel* v. *Loudin* and attempted to censor college library materials.[24]

Those at the ceremony heard speakers repudiate the college's recent past administration and what it had stood for. State school superintendent W. W. Trent reaffirmed his belief that the state colleges were extended high schools. He expressed regret that the legislature had seen fit to have the "teachers" removed from the names of the state colleges. Whatever they were called, he asserted, training teachers remained their primary function.

In his address, Pence bowed to both local and national political realities. After proposing generally popular expansion and beautification of the college physical facilities, he turned to sensitive matters. Renouncing a liberal arts emphasis and free thinking, he defined the mission of the college as to "provide vocational competence and to assist [students] in developing useful social attitudes." On the politically tender issue of the prerogatives of West Virginia University he pledged that Fairmont State would not compete for students or duplicate the curriculum of the Morgantown school. Fairmont would be content, he said, to be a "good college" whose task was to furnish education at a "modest cost . . . which the vast majority of these students could not obtain any other way."[25]

On the most inflammatory issue of all, Pence pledged to keep the campus quiet and the faculty members in line. He promised to "support freedom in the classroom and in research" but added, paraphrasing and extending the AAUP academic freedom guideline: "In discussing other matters of a controversial nature the welfare of the institution should be considered and no position of any faculty member should be such as to embarrass the college before its clientele and the general public from which its support is drawn. In our opinion there is no place on any faculty for persons with membership in or affiliation with subversive organizations."[26]

Until his death in 1959, President Pence avoided controversy and kept the college out of the headlines. He oversaw minor reforms. The many one- and two-teacher academic departments that had bred bickering and jealousy were combined into five more manageable divisions. The conventional academic ranks, instructor through professor, replaced the general designation of teacher to provide recognition for service and accomplishment and incentive to perform. For the first time a sabbatical leave policy was put in place. Pence also quietly retained many of Hand's academic innovations and continued to seek teachers with doctorates. But he was careful to make plain that Fairmont State would remain a teachers college and that in hiring new faculty members he would give priority to "those who have had public school training and teaching experience and who are in sympathy with such a program."[27]

This policy, in combination with the expansion of nearby West Virginia University's graduate programs, Fairmont State's slight notoriety among academic liberals,[28] and a favorable academic job market that made recruiting and retaining out-of-state faculty difficult, fostered academic inbreeding and provincialism. The educational effects of the relatively narrow range of outlook and experience of the faculty were magnified by the gray homogeneity of the student body. In the years immediately after 1952 the never very large out-of-state contingent of students, which had been growing under Hand, declined by half, although this narrowing was partially offset by the enrollment of a few black students in the wake of *Brown* v. *Board of Education of Topeka* (1954).[29]

Dire predictions that the Mundel controversy would destroy the college proved false. The sky did not fall, although for a time town-gown relations remained correct but cool in spite of Pence's efforts to "build the college more and more into the life of the community it serves." The school kept its accreditation with the North Central Association of Colleges and Secondary Schools even though evaluators in 1952 faulted it for the very deficiencies, endemic at similar institutions everywhere, that Hand had tried to correct. Specifically their report noted that faculty members tended to underuse the library, to devote little time to scholarship or learned society activities, and to attempt a curriculum too ambitious for their qualifications. Ironically, it excused most deficiencies as the result of the "recent distractions."[30]

After 1960, following the national trend, the college grew. Of course it grew without benefit of the considerable talents of George Hand, Luella Mundel, Harold Jones, Eric Barnitz, Dorothy Lucker, Spaulding Rogers, and the others who left because of the crisis. Their subsequent record offers little support to the contention that the so-called clique at Fairmont State was anything but a group of loyal and competent professional educators. Had it not been for the Red Scare hysteria, its members might have made their contributions at Fairmont State.

Eric Barnitz left teaching after the Mundel affair ended, but the others whom I have managed to trace built worthy careers including long service at a college or university. Hand remained for the rest of his academic life as an administrator at Southern Illinois University, which expanded very dramatically in the 1950s and 1960s. Jones spent the rest of his career on the library staff at Brooklyn College and served on a commission that helped to plan academic libraries throughout the country.[31] Dorothy Lucker taught until her retirement in the Pennsylvania state college system. Luella Mundel served a year at Goddard College in Vermont after regaining her health. Then for several years she was an art professor at Nebraska's Kearney State College. She finished her academic career in 1975 after seventeen years as head of the art department at Mayville State College in North Dakota.[32]

The AAUP's Ralph Himstead, whose health had already begun to fail at the time of the Mundel affair, died in 1955.[33] In the mid-1950s Louis Joughin left the ACLU for the AAUP, where he is remembered as a leading advocate for academic freedom and academic due process.[34] William Manchester went on to greater fame as a journalist-historian.

Most of Mundel's and Hand's foes departed Fairmont State within a decade. C. Moore Roberts died in 1953. Thelma Brand Loudin left the state board of education in 1955 and eventually, widowed and remarried, moved to Florida.[35] Robert L. Carroll left the college in 1956. After nine years in impressive military and private engineering positions, in 1965 he became head of the physics department at Baptist College, Charleston, South Carolina. Since his retirement in 1977, through the Carroll Research Institute of Columbia, South Carolina, he has issued several publications. According to the dust jacket of one of them he has devised a means other than fission or fusion to "convince the atom to give up its energy." He claims this theoretical process, called "disruption," will be "100 percent efficient and leave no radioactive waste."[36]

Schroder moved on in the late 1950s. House was the last of the anti-Hand activists to leave, remaining at his journalism post until the early 1960s. He is the only major participant in the affair to hold emeritus status at the college.

The trial lawyers have all since died. *Mundel* v. *Loudin* marked Matthew Neely's last major appearance as a lawyer, but he remained West Virginia's most powerful Democrat until he became ill in 1956. He died in 1958 of cancer with his national liberal reputation intact. The funeral and interment attracted the largest gathering of political and labor union notables in the town's history. In a eulogy Senate chaplain Frederick Brown Harris recalled visiting the hospitalized senator. Harris said that "when toward the end, his mind was at times clouded, . . . [Neely] talked . . . about the Old McGuffey Readers. . . . [There] one glimpsed the source of much of his love of great literature. In the country schools of his native State he had studded his memory with choice gems from these old readers." Eighty-four-year-old Tusca Morris played a prominent part in Fairmont's final salute to Neely, his friend since 1903, by offering eulogies at the Elks club and at the memorial service.[37]

Horace Meldahl survived until 1983. In the 1960s he made several visits to the Soviet Union. Long after that he continued to practice law in West Virginia and to advocate "maximum welfare" until a very high age. He was 93 when he died.[38] Trial judge J. Harper Meredith outlived all the lawyers. In fact he was a pallbearer for Matthew Neely. He remained on the bench until his death in 1985. Marion County's new City-County Annex to the venerable courthouse where he presided over the Mundel-Loudin case is named in his honor.

No one visiting Fairmont in the 1980s would see the bustling market town portrayed by the *Christian Science Monitor* reporter in 1952. Merchants and shoppers long ago deserted Adams (Main) Street for the ubiquitous malls. The Fairmont Hotel where Mundel challenged Lasky has been converted to low-cost housing. Across from it, guarding a once splendid and strong, now dangerously decayed bridge over the Monongahela, Legion Post 17 still stands, its grounds graced by a miniature replica of the Statue of Liberty. Were he to come to Fairmont today, William Manchester would not choke on soot and smoke, for it is gone with the coal-fired locomotives and the industrial activity that produced it. His description of a vista of "sore-eyed houses" is nearer the mark than it was in 1952. The town, like other rust-bowl communities, has declined and lost population in recent years as it endures a painful economic transition.

On June 23, 1983, the ABC Television Network aired "The American Inquisition," a one-hour documentary about the victims of McCarthyism, of whom one was Luella Mundel. ABC filmed much of the Mundel segment in Fairmont and brought back some of the central figures to the courtroom where the slander case was tried. William Manchester narrated part of the segment. Several former jurors and Legionnaires discussed the case and its atmospherics. So did Jeanne Barnitz and an obviously uncomfortable Mundel, haunted by Fairmont's "bad vibes." Filmed elsewhere, George and Madelaine Hand, Father Luckenbill, and Victor Lasky spoke. As a whole the program was less of a factual historical narrative than an evocation of visual impressions and recollections of the feelings of the time, when as the Fairmont paper put it, America was suffering from a mild case of insanity.[39]

In the days before the program was broadcast, the now combined *Fairmont Times–West Virginian* ran several articles summarizing the Mundel affair for the majority of local citizens who were too young to remember or whose recollections were hazy. In an editorial published the day of the broadcast, the paper worried that ABC might "do a job on us," since it believed the film crew that visited the Friendly City had been excessively "tight-lipped" about the show's content and purpose. The editor acknowledged the need to examine the past in order to plan for the future but admitted he was glad the affair had been largely forgotten. He hoped for a balanced presentation.[40]

Once the program had been seen it became obvious that national and local perspectives remained as much at odds as in 1951. A *New York Times* reviewer thought the Mundel segment of the program was quite well done. He believed Mundel attained a "mythic" quality and that the viewer felt a deep sadness when the Fairmont participants seemed embarrassed but not sorry for what had happened to the art teacher in their community. On June 24 the *Times–West Virginian* judged the local reaction to the show to have been surprisingly mild.[41] Some parents expressed disappointment at how briefly a local high-school band had been seen. Others felt that a scene in which the camera lingered on Fairmont's Adams (Main) Street peopled principally by a strolling pigeon (the scene was shot very early in the morning) did not reflect favorably on their fair city. Several local residents who had been on the show were moderately critical. One denied that the Legion had engaged in a witch hunt and asserted that in 1951 some of the people at the college belonged in Greenwich Village. Another felt that the charms of the town and the growth of the college had not received adequate coverage in the piece. The then president of Fairmont State was quoted to the effect that because of the development of academic due process what had happened to Mundel could no longer occur.[42]

The paper printed a single letter to the editor pertaining to the show. It came from Harold Jones in Brooklyn. In it he commended the Fairmont paper's objectivity, described his own firing from the college, and denied that there had been, as one program participant claimed, Antioch Communists there. The paper also reported that Victor Lasky had telephoned several Fairmont citizens and a local reporter to say the program had misrepresented him and his role in the affair. He would later unsuccessfully sue ABC for libel.[43]

All in all, self-absorbed townsfolk responded to the program's revelations with a polite yawn. One might conclude that the documentary had taught the Fairmont community less about the true value of thinking and speaking freely and about tolerance than about the utility of clever town public relations.

However blasé the general reaction, over the years and through all the changes many older Fairmonters remember the Mundel case as vividly as yesterday. A few who are sure that she was an immoral woman and a Communist continue to see her expulsion as good riddance. A few more who knew and did not like her lament the affair but believe she received what she deserved for her foolish behavior. Some, not many, defend her and believe that a grave injustice was done to her and those who helped her. Others seem to be not sure who was right. They are only sure that the affair at the college and the trials were among the more exciting and unsettling events they can recall. It was an affair that never had a proper ending. The court spoke; Mundel and her ilk left town; life went on. But was justice done?

A Note on Sources and Method

The careful reader will discover that the end notes to the text contain bibliographical information. Some are mini-bibliographies that enumerate primary and/or secondary sources for specific secondary topics such as higher education and West Virginia politics, institutions such as the American Legion, or key characters such as Matthew Neely. Detailed examination of the notes will show the reader that the manuscript is constructed mostly from conventional written documents—letters, court records, newspaper accounts, institutional minutes and memos, and, of course, secondary articles, monographs, and general histories. Because the Mundel affair attracted much attention, a rich cache of contemporary documents remains.

I formally interviewed and/or corresponded with about twenty-five surviving participants, witnesses, or authorities for this study and spoke informally with many more Fairmonters. For several reasons I have relied less directly on oral history than some might prefer (or I had expected) in describing and analyzing events of less than forty years ago. The research evolved as it did in the first place because death had taken many of the key figures—Neely, Meldahl, Morris, Meredith, Rogers, Mr. and Mrs. Roberts, Luckenbill. Also, I soon discovered that some of the survivors remembered little. Others, mostly among those opposed to Mundel and/or Hand, politely refused to be interviewed or ignored my letters. To complicate matters, participants had long since scattered across the continent, and my financial resources for travel were limited. Thelma Loudin lived in Florida and apparently continued her practice since 1952 of refusing interviews about the trial. Dr. Mundel lived in California, had already told her story for television, and was understandably wary of an inquisitive Fairmont State professor, although she was kind enough to answer questions about events from my written inquiry. More generally among Mundel-affair cognoscenti a barrier to candor was raised by Victor Lasky's pending lawsuit against ABC. The suit kept alive interest in the affair, but the legal proceedings dragged on from 1984 to 1988, making some reluctant to discuss the case lest they somehow be drawn into it, or leading them to suspect that I was working for one side or the other. A not unexpected obstacle came from isolated individuals in the

Fairmont community. Although many encouraged my research and no one openly tried to censor or interfere with it, I soon learned that not everyone approved of my topic. Some thought it would be best for everyone to forget the Mundel affair. The result was that although several of Mundel's former opponents were frank, cordial, and helpful, it was impossible to obtain much interview data from that side.

On the other hand, when I began this work many of the surviving participants, most of them Mundel allies, had already told their story to ABC for its 1983 documentary about the affair and several others were eager to describe their experiences. I made use of that material. Furthermore, I had lived in Fairmont and taught at the college since 1970. Although no insider and certainly not a member of the local elite, I had for many years been a somewhat bemused observer of the scene of the crime, so to speak. Armed with my own experience, a transcript and tape of the documentary, and my own interview results, I set out to compare participant recollections and contemporary documents. I found the documents to be much more trustworthy as to the facts. The interviews seemed best for establishing leads to documents, for gauging emotional reactions to events, for formulating subjective estimates of the personality and character of participants, and above all, for documenting local lore and mythology. In the process I became increasingly wary of oral history's pitfalls and more aware of what seemed to me its limitations. And so while oral history *colors* much of the narrative, written sources most often *inform* it.

The end result of this project is, I hope, a useful and scholarly contribution to the study of McCarthyism and a reasonably complete and accurate narrative of the Mundel affair. It is in no way court history or anyone's authorized version. As I am sure all parties will agree, I do not speak for Fairmont State College, the Fairmont community, or any of those involved in the events here described.

Abbreviations and Short Titles
Used in the Notes

AAUP: American Association of University Professors, Archives, Luella Mundel File; Washington D.C.

ACLU: American Civil Liberties Union, Archives; Princeton University, Princeton, N.J.

A & M: *See* WVU.

ALM: American Legion Magazine.

AL PROC [various dates]: U.S. Government, *Proceedings of the . . . National Convention of the American Legion. . . .*

Board Minutes: Minutes of the West Virginia State Board of Education, 1945–53.

CG: Charleston [West Virginia] *Gazette.*

Columns: The Fairmont State College student newspaper.

FBI–ALCP: "FBI American Legion Contact Program." Athan Theoharis, comp. Wilmington, Del.: Scholarly Resources, 1984 (microfilm).

FT: Fairmont Times.

Hand, "Report": George H. Hand, "A Report on the Fairmont State College Case [to the AAUP and AACTE]." [Fairmont, W.Va., Apr. 15, 1952]. AAUP Archives, Mundel File.

JP: Private papers of Harold D. Jones, Brooklyn, N.Y.

MCCC: Marion County [West Virginia] Clerk of Courts.

Mound: The Fairmont State College yearbook.

WV: [Fairmont] *West Virginian.*

WVSA: West Virginia State Archives, Charleston, W.Va.

WVU: West Virginia and Regional History Collection, West Virginia University Library, Morgantown. The particular collection is identified in each citation by its A. & M. (Archives and Manuscript) number(s).

Notes

INTRODUCTION

1. John Putnam Demos, *Entertaining Satan: Witchcraft and Culture in Early New England* (New York: Oxford University Press, 1982), pp. 394–400.

2. Robert H. Wiebe, *The Segmented Society: An Introduction to the Meaning of America* (New York: Oxford University Press, 1975), p. ix.

3. Demos, *Entertaining Satan*, pp. 399–400. He allows Emily Dickinson the last word to illuminate his insight:

> Witchcraft was hung, in History
> But History and I
> Find all the Witchcraft we need
> Around us every Day—
>   (c. 1883)

The classic discussion of paradigm shift is Thomas S. Kuhn, *The Structure of Scientific Revolutions.* 2d ed. (Chicago: University of Chicago Press, 1970). For a summary of criticism and applications of Kuhn's theories in the social sciences and religion see Gary Cutting, ed., *Paradigms and Revolutions: Appraisals and Applications of Thomas Kuhn's Philosophy of Science* (Notre Dame, Ind.: Notre Dame University Press, 1980), especially Cutting's introduction, pp. 1–22; Sheldon S. Wolin, "Paradigms and Political Theories," pp. 160–94; David Hollinger, "T. S. Kuhn's Theory of Science and Its Implications for History," pp. 195–222; and Ian Barbour, "Paradigms in Science and Religion," pp. 223–46.

4. Isaac Asimov, *A Whiff of Death* (New York: Fawcett-Crest, 1958), pp. 152–53.

5. David Caute, *The Great Fear: The Anti-Communist Purge under Truman and Eisenhower* (New York: Simon and Schuster, 1978), pp. 406, 410–21.

6. James T. Selcraig, *The Red Scare in the Midwest, 1945–1955* (Ann Arbor: UMI Research Press, 1982), pp. 69–74, 123–24, 132–34; Robert W. Iverson, *The Communists and the Schools* (New York: Harcourt, Brace and Co., 1959), pp. 361–64; Samuel A. Stouffer, *Communism, Conformity, and Civil Liberties: A Cross-Section of the Nation Speaks Its Mind* (Garden City, N.Y.: Doubleday and Co., 1955), p. 43.

7. The comprehensive study is Ellen W. Schrecker, *No Ivory Tower: McCarthyism and the Universities* (New York: Oxford University Press, 1986). It focuses on the cases of persecuted radicals and with few exceptions on the more visible colleges and universities. Among the better-known schools where professors felt the lash of the anticommunists were Harvard, MIT, Ohio State, University of Vermont,

Boston University, Michigan, Temple, Fisk, Washington, Colorado, and the California system. See Richard Pells, *The Liberal Mind in a Conservative Age: American Intellectuals in the 1940s and 1950s* (New York: Harper and Row, 1985), p. 289; Allen Weinstein, "The Symbolism of Subversion: Notes on Some Cold War Icons," *Journal of American Studies* 6 (Aug. 1972): 179.

8. Paul F. Lazarsfeld and Wagner Thielens, Jr., *The Academic Mind: Social Scientists in a Time of Crisis* (Glencoe, Ill.: Free Press, 1958), pp. 3–6, 21, 26–27, 41, 128, 189, 337–42; President's Commission on Higher Education, *Higher Education for American Democracy*, (New York: Harper and Brothers, [1947]), vol. 3, pp. 59–61.

9. The literature of McCarthyism is voluminous and growing. A sampling of the newer scholarship might include Edwin R. Bayley, *Joe McCarthy and the Press* (Madison: University of Wisconsin Press, 1981); Donald F. Crosby, *God, Church, and Flag: Senator Joseph R. McCarthy and the Catholic Church, 1950-57* (Chapel Hill: University of North Carolina Press, 1978); Richard M. Fried, *Men against McCarthy* (New York: Columbia University Press, 1976); Robert Griffith, *The Politics of Fear: Joseph R. McCarthy and the Senate* (Lexington: University Press of Kentucky, 1970); Robert Griffith and Athan Theoharis, eds. *The Specter: Original Essays on the Cold War and the Origins of McCarthyism* (New York: New Viewpoints, 1974); Michael Paul Rogin, *McCarthy and the Intellectuals* (Cambridge, Mass.: Harvard University Press, 1967). Earl Latham, ed. *The Meaning of McCarthyism*, 2d ed. (Lexington, Mass.: D. C. Heath and Co., 1973), is particularly useful for its wide sampling of scholarly interpretations of McCarthyism, as is a collection of articles by Les K. Adler, Robert L. Branyan, Richard M. Fried, James Hitchcock, Warren L. Vinz, and Daniel F. Whiteford in *Continuum* 6 (Autumn 1968). The few subnational studies of McCarthyism include Dale R. Sorenson, "The Anticommunist Consensus in Indiana, 1945–1958" (Ph.D. diss., Indiana University, 1980); and Don E. Carleton, *Red Scare! Right-Wing Hysteria, Fifties Fanaticism, and Their Legacy in Texas* (Austin: Texas Monthly Press, 1985). A most valuable bibliographical resource is John Earl Haynes, ed., *Communism and Anti-Communism in the United States: An Annotated Guide to Historical Writings* (New York: Garland Publishing, 1987).

CHAPTER 1

1. Mundel's B.A. degree is from Iowa Northern University. *Traill County* (N. Dak.) *Tribune,* June 4, 1975; Norman C. Meier to Ralph E. Himstead, Jan. 9, 1952; Luella Raab Mundel to Himstead, July 16, 1951, both AAUP. Mundel's article appeared in *Psychological Monographs*, vol. 51, no. 5, which was a unit of *Studies in the Psychology of Art* 3 (1939).

2. Mundel to Himstead, July 16, 1951, AAUP. For her ex-husband, Marvin E. Mundel, see *Who's Who in Science* (1972), p. 4453.

3. The place to start research on West Virginia is with Harold M. Forbes, ed., *West Virginia History: A Bibliography and Guide to Research* (Morgantown: West Virginia University Press, 1981). The place to begin analysis of the physical development of Fairmont in the twentieth century is the Sanborn Fire Insurance

Maps of the city and its environs (West Virginia, reel 3), microfilm from Chadwyck-Healy, Alexandria, Va.). Detailed plats showing structures, streets, and their use exist for 1884, 1902, 1906, 1912, 1918, 1927, and 1950 and confirm, at best, slow development between 1927 and 1950.

Data for these three paragraphs are from U.S. Department of Commerce, Bureau of the Census, *City and County Data Book* (1952) (Washington, D.C.: U.S. Government Printing Office, 1953), p. 498; Harry M. Caudill, *Theirs Be the Power: The Moguls of Eastern Kentucky* (Urbana: University of Illinois Press, 1983), pp. 45–56; Joseph E. Hoffmann, comp., *Marion County Centennial Yearbook, 1863–1963*, ([Fairmont, W.Va.]: Marion County Centennial Committee, 1963), pp. 28–32, 105. A fictionalized portrait of life during the heyday of the Fairmont coal barons is John Knowles, *A Vein of Riches* (Little, Brown, and Co., 1978). Knowles's boyhood home was but a short distance from Fairmont Farms and Highgate.

4. Janet B. Welch, "A Study of Appalachian Cultural Values as Evidenced in the Political and Social Attitudes of Rural West Virginians" (Ph.D. diss., University of Maryland, 1984), p. 279; Gerald W. Johnson, "West Virginia Politics: A Socio-Cultural Analysis of Political Participation" (Ph.D. diss., University of Tennessee, 1970), p. 168. Welch provides a convenient summary of the many definitions of Appalachia, which seem to agree only that the region is somehow different from the rest of the nation. At one extreme is the oversimplified media image of people who talk funny; dirty-faced, hollow-eyed coal miners; mountain women old before their time with unkempt children peering from behind their flour-sack skirts. Or there is the cartoonist's hillbilly lolling on the broken-down porch of a primitive cabin pulling on a jug of mountain dew. At the other extreme is the notion of a beautiful ancient land inhabited by a noble people savaged and exploited by the greed of urban individuals and corporations or (as a variant) a land of simple people whose way of life and art is threatened with extinction by the incursion of the modern world. In between lie several different outsiders' concepts: a place to escape the conformity imposed elsewhere by mass culture and gigantic national institutions; the "do gooders' " view that it is where "our contemporary ancestors" live and need help to progress into the modern world. Ibid., pp. 2–4.

5. *Fairmont, W.Va. Telephone Book* (1952). Robert T. Handy, *A Christian America: Protestant Hopes and Historical Realities*, 2d ed. (New York: Oxford University Press, 1984), pp. 159–90; and Grant Wacker, "Uneasy in Zion: Evangelicals in Postmodern Society," in *Evangelism in Modern America*, ed. George Marsden (Grand Rapids, Mich.: William B. Eerdmans Publishing Co., 1984), pp. 17–28. The battle over the role of Protestant Christianity in the public schools is as old as the public schools themselves. Compulsory prayer or Bible-reading was most often the focus of the debate. West Virginia's neighboring states represented sharply conflicting traditions in that regard. For example, since 1872 Ohio had forbidden the promotion of religion in the schools, the brief in the precedent-setting case noting that the words "Christian," "Protestant," or "Bible" do not appear in the United States Constitution. On the other hand, Pennsylvania legislators in 1913 had passed a law requiring daily Bible-reading in the public

schools in the interest of moral training and character building. For convenient excerpts of these and other relevant laws and opinions see Robert H. Bremner, ed., *Children and Youth in America: A Documentary History* (Cambridge, Mass.: Harvard University Press, 1971), vol. 2, pp. 1463–68.

6. U.S. Department of Commerce, *City-County Data Book* (1952), pp. 419, 498; *Fairmont, W.Va., Telephone Book* (1952).

7. Robert E. Lanham, "The West Virginia Statehouse Democratic Machine: Function and Process" (Ph.D. diss., Claremont Graduate School and University Center, 1971), pp. 76, 107–15; Leonard M. Sizer, *Estimates of the Population of West Virginia Counties, July 1, 1950-1962* (Morgantown: Office of Research and Development Appalachian Center, West Virginia University, 1969), pp. 6, 8; Sizer, *Population Change in West Virginia with Emphasis on 1940-1960* (Morgantown: West Virginia University Agricultural Extension Station Bulletin 563, May 1968), pp. 7–8, 11. A scholarly assessment of Marion County's economic base in 1952 correctly pointed to weaknesses. These included a lack of economic diversification, the volatility of the coal market and the stagnancy of local farming and retailing sectors. On balance, however, the study was upbeat about the future. The county had a four-hundred-year coal reserve; miners' wages were up; state agencies were actively seeking to enlarge the coal market, and manufacturing, even if it was concentrated in two large employers, was rapidly expanding. William G. Pinnell, "A Survey of the Economic Base of Marion County" (M.A. thesis, West Virginia University, 1953), pp. 23, 70–73.

8. Hoffman, comp., *Marion County... Yearbook,* pp. 99, 105; Welch, "Appalachian Cultural Values," pp. 174–76, 196–97, 206, 208–9, 242–43. Stephan Thernstrom, ed. *Harvard Encyclopedia of American Ethnic Groups* (Cambridge, Mass.: Harvard University Press, 1980), pp. 125–28. Coal-camp cultural values are chillingly delineated in Herman R. Lantz, *People of Coal Town* (Carbondale: Southern Illinois University Press, 1958), pp. 162–64; 246–74. The sharp decline in local mine employment did not begin until the Mundel affair was over. From 1948 to 1952 it remained fairly stable in the Fairmont area. Marion County mines employed 5,135 miners in 1948 and 4,966 in 1952—a relatively insignificant decline. State of West Virginia, *Annual Report of the Department of Mines* (Charleston: Jarrett Printing Co., 1949–52); (1949), pp. 44, 109; (1950), pp. 45, 121; (1951), pp. 35, 95; (1952), pp. 37, 87. U.S., Department of Commerce, *City and County Data Book* (1952), pp. 418–21, shows the nonfarming rural population of Marion County to be nearly equal to that of Fairmont itself. Fairmont State College lies within a few miles of the sites of two terrible mine disasters—Monongah Mines (December 1907, more than four hundred killed) and Farmington No. 9 (November 1968, seventy-eight dead).

9. *Fairmont, W.Va., Telephone Book* (1952).

10. Ibid.; *Columns,* Apr. 29, 1950; *Mound* (1949), p. 62.

11. John Gaventa, *Power and Powerlessness: Quiescence and Rebellion in an Appalachian Valley* (Urbana: University of Illinois Press, 1980), pp. 130–31, 258–59; John Alexander Williams, *West Virginia: A Bicentennial History* (New York: W. W. Norton and Co., and American Association for State and Local History, 1976), pp.

155–56. Charles A. Lord, *Years of Decision: A History of an Organization* (Charleston: West Virginia Education Association, 1965), pp. 215–17; David O. Levine, *The American College and the Culture of Aspiration, 1915-1940* (Ithaca, N.Y.: Cornell University Press, 1986), pp. 127–61, 211–20; Colin B. Burke, *American Collegiate Populations: A Test of the Traditional View* (New York: New York University Press, 1982), pp. 212–62.

12. Caudill, *Theirs Be the Power,* pp. 45–47; Williams, *West Virginia,* p. 146; John H. Fenton, *Politics in the Border States* (New Orleans: Hauser Press–Galleon Books, 1957), pp. 87, 104, fig. 14 (opp. p. 112); William E. Carrico, "Political Party Strength in West Virginia, 1920–1968" (M.A. thesis, West Virginia University, 1972), p. 129. For Neely see below, especially chapter 4.

13. Johnson, "West Virginia Politics," pp. 168, 170–71; Welch, "Appalachian Cultural Values," pp. 189–90. Fenton, *Border States,* presents perhaps an overly schematic portrait of four-party Mountain State political factionalism. He divides the Democrats into three parties: southern Bourbons; labor, represented by the United Mine Workers of America (UMWA) bloc vote; and the thoroughly pragmatic statehouse machine headed by Neely. The fourth party was the Republican, pp. 96–103, 108. Gaventa, *Power and Powerlessness,* pp. 14, 253–61. For a vivid description of the coal miner's life and culture in the late 1940s see Saul Alinsky, *John L. Lewis: An Unauthorized Biography* (New York: G. P. Putnam's Sons, 1948), pp. 3–9. The oral history collection at the West Virginia and Regional Collection at Morgantown also has a most interesting assemblage of interviews with coal miners on their twentieth-century experience.

14. Christopher Jencks and David Riesman, *The Academic Revolution* (Garden City, N.Y.: Doubleday and Co., 1968), pp. 1–5, 12–27, 155–57, 167. For "gatekeeping" powers of higher education curriculum and admissions see Levine, *American College,* pp. 242–43.

15. Ibid., pp. 232–33; William P. Turner, *A Centennial History of Fairmont State College* (Fairmont, W.Va.: Fairmont State College, 1970), pp. 1–5.

16. Charles H. Ambler, *A History of Education in West Virginia* (Huntington, W.Va.: Standard Printing and Publishing Co., 1951), p. 789; Medora Mason, "Joseph Rosier, Teacher-Senator," *West Virginia School Journal* (Sept. 1941), 5–6.

17. Ambler, *History,* pp. 789, 487.

18. Turner, *Fairmont State,* pp. 64–65. For Rosier's folksy ways see *FT,* Oct. 7, 8, 1951.

19. Ambler, *History,* p. 792. For the roseate details of Fairmont college and community life in the 1930s and 1940s see the astonishing letters and clippings of Berlin Basil Chapman, A. & M. 1668, WVU, particularly his letter to a Fairmont newspaper of Feb. 10, 1956. The campus character stories are inexhaustible and predictable. For example, there is the legendary absentmindedness of Dr. Paul Opp, who it is claimed on occasion would take colleagues on car trips to such distant locations as Pittsburgh and then forget to bring them back home with him. Then there was the professor who while waiting for a streetcar liked to pass the time climbing up and down a convenient utility pole. Or who could forget the ghastly story of the history teacher who died by walking in front of a truck in the

college parking lot while engrossed in his lecture notes? I have heard these stories during more than seventeen years at the college. I do not doubt that they have gained something in the retelling.

20. Turner, *Fairmont State,* p. 60; Chapman, A. & M. 1668, WVU. For the dominance of middle-class culture in pre–World War II American colleges see Levine, *American College,* pp. 113–35, 215–20.

21. Whether higher education should be "safe" or stimulating for young people is of course a perennial source of dispute. For a convenient and enlightening nineteenth-century exposition of the issue see Bremner, ed., *Children and Youth,* vol. 2, pp. 1490–91.

22. The findings of the Commission on Higher Education are quoted and summarized in Levine, *American College,* p. 216. State Department of Education, *The School Laws of West Virginia* (Reprinted from Michie's *West Virginia Code of 1949* and cumulative supplement, 1953) (Charlottesville, Va.: Michie Co., 1954), p. 77; Albert L. Sturm, *State Administrative Organization in West Virginia* (Morgantown: West Virginia University, Bureau for Government Research, Publication 7, 1952), pp. 52–55; Joseph Rosier, "The Status of Higher Education in West Virginia," *West Virginia School Journal* 74 (Sept. 1946): 5, 31.

23. Turner, *Fairmont State,* pp. 69–70; State Board of Education, *Biennial Report* (1944), pp. 31–34. In 1951 West Virginia's per pupil expenditure was $142.32, well below the national mean of $181.48 but still greater than ten states', including neighboring Virginia and Kentucky. U.S., Department of Commerce, *Statistical Abstract of the United States* (1951), p. 104.

24. George D. Strayer, *A Report of a Survey of Public Education in the State of West Virginia* (Legislative Interim Committee, State of West Virginia, 1945), pp. 641, 665–69, 671–75, 684, 687, 698–99. The state board of education formally discussed and asked each state college president to report within sixty days on the Strayer report and its projected impact on his institution. Board Minutes, Nov. 20–21, 1947, WVSA. I was unable to locate the reports of the presidents. Strayer's recommendations divided Democratic political factions in 1947 and 1948, pitting Gov. Clarence W. Meadows, who favored the proposed reforms, against popular state school superintendent W. W. Trent. Among other things, Strayer proposed making Trent's office appointive, thus earning the superintendent's ire with the result that the Strayer report failed to change much in West Virginia education. Paul D. Casdorph, "Clarence W. Meadows, W. W. Trent and Educational Reform in West Virginia," *West Virginia History* 41 (Winter 1980): 132–40.

25. State Department of Education, *School Laws,* 1949, and 1953 supplement, pp. 6–7, 9, 13; Author's interview with Harry B. Heflin (1985); William P. Jackameit, "The Evolution of Higher Education Governance in West Virginia: A Study of Political Influence," *West Virginia History* 36 (Jan. 1975): 97.

26. *FT,* May 20, 1941; July 15, 1952.

27. George H. Hand, "A Report on the Fairmont State College Case [to the AAUP and AACTE]" [Fairmont, W.Va.: April 15, 1952], typescript, hereafter referred to as Hand, "Report," pp. 5–6A; Turner, *Fairmont State,* p. 72; Interview with Heflin (1985). In 1947 the power of the board was increased when financial

control of the colleges was transferred to it from the state board of control. Thus ended a long-standing bifurcation of oversight.

28. Turner, *Fairmont State,* p. 70; *Who's Who in America,* 37th ed., vol. 1, p. 1311.

29. Jencks and Riesman, *Academic Revolution,* pp. 12–27; Theodore Caplow and Reece J. McGee, *The Academic Marketplace* (New York: Basic Books, 1959), pp. 167–68.

30. Interview with Heflin (1985); President's Commission, *Higher Education,* vol. 3, pp. 59–61; vol. 1, pp. 8–20, 25–43, 77, 103. The commission was chaired by George F. Zook. Among its distinguished members were Milton S. Eisenhower, Douglas Southall Freeman, Rabbi Steven Wise, Mark Starr, George Stoddard, and Bishop G. Bromley Oxnam. For criticism of the commission report see Diane Ravitch, *The Troubled Crusade: American Education, 1945–1980* (New York: Basic Books, 1983), pp. 15–18. The most common fault found by critics was that if implemented the proposed expansion of enrollment would undermine academic standards and perhaps destroy many private colleges.

31. See S. M. Vinocour, "The Veteran Flunks the Professor: A G.I. Indictment of Our Institutions of Higher Education!" *School and Society* 66 (1947): 289–92. See also the sputtering rejoinder from Brooklyn College professors Thomas E. Coulton and Joseph Justman in the same volume, pp. 446–47. Thomas R. Bennett to Post Commanders, mimeograph, [1947], A. & M. 537, 139, WVU. Some college staff members who had to deal with returning GIs (and their wives) thought some of them made arrogant and unreasonable demands for college services. Several others thought that they lowered the tone of the place. Obviously the GI bill and their numbers gave veterans considerable influence and aroused jealousy among some of the more traditional students and faculty.

32. Ambler, *History,* p. 794.

33. Hand, "Report," p. 3.

34. Ambler, *History,* p. 794; Hand, "Report," pp. 50A, 51–52, 1–2; Turner, *Fairmont State,* pp. 71–72. Thirty-four semester hours of B.A. and B.S. core courses were required. Also put in place were a major and minor system and foreign language requirements for some degrees.

35. Hand, "Report," p. 51; *FT,* Sept. 28, 1945.

36. *FT,* Apr. 27, 1946. Hand actually took over the administration of the college in the summer of 1945 even though his formal inaugural did not take place until April 1946. Phares Reeder, "The Passing of Joseph Rosier," *West Virginia School Journal* (Nov. 1951): 17.

37. Ambler, *History,* p. 794; George H. and Madelaine R. Hand to the author, July 12, 1984. With the phasing out of teachers colleges and their replacement by more comprehensive state institutions after the war the debate between liberal arts advocates and educationists grew heated on many campuses. For an educationist's attack on what he deemed the unwarranted worship "at the shrine of the Goddess of Academic Scholarship," see Edwin H. Reeder, "The Quarrel between Professors of Academic Subjects and Professors of Education: An Analysis," AAUP *Bulletin* (Autumn 1951): 506–21.

38. *FT,* Apr. 25, 1947.

39. For Hand's anticommunism, liberalism, and reaction to the Legion's Americanism, see below especially chapters 2, 5, and 7. Rosier had recently finished reading Marion L. Starkey, *The Devil in Massachusetts: A Modern Inquiry into the Salem Witch Trials* (New York: Alfred A. Knopf, 1949) and wrote to Kilgore that McCarthy had only spectral, *i.e.*, ghostly, evidence to support his claims. Rosier to Kilgore, Apr. 25, May 1, 1950, box 74, Harley M. Kilgore Mss., Franklin D. Roosevelt Library (I am indebted to Richard M. Fried, who shared with me his research notes on the Kilgore Papers at Hyde Park, N.Y.); State Board of Education, *Biennial Report* (1947–48), p. 39; *Columns*, Dec. 12, Sept. 25, 1950; *WV*, May 28, 1951.

40. *WV*, July 28, Aug. 29, 1947; Ambler, *History*, pp. 714–15; State Board of Education, *Biennial Report* (1949–50), p. 41.

41. *WV*, July 28, Aug. 29, 1947.

42. George H. and Madelaine L. Hand to author, July 12, 1984; *WV*, Aug. 18, 24, 1947; clipping from *WV* [Dec. 24? 1948] in Chapman, A. & M. 1668, WVU; *FT*, May 11, 1947; Ned Smith, typescript for "Good Morning," *FT*, [n.d.] C. E. Smith Papers, A. & M. 1604, 1606, WVU.

43. Board Minutes, Aug. 15–16, 1947, WVSA.

44. *WV*, Aug. 18, 1947. In September state auditor Edgar B. Sims refused to issue paychecks for the two women and told the board of education that they could not be paid for the following year. *WV*, Sept. 9, 1947. Mason was eventually paid for August and Price for August and September, but neither was paid for the rest of the year. See West Virginia Department of State Tax Commissioner, *Thirty-fourth Annual Report, Audit of Finances of the State of West Virginia Showing in Detail the Sources of Revenue and the Purposes for Expenditures for the Fiscal Year Ended June 30, 1948* (Charleston: Mathews Printing and Lithography Co., [1948]), p. 421.

45. Hand to Himstead, May 27, 1952, ACLU.

46. Clipping from *WV* [Dec. 24? 1948] in Chapman, A. & M. 1668, WVU; Hand, "Report," pp. 6A–7.

47. Hand, "Report," p. 2; Board Minutes, May 7–8, 1951, WVSA. Hand claimed that the faculty represented "more than 50 colleges and universities." If one counts undergraduate and intermediate degrees he is correct. Actually their highest degrees were from only twenty graduate schools.

48. Hand, "Report," pp. 2, 51–53; Board Minutes, May 7–8, 1951, WVSA.

49. See Mary McCarthy, *The Groves of Academe* (New York: Harcourt, Brace and World, 1952); Asimov, *A Whiff of Death* (Original title, *The Death Dealers*); Logan Wilson, *The Academic Man: A Study in the Sociology of a Profession* (New York: Oxford University Press, 1942); Jacques Barzun, *Teacher in America* (Boston: Little, Brown and Co., 1945).

50. See Asimov, *A Whiff of Death;* Barzun, *Teacher in America,* especially chapters 14, 19; Caplow and McGee, *The Academic Marketplace;* Reeder, "Quarrel," pp. 506–19; and William Fisher, "Progress and the Demise of Teachers Colleges," *School and Society* (1951): 149–51.

51. Wilson, *Academic Man*, pp. 19–20. Wilson based his analysis on B. W. Kimball, "A Survey of College Teachers," AAUP *Bulletin* (1938): 262; Stouffer,

Communism, Conformity, and Civil Liberties, pp. 116–17, 119–22, 132–33, 142–50. On the status difference between university professors and public school instructors see President's Commission, *Higher Education,* vol. 6, p. 44. In a 1947 poll, a national sampling of the public was asked to rank some ninety occupations according to prestige. College professor ranked near the top (seventh) while public school teachers ranked above the middle at thirty-sixth, well above small businessmen, bookkeepers, insurance agents, and small store managers—much of Fairmont's town elite. Professors ranked above the lawyers (fifteenth), who were near the top echelon of the town's elite.

52. The information on Rogers is constructed from a number of interviews with those who were at the college either as students or faculty in the Hand era. Some of it may be legend, but it is useful nevertheless for understanding the impression some new faculty made on college and community. *WV,* Aug. 29, 1947, summarized Rogers's professional background.

53. e.e. cummings, *Poems* (1921; reprint ed., New York: Harcourt, Brace and World, 1953).

54. Mundel to author, Aug. 21, 1984; Eric Barnitz to Louis Joughin, May 3, 1952, ACLU; Hand, "Report," p. 23; *Columns,* Apr. 30, 1951; *FT,* June 24, 1983.

55. Hand, "Report," p. 38; The unsubstantiated and anonymous charges focused particularly upon the University of Iowa graduates on the faculty. See also Barnitz to Joughin, Jan. 29, 1952, ACLU, who reported that of seven rumors circulating about Mundel and her faculty supporters, three focused on communism and the rest on moral transgressions. Jones to Tusca Morris and Horace Spencer Meldahl, June 30, 1952, JP, reporting the rumor and denying that Mundel was homosexual.

56. *Columns,* Apr. 10, Mar. 6, May 15, 1951; Author's interview with Jack Sandy Anderson (1985).

57. ABC News, *The American Inquisition* (transcript; New York: Journal Graphics, 1983), p. 8; *Fairmont Times-West Virginian,* June 21, 1983. Schrecker, *No Ivory Tower,* pp. 118–19, 126, 132, 134, 140. For a 1952 analysis of the sexual behavior of Communists see the ACLU's Morris L. Ernst with David Loth, *Report on the American Communist* (New York: Holt, Rinehart and Winston, 1952), pp. 162–80. Leslie K. Adler, "The Red Image: American Attitudes toward Communism in the Cold War Era" (Ph.D. diss., University of California at Berkeley, 1970), pp. 7, 10–11, 15, 18–19. Adler argues that Communist ideology was less the issue than Americans' national self-image. He follows Talcott Parsons in calling postwar communism the "symbolic intruder." He adds that the Red image stood for the violation of natural order and human law and for complete materialism. Communists were assumed to be totally controlled by ideology. This view was facilitated by contrasting Communist practices with American ideals.

58. Hand, "Report," pp. 20–21; *FT,* Jan. 16, 1951.

59. *Columns,* Oct. 2, 1947; Nov. 18, 1949; Fridtjof Schroder, "Off Main Street: In Which Local College Teacher Discusses the Pseudo-Liberal," parts 1–3, *WV,* May 7, 8, 9, 1952; Fridtjof Schroder, "The Nature and Meaning of Art" (Fairmont, W.Va.: Privately Printed, 1955), pp. iii–iv.

60. *WV,* May 7, 8, 9, 1952.

61. Jane De Hart Mathews, "Art and Politics in Cold War America," *American Historical Review* 81 (Oct. 1976): 762–63, 772–76, 783–87. See also Max Kozloff, "American Painting during the Cold War," *Artforum* 12 (Oct. 1973): 39–41; William Hauptman, "The Suppression of Art in the McCarthy Era," *Artforum* 12 (Oct. 1973): 48–52.

62. Hand, "Report," pp. 26–27, 29, 31–33. Schroder's "Beasts of Prey" was at Youngstown and his "Christmas Eve" was in the Hallmark exhibition in New York. *Columns,* Jan. 18, Nov. 18, 1949.

63. Author's interview with Harold Jones (1984); *WV,* May 7, 8, 9, 1952; *Columns,* Sept. 30, 1949; Mundel to Joughin, Sept. 11, 1951, ACLU.

64. Hand, "Report," pp. 26–27, 29, 31–33; W. H. Cramblet, "The Future of Higher Education," *West Virginia School Journal* (Sept. 1952): 7–8.

65. *WV,* Aug. 15, 1951; *FT,* July 15, 1952; Schroder to Himstead, Aug. 20, 1951, AAUP.

66. *WV,* Aug. 15, 1951. For Mundel's complaints about Schroder as a teacher, see Mundel to Joughin, Sept. 9, 1951, ACLU.

67. *FT,* July 15, 1952; Ned Smith, "Good Morning" column [typescript], [n.d.], C. E. Smith Papers, A. & M. 1604, 1606, WVU.

68. Biographical information on dust jacket of Robert L. Carroll, *The Energy of Physical Creation* (Columbia, S.C.: Carroll Research Institute, 1985); See also "The Cover," n.p., in his suitably slim *West Virginia Wit and Wisdom* (n.p.: Robert L. Carroll, 1986); Script by Carroll for "Campus Highlights" radio program on WMMN (Fairmont), 1949–50 series, pp. 4–11, 14, ACLU; Hand, "Report," pp. 27–30; *FT,* July 15, 1952.

69. William Manchester, "The Case of Luella Mundel," *Harper's Magazine* (May 1952): 55.

70. Jones to Meldahl and Morris (copy), Nov. 19, 1951, JP. The simple explanation for Mundel's remark is that she was telling students that she graded tests blindly in the interest of objectivity, *i.e.,* without knowing the name that belonged to a particular paper when she was looking at it.

71. Richard Hofstadter and Walter Metzger, *The Development of Academic Freedom in the United States* (New York: Columbia University Press, 1955), p. 492.

CHAPTER 2

1. Harold Jones reported to Mundel's lawyers the gist of a June 1951 conversation over coffee with a locally connected colleague who supposedly said, "It was the Legion that done it." Jones wrote to Helen Fuller of the *New Republic* in October 1951 that he had "no proof" of the campaign. See Jones to Morris and Meldahl, Nov. 21, 1951; same to same, Dec. 13, 1951; same to Helen Fuller, Oct. 2, 1951, all copies, all JP.

2. Legion activity was the subject of persistent rumor throughout the affair. Jones suspected that Legionnaires carried on a clandestine letter-writing campaign to the state board of education against Mundel and were spreading mali-

cious gossip about her. The Post 17 commander denied it to Jones in July 1951 and to the author in 1984. Board of education member Lawrence R. Lynch denied it under oath in July 1952. I was unable to locate the correspondence of the board of education for this period. All of the board members from that time are deceased excepting Loudin (now remarried) and board secretary Herbert K. Baer. Both declined to participate in this study. Sorenson, "Anticommunist Consensus," passim and especially pp. 27–30, 212–13; Daniel F. Whiteford, "The American Legion and McCarthyism," *Continuum* 6 (Autumn 1968): 326–27. Carleton, *Red Scare,* pp. 101–2, 126, 134; W. Lloyd Warner, *Democracy in Jonesville: A Study of Quality and Inequality* (New York: Harper and Brothers, 1949), pp. 284–86. In his study of anticommunism in the Midwest, James T. Selcraig grants substantial power to the Legion at the community level. He notes, however, that the Legion lacked uniformity of policy and a formal structure. He is certainly correct to say that there was no liberal organization that could match the Legion's local operations. Selcraig, *Red Scare,* p. 99.

3. Seminal and controversial works that illuminate American historical attitudes toward internal subversion are Richard Hofstadter's collection of essays, *The Paranoid Style in American Politics and Other Essays* (New York: Alfred A. Knopf, 1965) and David Brion Davis, ed., *The Fear of Conspiracy: Images of Un-American Subversion from the Revolution to the Present* (Ithaca: Cornell University Press, 1971).

4. William Gellermann, *The American Legion as Educator* (New York: Columbia University Press, 1938), pp. 246, 254; Adler, "The Red Image," pp. 1–23, 43–44.

5. Adler, "The Red Image," p. 45; speech of Carl R. Gray, Jr., to Legion Convention, AL PROC (1951), p. 28.

6. Adler, "The Red Image," p. 45; *FT,* Mar. 24, 1951.

7. Sanford J. Ungar, *FBI* (Boston: Little, Brown and Co., 1976), pp. 129, 282–84; Kenneth O'Reilly, *Hoover and the Un-Americans: The F.B.I., H.U.A.C., and the Red Menace* (Philadelphia: Temple University Press, 1983), pp. 38–40, 170–77; Caute, *The Great Fear,* pp. 404–5.

8. Athan Theoharis, "The FBI and the American Legion Contact Program, 1940–1966," *Political Science Quarterly* 100 (Summer 1985): 271–73.

9. Theoharis, "Contact Program," pp. 273–80; Memo, L. J. Gauthier to M. R., Nov. 23, 1945; Memo, A. H. Belmont to D. M. Ladd, July 31, 1950, both FBI–ALCP.

10. Memo, [FBI] Executives' Conference to Director, July 17, 1950, FBI–ALCP. For FBI difficulties with a VFW post apparently jealous of the ALCP see Memo, D. M. Ladd to C. A. Tolson, Feb. 4, 1954, FBI–ALCP.

11. Harry S Truman, Information Relating to Domestic Espionage, Sabotage, Subversive Activities and Related Matters, July 24, 1950, FBI–ALCP.

12. Bureau Bulletin no. 43, ser. 1950, Aug. 14, 1950, FBI–ALCP.

13. Theoharis, "Contact Program," pp. 273–80.

14. Ibid., pp. 280–84. The quotations are from portions of a Dec. 22, 1965, internal memo from FBI Supervisor F. J. Bumgardner reprinted in ibid., pp. 283–84.

15. Ibid., p. 281.

16. Memos from D. M. Ladd to Hoover, Apr. 11, July 18, and Oct. 29, 1951; Jan. 25, Apr. 28, July 29, and Oct. 24, 1952; Jan. 28, Apr. 9, 1953, all FBI–ALCP. Generally the field office summaries of ALCP progress were accompanied by bar graphs illustrating the average number of contacts per post.

17. Memo, SAC [Special Agent in Charge] New York to Director, Apr. 30, 1951; Memo, SAC Philadelphia to Director, June 16, 1951, both FBI–ALCP.

18. Wilson should be considered a protégé of Louis A. Johnson since he was a *wunderkind* of Johnson's law firm. For Johnson see Robert J. Donovan, *The Tumultuous Years: The Presidency of Harry S Truman, 1949–1953* (New York: W. W. Norton and Co., 1982), pp. 61–63, 266–67; Ken Hechler, *Working with Truman: A Personal Memoir of the White House Years* (New York: G. P. Putnam's Sons, 1982), pp. 148–50.

19. For a summary of the shocks see Eric F. Goldman, *The Crucial Decade—and After: America 1945–1960* (New York: Alfred A. Knopf, 1966), pp. 174–219. The status insecurity argument to explain the early Cold War Right is made most elaborately in Seymour M. Lipset and Earl Raab, *The Politics of Unreason: Right Wing Extremism in America 1790–1970* (New York: Harper and Row, 1970), pp. 209–12.

20. AL PROC (1951), p. 101. The speech was delivered on October 18, 1951. For a profile of Wilson, see R. B. Pritkin, "The Legion's New Commander," *ALM* (Apr. 1952): 20.

21. Wayne E. McKinley, "A Study of the American Right: Senator Joseph McCarthy and the American Legion, 1946–1955" (M.S. thesis: University of Wisconsin, 1962), p. 117; AL PROC (1951), pp. 100–102.

22. AL PROC (1951), pp. 100–102. The Americanism crusade waxed after 1947. See Karl Baarslag, "How to Spot a Communist," *ALM* (Jan. 1947): 9–11, 44–47; "List of Subversive Organizations" and related correspondence in the files of the American Legion Mountaineer Post 127, A. & M. 139, 537, WVU. The FBI also sought to use many other volunteer associations in its fight against disloyalty, but to a lesser extent. Included among them were the American Bar Association, B'nai B'rith, Boy Scouts of America, the Chamber of Commerce, VFW, Optimist Clubs, Kiwanis, and Rotary. O'Reilly, *Hoover,* p. 88.

23. McKinley, "American Right," pp. 17–18.

24. See John Edgar Hoover, "Civil Liberties and Law Enforcement: The Role of the F.B.I.," *Iowa Law Review* (Winter 1952):194. See also Sen. Pat McCarran's speech to the Legion Convention, in AL PROC (1951), pp. 17–18.

25. Clarence Manion, *The Key to Peace* (Chicago: Heritage Foundation, 1953), pp. 38–39; Speech, Mayor Fletcher Bowron [of Los Angeles], AL PROC (1951), p. 1; Adler, "The Red Image," pp. 15, 26, 29, 146–49, 154.

26. AL PROC (1951), pp. 6–8, 46–50; Victor S. Navasky, *Naming Names* (New York: Viking Press, 1980), pp. 86–91, 415; Selcraig, *Red Scare,* pp. 90–91.

27. Clarence Manion, "We Can Win on These Terms," *ALM* (July 1951): 9.

28. McKinley, "American Right," p. 17; Caute, *The Great Fear,* pp. 404–5; AL PROC (1950), p. 31; AL PROC (1951), pp. 40–41; Arthur Zilversmit, "The Failure of Progressive Education, 1920–1940," in *Schooling and Society,* ed. Lawrence Stone

(Baltimore: Johns Hopkins University Press, 1976), pp. 260–61; Ravitch, *The Troubled Crusade*, chapter 2; Irene Corbally Kuhn, "Your Child Is Their Target," *ALM* (June 1952): 18–19, 54–56; J. B. Matthews, "Communism and the Colleges," *American Mercury* (May 1953): 111–15, 134; Selcraig, *Red Scare*, pp. 69–70. U.S., Congress, House, Committee on Un-American Activities, *Annual Report for the Year 1953*, 83d Cong., 2d sess., H. Rept. 1192, p. 9. The most elegant argument against uncapitalist, un-American, and anti-Christian influences and against twentieth-century liberal concepts of academic freedom in higher education was young William F. Buckley, Jr.'s *God and Man at Yale* (Chicago: Henry Regnery Co., 1951). The book came out in September 1951 just before Mundel filed suit against Thelma Loudin. By the time of the suit's completion in the summer of 1952 it was in its fifth printing.

29. AL PROC (1951), p. 144; AL PROC (1952), pp. 15–19; American Legion Papers, Post 127, A. & M. 537, 139, WVU; Manion, *The Key to Peace*, preface, n.p.

30. *ALM*, (Nov. 1951): 12–13, 40–43; (June 1952): 18–19, 54; (Dec. 1952): 18–19, 56–59.

31. McKinley, "American Right," pp. 7–8; AL PROC (1951), p. 143.

32. For an example of Legion local mischief, see the 1950 "Red Takeover" of Mosinee, Wisconsin, in Fried, *Men against McCarthy*, pp. 1–2.

33. *FT*, May 22, 1950; *Fairmont Times–West Virginian*, May 21, 1950.

34. Iverson, *The Communists and the Schools*, pp. 243–44, 277–79. Matthews claimed to have taught at forty-two colleges and universities and included among his 3,500-name list of fellow travelers in academe Thomas Mann and Albert Einstein. See Matthews, "Communism and the Colleges," pp. 111–15.

35. *FT*, May 22, 1950; *Fairmont Times–West Virginian*, May 21, 1950. Matthews's special field was campus communism, although he occasionally branched out, as for instance when he campaigned to prove that the Consumers Union was a Communist group. See O'Reilly, *Hoover*, pp. 54–55. See also *WV*, May 22, 1950; *Fairmont Times–West Virginian*, May 21, 1950; Hand, "Report," p. 20; Author's interview with Edgar Jaynes (1984).

36. Hand, "Report," pp. 8, 22; *FT*, May 22, 1950.

37. *WV*, May 22, 1950. Adding to the idea of anticommunism as a partisan Republican issue was another Fairmont meeting that weekend. It was a tea for the Marion County Republican Women's Club and featured Mrs. E. Wyatt Payne in an address against communism. *Fairmont Times–West Virginian*, May 21, 1950.

38. Alonzo L. Hamby, *Beyond the New Deal: Harry S. Truman and American Liberalism* (New York: Columbia University Press, 1973), pp. 418–22.

39. Harold F. Gosnell, *Truman's Crises: A Political Biography of Harry S. Truman* (Westport, Conn.: Greenwood Press, 1980), p. 458. Donovan cites a Truman confidant who said the only time he saw the President overimbibe was after the Democratic defeat in the 1950 election. Donovan, *The Tumultuous Years*, pp. 297–98.

40. Fried, *Men against McCarthy*, pp. 119–22; Hechler, *Working with Truman*, pp. 160–66.

41. Hechler, *Working with Truman*, pp. 167–69; Donovan, *The Tumultuous Years*,

pp. 321–62, 366; Gosnell, *Truman's Crises,* pp. 483–86; Bert Cochran, *Harry Truman and the Crisis Presidency* (New York: Funk and Wagnalls, 1973), pp. 338–40. For Democratic efforts to show their party as the greatest enemy of the American Communist, see "Democratic Fact Sheet," Dec. 1953, Harley M. Kilgore Papers, A. & M. 1068, WVU. See Athan Theoharis, *Seeds of Repression* (Chicago: Quadrangle Books, 1971), pp. 123–81. For the Truman administration's perceived need to answer allegations that domestic communism was running rampant, see Michal R. Belknap, "Cold War in the Courtroom: The Foley Square Communist Trial," in *American Political Trials,* ed. Belknap (Westport, Conn.: Greenwood Press, 1981), p. 237.

42. Mundel to author, Aug. 21, 1984; *FT,* Apr. 29, 1951.

43. Harold Jones named the Fairmont State faculty members present at the seminar as Dr. Dorothy Lucker (English) and H. Norman Taylor (history), who sat with him and Dr. Mundel. Jones also saw Dr. George Hunt (science), Paul Davis (recreation), Regis Larkin (business), and "Squibb" Wilson (physical education). President Hand did not attend; others may have. See Jones to Meldahl and Morris, Nov. 19, 1951 (copy), JP. See also *Fairmont Times—West Virginian* Apr. 1, 1951; *FT,* Mar. 24, 1951.

44. Karl Baarslag and Donald Wilson cancelled their speeches. Wilson, of nearby Clarksburg and the powerful law firm of Steptoe and Johnson, was in the midst of his successful campaign to become national commander of the American Legion. *Fairmont Times-West Virginian,* Apr. 1, 1951; *FT,* Mar. 29, 1951.

45. *Fairmont Times-West Virginian,* Apr. 1, 1951; *FT,* Mar. 29, 1951.

46. *Fairmont Times-West Virginian,* Apr. 1, 1951; ABC News, *The American Inquisition,* p. 7; Mundel's quoted testimony, *WV,* Dec. 20, 1951; *FT,* Dec. 21, 1951; Mundel to author, Aug. 21, 1984.

47. Jones to Morris and Meldahl, Nov. 19, 1951 (copy), JP; Eric Barnitz to the ACLU, Aug. 12, 1951, ACLU.

48. ABC News, *The American Inquisition,* p. 7 and especially p. 10, for Lasky's denial and ABC's response. Author's conversation with Victor Lasky, Nov. 5, 1985; *Variety,* Feb. 17, 1988, pp. 158, 163.

49. Jones to Morris and Meldahl, Nov. 19, 1951 (copy), JP; Jones to Ralph E. Himstead, July 19, 1951, AAUP; Jones to Lasky, Nov. 14, 1951 (copy provided to the author by Mr. Lasky); Mundel's testimony quoted, *WV,* Dec. 20, 1951; *FT,* Dec. 21, 1951. The reporters for the Fairmont papers, William Evans for the *Times* and Logan Carroll for the *West Virginian,* organized their trial notes differently. Sportswriter Evans used a straight chronological narrative while Carroll, who also wrote short stories and novels, tended to arrange the events topically. Their reports of the day's courtroom activities differ in some details. For example, Carroll adopted "Laski" as the spelling of the anticommunist speaker's name, and heard Benjamin Mandel's name as "C.Q. Mandel." He reported that Mundel said there were about fifty people at the Legion meeting when other accounts place the number at two or three times that many. But his version of Mundel's testimony about Lasky's statement is almost exactly the same as Evans's: "I know you are not a Communist. You shot off your mouth. Communists keep quiet." It

appears that Lasky's first public reaction to the Mundel affair was a letter to the editor of *Harper's* (published in the June 1952 issue, p. 16) denying that he had ever been a Communist and taking exception to William Manchester's characterization (May 1952) of speakers at the Fairmont Legion meeting as ex-Communists. Manchester stuck by his description but denied any intent to portray Lasky as a Communist or ex-Communist. The *Harper's* editor apologized to Lasky.

50. Jones wrote at the time and several interviewees vaguely recalled later that Hartnett as well as Matthews had made disparaging remarks about the college liberals at the 1950 meeting. Hartnett was alleged to have suggested that faculty member Regis Larkin, a mild liberal and devout Catholic, might be the head of a Communist cell. Asked to recall the Legion antisubversive seminars, some of those interviewed did not distinguish between the 1950 and 1951 meetings, remembering them as part of a continuum rather than discrete events.

51. Whatever was actually said, many sources mentioned rumors that Mundel had been branded a Communist at the Legion meeting.

52. *Fairmont Times-West Virginian,* Apr. 1, 1951.

53. *WV,* Apr. 3, 4, 12, 1951.

54. *WV,* Apr. 12, 1951. Cvetic's story, as dramatized in the film *I Was a Communist for the F.B.I.,* premiered in early April 1951. It was a major story at the time. For a jaundiced view of Cvetic see Caute, *The Great Fear,* p. 220.

55. Helen MacInnes, *Neither Five nor Three* (New York: Harcourt, Brace, 1951). Sokolsky seems to have believed that liberalism, sexual permissiveness, progressive education, atheism, and communism were part and parcel of a massive evil force undermining young American womanhood. The book by MacInnes received generally favorable notices despite its apparent premise that American intellectuals were mostly fellow travelers or Communists.

56. William H. Chafe, *The American Woman: Her Changing Social, Economic, and Political Role, 1920-1970* (New York: Oxford University Press, 1972), pp. 174–81. See also Barbara M. Solomon, *In the Company of Educated Women: A History of Women and Higher Education* (New Haven: Yale University Press, 1985), pp. 191–94; and Mabel Newcomer, *A Century of Higher Education for American Women.* (New York: Harper and Brothers, 1959), pp. 210–32, 245–56.

57. Chafe, *American Woman,* pp. 181–84; Gertrude Samuels, "Why Twenty Million Women Work," *New York Times Magazine,* Sept. 9, 1951; Dorothy Barclay, "What's Wrong with the Family," Ibid., Sept. 16, 1951; *New York Times,* Sept. 19, 1951.

58. Mirra Komarovsky, "Cultural Contradictions and Sex Roles," *American Journal of Sociology* 52 (Nov. 1946): 184–89.

59. Ibid., p. 189.

60. Evelyn Ellis, "Social Psychological Correlates of Upward Social Mobility among Unmarried Career Women," *American Sociological Review* 17 (Oct. 1952): 563.

61. Summarized in Chafe, *American Woman,* pp. 202–6.

62. Ibid., pp. 207–8; George D. Stoddard, *On the Education of Women* (New York: Macmillan Co., 1950); Anne G. Parnell, "A Nation's Strength Begins at

Home," *Vital Speeches* 18 (Dec. 15, 1951); Lynn White, Jr., *Educating Our Daughters* (New York: Harper and Brothers, 1950).

63. White, *Daughters,* p. 128.

64. Ibid., pp. 129–31.

65. *FT,* Apr. 14, 1951; *WV,* Apr. 14, 1951; *Columns,* May 30, 1949; Patricia Albjerg Graham, *Progressive Education: From Arcady to Academe* (New York: Teachers College Press, 1967), pp. 62–74, 128–30; Iverson, *The Communists and the Schools,* pp. 64–67, 115–16.

66. Gerald L. Gutek, *George S. Counts and American Civilization: The Educator as Social Theorist* (Macon, Ga.: Mercer University Press, 1984), pp. 10, 33–34, 154–57, 160–62. William Gellermann's *The American Legion as Educator* is inscribed on its title page with Counts's name as "sponsor." On the Legion's reaction to the book, see Iverson, *The Communists and the Schools,* p. 200. In the 1953 right-wing attack on Houston, Texas, public school official George Ebey, much was made by his attackers of his association with Columbia Teachers College and progressive education. As with Mundel, Ebey's contract was not renewed by the school board. Don E. Carleton, "McCarthyism in Houston: The George Ebey Affair," *Southwestern Historical Quarterly* 80 (Oct. 1976): 174–75.

67. Bayley, *Joe McCarthy and the Press,* p. 67.

68. *FT,* Apr. 2, 30, 1951; *WV,* Apr. 3, 5, 6, 11, 1951.

69. *FT,* May 3, 1951; *WV,* Apr. 2, May 2, 4, 1951.

70. *FT,* Apr. 3, 4, 7, 1951; *WV,* Apr. 5, May 5, 1951.

71. *FT,* Apr. 9, 10, 1951.

72. *FT,* Apr. 5, 7, 11, May 2, 1951; *WV,* Apr. 4, May 2, 1951.

73. The sample was both papers daily Apr. 11–May 5, 1951.

74. *FT,* Apr. 12, May 3, 4, 1951; *WV,* May 5, 1951.

75. U.S., Congress, Senate, *Congressional Record,* 82d Cong., 1st sess., p. 4709 (May 2, 1951). Neely's remarks were featured in the *New York Times,* May 3, 1951.

76. *WV,* Apr. 11, 12, May 2, 3, 5, 1951.

77. Bayley, *Joe McCarthy and the Press,* pp. 25, 66, 68, 87–88.

78. *FT,* Apr. 4, 5, 10, 11, 30, May 4, 5, 1951; *WV,* Apr. 3, 4, 7, 8, May 2, 3, 4, 5, 1951.

79. *FT,* Apr. 17, 1951.

CHAPTER 3

1. *Columns,* Sept. 26, 1950; Hand, "Report," pp. 22–23; Board Minutes, May 7–8, 1951, pp. 22–23, WVSA. Dr. Schoeck held a sociology degree from Tübingen yet he was not permitted to teach that subject. Hand later explained to the AAUP that he had defended Schoeck as an erudite, perhaps too erudite, scholar who spoke excellent English against some unspecific complaints by Board Secretary Baer. In the wake of several resignations Hand wanted to consolidate psychology, philosophy, and religion into one department with Schoeck teaching them all plus German. Hand, "Report," p. 4A. One might suspect the American Legion here. In 1947 the West Virginia Legion at its state convention had recommended legislation to bar aliens from teaching in the state. Minutes of the Executive

Committee of the State American Legion, Oct. 17–18, 1947, in A. & M. 139, WVU. Loudin also brought up a fourth name, that of Albert Greco, a music teacher whose services, Hand said, were no longer needed. *FT,* July 12, 15–16, 1952.

2. Hand, "Report," pp. 22–23; *WV,* July 14, 1952. Hand's version of Loudin's words was "Well, let us put it this way, let us say she is a poor security risk." At the July 1952 trial several board members testified that Hand had said Mundel should receive another year's employment to give her enough rope to hang herself. In sworn testimony at the trial Hand admitted he might have said something like that. *FT,* July 11–12, 15–16, 1952.

3. With the passage of the Hatch Act in 1939, loyalty became a condition of employment in the federal government. The Smith Act the next year established federal predominance in the field of antisubversive legislation. In 1946 there was created the President's Temporary Commission on Employee Loyalty. Presidential Executive Order 9835 (1947) formally married loyalty to security and greatly expanded the scope of inquiry. Alan D. Harper, *The Politics of Loyalty: The White House and the Communist Issue, 1946–52* (Westport, Conn.: Greenwood, 1969), pp. 14–15, 20–45. In late 1947 local Legion posts were enlisted in the antisubversive campaign. Under a cover letter from Seth Richardson (December 4), lists of subversive organizations were sent to them. See "List of Subversive Organizations," American Legion Mountaineer Post 127, A. & M. 139, 537, WVU. J. Edgar Hoover reported on April 28, 1951, that since 1947 the FBI had checked 3,325,000 federal workers and had received "derogatory information" in 14,484 cases. As a result 299 employees had been removed or denied employment, 2,941 had resigned under scrutiny, and 8,060 had returned after investigation. *New York Times,* Apr. 28, 1951. As of March 1952 some 4,000,000 federal employees had been checked by various agencies. One in 200 had been investigated, 1 in 2,000 had been removed. Charges had been brought against 9,077; 2,961 hearings had been held; 378 had been dismissed and 145 had been denied employment. See Eleanor Bontecou, *The Federal Loyalty-Security Program* (Ithaca, N.Y.: Cornell University Press, 1953), p. 145.

4. Federal loyalty-security investigation procedures contained a narrow definition of disloyalty and stipulated that subjects' due process was to be protected by requiring the government to file written charges and grant hearings and the right to legal counsel to the accused. See Bontecou, *Federal Loyalty-Security Program,* pp. 275–88, 310–12. These procedures, however, were soon set aside as a multiplicity of regional and agency loyalty review boards interpreted the idea of disloyalty with considerable latitude. *New York Times,* Apr. 28, 1951.

5. Bontecou, *Federal Loyalty-Security Program,* p. 104. The courts generally supported the principle that employment was a privilege, not a right. See Alfred H. Kelly, Winfred A. Harbison, and Herman Belz, *The American Constitution: Its Origins and Development,,* 6th ed. (New York: W. W. Norton and Co., 1983), p. 594.

6. Bontecou, *Federal Loyalty-Security Program,* p. 105. The FBI and J. Edgar Hoover, searching for those employees vulnerable to blackmail, took the lead in broadening the definition of loyalty by identifying, as of April 1950, 406 so-called "sexual deviates in government service." *New York Times,* Apr. 28, 1951. For a

detailed discussion of antisubversive legislation by the states see Walter Gellhorn, ed., *The States and Subversion* (Ithaca, N.Y.: Cornell University Press, 1952). Page 439 of that book summarizes relevant West Virginia legislation.

7. State Department of Education, *School Laws* (1952), item 1807. Passed by the New York legislature in 1949, the Feinberg law required the state board of regents to compile a list of subversive organizations, membership in any of which was grounds for a professor's dismissal. There was to be a report on the loyalty of every teacher. The U.S. Supreme Court upheld the law's constitutionality in 1953. California's Tenney Committee (Fact-Finding Committee on Un-American Activities), organized in 1941 as a sort of state HUAC, focused intensively in the late 1940s on alleged subversion among faculty members of the state's colleges and universities. Iverson, *Communists and the Schools,* pp. 265–72. For actions in other states see Gellhorn, ed., *States and Subversion,* especially pp. 55–61, 140–42, 157–59, 196–98, 241–81, 375–77.

8. Bontecou, *Federal Loyalty-Security Program,* pp. 280–82. Kelly, Harbison, and Belz, *American Constitution,* pp. 593–94. The justification for the new "reasonable grounds" standard was that since the CPUSA had gone underground in 1949 it was impossible to remove Communists in government service because they were now behaving as loyal citizens. The new standard made it possible for loyalty review boards to fire employees for past actions. Executive Order 10241 led to the reopening of about 10,000 cases in various government agencies. *New York Times,* Apr. 29, May 1, 10, 11, 19, 1951.

9. Bontecou, *Federal Loyalty-Security Program,* pp. 223–32; Kelly, Harbison, and Belz, *American Constitution,* pp. 593–94; *New York Times,* May 1, 11, 19, 1951.

10. Defendant's Plea of Special Privilege and Defendant's Specification of Defense, *Mundel* v. *Loudin,* MCCC.

11. Schrecker, *No Ivory Tower,* pp. 93–95, 106–12, 126–27.

12. *FT,* July 11, 12, 1952; Hand, "Report," pp. 22–23.

13. *FT,* July 11, 12, 1952.

14. Hand, "Report," pp. 22–23; Board Minutes, May 7–8, 1951, p. 26, WVSA; *WV,* July 11, 14, 1952.

15. Hand, "Report," pp. 11–15, 23–24.

16. Ibid., p. 24; Mundel to Himstead, July 16, 1951, AAUP. Jones used these exact words in writing to Mundel's lawyers in November 1951, but in December had adopted the wording Hand used in his 1952 report. Jones to Morris and Meldahl, Nov. 19, 1951 (copy); typed notes to [Morris and Meldahl?], Dec. 18, 1951, JP.

17. Hand, "Report," p. 24; Jones to Morris and Meldahl (copy), Nov. 19, 1951, JP. I was unable to determine whether or not Mundel was actually investigated by the FBI.

18. Jones to Morris and Meldahl (copy), Nov. 19, 1951, JP; *WV,* July 14, 1952.

19. Hand, "Report," pp. 24–25. The length of Hand's report on Mundel to the board has variously been given as eight, eight and a half, nine, or eleven pages. It is five and a half single-spaced pages or about 2,200 words in the version used for

this study, which appears on pp. 25–30 of Hand's "Report" to the AAUP and AACTE under the heading "Report to the West Virginia Board of Education on Dr. Luella Raab Mundel Chairman [*sic*] Department of Art Fairmont State College."

20. Ibid., pp. 25–26.

21. Ibid., pp. 27–28.

22. Ibid., pp. 28–30.

23. Ibid., p. 30.

24. Ibid., pp. 30–31.

25. Ibid., p. 33.

26. Mundel to Louis Joughin, Aug. 31, 1951, ACLU; Spaulding Rogers to Himstead, July 14, 1951, AAUP. *The West Virginia Code of 1949* (Charlottesville, Va.: Michie Co., 1949). (Section 1810, no. 6, details the rules for firing public school employees generally, although not public college professors specifically.) Hand, "Report," p. 37. Hand's vacation was extraordinary not only because of when he chose to take it, but because a month was exactly twice the time allowed to West Virginia state college presidents in 1951. Memo, Jones to Hand (endorsed with Hand's disapproval), July 11, 1951, JP.

27. Hand, "Report," p. 34; Barnitz to ACLU, Aug. 12, 1951, ACLU. My interviews indicate that Mundel was disliked by some and unknown to many others of her colleagues. Schrecker, *No Ivory Tower,* pp. 308–37.

28. Mundel to Dunn, July 14, 1951 (copy); same to Trent, July 14, 1951 (copy), both JP.

29. *WV,* July 15, 1952.

30. AAUP *Bulletin* (Spring 1951): 170, 185; Hofstadter and Metzger, *Academic Freedom,* pp. 487, 491.

31. Appendix 4 in Wilson, *Academic Man,* pp. 237–39.

32. Ibid., p. 237.

33. Ibid., p. 239.

34. Himstead to West Virginia State Board of Education (night letter—copy), July 17, 1951, AAUP.

35. Hand, "Report," p. 34; Dunn to Mundel, July 19, 1951 (copy), JP; Mundel to Himstead, July 16, 1951, AAUP.

36. Trent to Mundel, July 19, 1951 (copy); Same to Himstead, July 20, 1951, both AAUP; State Department of Education, *School Laws* (1949), (1953), pp. 30–31.

37. Wilson, *Academic Man,* p. 120, 120n.; R.H. Freer, comp., *Reports of Cases Determined by the Supreme Court of Appeals of West Virginia from January 19, 1901, to September 7, 1901,* vol. 49 (Charleston: Charleston Daily Mail Printing Co., 1902), pp. 18–24. The board did hear oral charges against Hartigan for "untruthful, unscientific" behavior, waste of university property, and inefficient teaching— after he had been dismissed. The real issue in the case was the personality and administration of President J. H. Raymond (1897–1901) and the resulting politicization of the regents. Ambler, *History,* pp. 323–39.

38. R. H. Freer, comp., *Reports of Cases* (49), pp. 32, 34, 37, 39, 42, 51. Dent in his written opinion claimed his colleagues on the bench had refused to allow him to share in their deliberations or have access to case files. He bemoaned the fact that

the abolition of duelling left him with no redress. For Dent see John Philip Reid, *An American Judge: Marmaduke Dent of West Virginia* (New York: New York University Press, 1968).

39. Mundel to Dunn, July 21, 1951 (copy), JP.

40. Mundel to Phares H. Reeder, Aug. [5?], 1951, JP; same to Himstead, July 16, 1951, AAUP.

41. The relevant passage of the board minutes is quoted verbatim in Jones to Himstead, July 23, 1951, AAUP; WVEA, *Annual Report of the Secretary, 1951* (Charleston: WVEA, [1951]), p. 14.

42. Barnitz to ACLU, Aug. 12, 1951, ACLU; *WV,* July 29, Aug. 1, 2, 1951.

43. *WV,* Aug. 2, 1951.

44. *WV,* Aug. 3, 1951.

45. Mundel to Himstead, Aug. 2, 1951, AAUP.

46. George Marsden, *Reforming Fundamentalism: Fuller Seminary and the New Evangelicalism* (Grand Rapids, Mich.: William B. Eerdmans Publishing Co., 1987), pp. 4–7, 32–37.

47. Ibid., pp. 10–11, 29, 60–63, 154–55.

48. Carleton, *Red Scare,* pp. 103–10, 142–43; *Christian Century,* Apr. 23, 1952, pp. 486–93; May 16, 1952, pp. 630–31; Stanley High, "Methodism's Pink Fringe," *Reader's Digest,* Feb. 1950, pp. 134–38.

49. Telegram, Jones to Okey Patteson, Aug. 7, 1951 (copy); Patteson to Jones, Aug. 11, 1951, both JP.

50. Paul Allen to Jones, Aug. 8, 1951; Jones to Allen, Aug. 10, 13, 1951 (copy); Mundel to Allen, Aug. [?], 1951 (copy), all JP.

51. *WV,* Aug. 15, 1951. Mundel then wrote to Loudin charging her with lying. Apparently Loudin did not reply. Mundel to Loudin, Aug. 24, 1951 (copy), AAUP. Editor Boggs later testified that he had received the notes from Loudin. *WV,* July 9, 1952.

52. Himstead to Dunn, Aug. 20, 1951; Rogers to Hand, Aug. 21, 1951; Rogers to L. G. Boggs, Aug. 24, 1951 (all copies), all AAUP.

53. Fridtjof Schroder to Himstead, Aug. 20, 1951, AAUP.

54. Ibid.

55. Memo, GPS to REH, Aug. 31, 1951, AAUP.

56. Ibid.

57. Ibid.

58. Hand, "Report," pp. 35–36, AAUP. The clergyman was J. Clair Jarvis, Hand's pastor at Fairmont's First Methodist Church. *WV,* July 9, 1952.

59. Board Minutes, Sept. 5, 1951, WVSA.

60. Author's interviews with former faculty members Regis Larkin and Edgar Jaynes (1984) and newspaper coverage confirm that others on the faculty who spoke out against the anticommunists or wrote letters to the newspapers were not punished. It is also certain that Mundel was not the only admitted agnostic at the college.

61. Hand, "Report," pp. 37–39.

62. Ibid.

CHAPTER 4

1. *Charleston Daily Mail*, Sept. 23, 1951. This paper also published pro-Mundel editorials Aug. 29 and Sept. 14. An editorial defending the board against Mundel appeared in the *Morgantown Post*, a paper edited by former board member Brooks Cottle.

2. Mundel to Himstead, Sept. 25, 1951, AAUP.

3. Joughin to Mundel, Sept. 9, 13, 1951 (copies); same to Jones, Sept. 26, 1951; Mundel to Joughin, Sept. 27, 1951 (copy); Eric Barnitz to same, Aug. 12, 1951; Meldahl to same, Sept. 20, 1951, all ACLU; Meldahl to Jones, Sept. 9, 1951, JP. For Joughin's concept of academic due process see Clark Byse and Louis Joughin, *Tenure in American Higher Education: Plans, Practices, and the Law* (Ithaca, N.Y.: Cornell University Press, 1959), pp. 93–98.

4. David R. Manwaring, *Render unto Caesar: The Flag Salute Controversy* (Chicago: University of Chicago Press, 1962), pp. 210–11, 214, 225–33, 303 (n. 17).

5. *WV*, Mar. 17, 1952; Horace S. Meldahl, *Maximum Welfare* (Charleston, W.Va.: Hood Hiserman-Brodhag Co., 1934), pp. 4–14, 197–208, 216–17, 260–75; "The Maximum Welfare Society Invites Mr. and Mrs. Eric Barnitz to Become Members," [1953], JP.

6. The Truman administration did not support the Nixon-Mundt bill in 1949 and it died in committee only to be revived the next year during the Korean conflict and passed as the notorious McCarran Internal Security Act. Meldahl portrayed the bill to Kilgore as the product of the evil influences of Wall Street financiers and American industrialists. Meldahl to Kilgore, June 18, 1949. See also same to same, June 22, 25, 1949; Kilgore to Meldahl, June 22, 1949 (copy), all in Harley M. Kilgore Papers, A. & M. 1068, WVU. For Meldahl's denial of Communist affiliations, see Meldahl to Morris, Mar. 20, 1952 (copy), JP. Kilgore was one of several members of Congress who often lent an ear to the old Left in the late 1940s. See O'Reilly, *Hoover*, p. 113; Joseph R. Starobin, *American Communism in Crisis, 1943–1957* (Berkeley: University of California Press, 1972), p. 256n.

7. Meldahl to Jones, Sept. 9, 1951; Jones to Meldahl, Sept. 13, 1951 (copy), JP. Jones pestered the WVEA in a series of letters. The quotation is from Phares Reeder to Jones, Nov. 6, 1951. See also Jones to Reeder, July 31, 1951 (copy); Reeder to Jones, Aug. 3, 15, 1951, all JP. Despite this correspondence, the WVEA Tenure and Ethics Committee made no mention of the Mundel case in its 1951–52 report. It noted ten "special problems," none of which involved college faculty. WVEA, *Annual Report* (1952), pp. 56–58; Lord, *Years of Decision*, p. 195.

8. Meldahl to Jones, Sept. 9, 1951, JP. Repeatedly pressed by the ACLU on the mandamus issue, Meldahl explained that he believed that a hearing would do no good because the board would act at such a hearing as "judge . . . , prosecutor, and persecutor." Meldahl to Joughin, Mar. 31, 1952, ACLU.

9. Mundel to Joughin, Sept. 25, 1951, ACLU.

10. Ironically, the station's call letters WMMN (Neely's initials) had been selected originally to honor the senator.

11. Mundel to Joughin, Sept. 25, 1951, ACLU; John C. McKinney, "The Black Hand," in Hoffman, comp., *Marion County . . . Yearbook*, pp. 76–77; *FT*, Mar. 31,

1940; Dec. 12, 1953; *CG,* Oct. 8, 1942. Meldahl agreed to try the case for expenses only, no fee.

12. Herbert Monte Levy to Meldahl, Sept. 28, 1951 (copy), ACLU.

13. Joughin to Mundel, Sept. 13, 1951 (copy), ACLU.

14. Joughin to Mundel, Oct. 4, 1951 (copy), ACLU.

15. Meldahl to Levy, Sept. 29, 1951, ACLU.

16. Meldahl to Joughin, Sept. 20, 1951, ACLU.

17. It was later established that Post 17 officers, apparently without informing their full membership, had underwritten Loudin's defense in the sum of $2,500. See below, chapter 7.

18. There is no scholarly biography of Neely. For a brief but perceptive assessment of Neely the politician see Williams, *West Virginia,* pp. 165–70, and also Lanham, "Statehouse Machine," pp. 198–210. One can also glean much from the voluminous collection of newspaper clippings on Neely's career in the West Virginia and Regional History Collection at West Virginia University, as well as from William A. Yaremchuk, "The Congressional Speaking of Matthew Mansfield Neely in Behalf of Cancer Research Legislation" (M.A. thesis, West Virginia University, 1964). Specific citations for the information presented are: Yaremchuk, pp. 1–7; Hoffman, comp., *Marion County Yearbook,* p. 61; undated clipping [1944?], Neely Scrapbooks, A. & M. 1414, WVU.

19. Yaremchuk, "Congressional Speaking," pp. 53–66; clipping, Holmes Alexander column, Jan. 25, 1950, Neely Scrapbooks, A. & M. 1414, WVU. The *Clarksburg* [W.Va.] *News,* June 11, 1947, compared Neely to Huey Long, Matt Quay, and Boss Platt, but the *Charleston Daily Mail,* July 10, 1951, likened him to great Senate orators such as William Borah and Robert La Follette, Sr. William Jennings Bryan was surely the most appropriate comparison. See also Yaremchuk, p. 86.

20. All of the epithets are found in a single campaign speech delivered by Neely on November 2, 1936, to a large audience at the Marion County Courthouse and carried by radio station WMMN. The title of the printed transcript of the speech catches its flavor: "Rush D. Holt, An Infamous Traitor to the Democratic Party; An Intolerable Abomination to the United States Senate; An Everlasting Disgrace to the People of West Virginia," C. E. Smith Papers, A. & M. 1604, 1606, WVU. Holt was a former political protégé of Neely. Neely continued to use this repertoire (and other terms) as the occasion seemed to warrant. For a broader sampling of Neely's rhetoric, see Matthew Mansfield Neely, *State Papers and Public Addresses* (Charleston, W.Va.: Mathews Printing and Lithographing Co., n.d.); Anon., comp., *Memorial Services Held in the Senate and House ... in Eulogy of Matthew Mansfield Neely ...* (Washington, D.C.: U.S. Government Printing Office, 1958), pp. 153–255.

21. Fried, *Men against McCarthy,* p. 78. Also *Washington Daily News,* May 3, 1951; *Washington Evening Star,* May 3, 1951; *FT,* Jan. 6, 1952; *New York Times,* Jan. 19, 1958. Griffith, *The Politics of Fear,* p. 105, counts Neely among a small group of openly anti-McCarthy Democratic Senate liberals that included Neely's West Virginia colleague Kilgore, Herbert Lehman of New York, William Benton of Connecticut, Clinton Anderson of New Mexico, Hubert Humphrey of Minnesota,

and Paul Douglas of Illinois. Whether Neely was actually an ideological liberal on noneconomic issues like Humphrey or Douglas for example, or simply a Truman administration loyalist is debatable.

22. Fenton, *Border States,* pp. 83–89, 100–103; Williams, *West Virginia,* pp. 169–70.

23. Anon., comp., *Memorial Services... Eulogy of... Neely,* pp. 153, 197–200.

24. For a provocative essay that relates McCarthyism to the defense of domestic ideology in Hollywood motion pictures, see Michael Rogin, "Kiss Me Deadly: Communism, Motherhood, and Cold War Movies," *Representations* 6 (Spring 1984): 1–35. (I am indebted to Richard M. Fried for calling it to my attention.)

25. U.S., Congress, Senate, *Congressional Record,* 82d Cong., 2d sess., May 14, 1952, pp. 5244–45. Neely maintained a fourteen-room frame house overlooking downtown Fairmont and continued a local law practice with his son. If Mundel belonged to no group in Fairmont, Neely seems to have belonged to them all. In 1941 he was a member of the Presbyterian Church, Junior Supreme Governor of the Loyal Order of Moose, Past Exalted Ruler of the Fairmont BPOE (Elks), life member 32d Degree Mason and Shriner, and member of Knights of Pythias, Odd Fellows, Delta Chi, Phi Sigma Kappa, and Phi Beta Kappa among others. Clipping, *West Virginia Review* (Jan. 1941), Neely Scrapbooks, A. & M. 1414, WVU; *CG,* Jan. 19, 1958.

26. *FT,* July 16, 1952; *FT,* May 17, 1948.

27. *CG,* May 13, Nov. 2, 1952; The 1952 primary is summarized in Fenton, *Border States,* pp. 100–103; and in Paul F. Lutz, "The 1952 West Virginia Gubernatorial Election," *West Virginia History* 39 (Jan.–Apr. 1978): 210–14, 221, 224. Neely's strategy may be divined from Lutz and from the editorials of Neely ally Bill Hart in the *Morgantown Dominion News,* particularly Dec. 21, 1951, and Jan. 4, 1952. In the general election West Virginia Republicans tried to paint Democratic Senator Kilgore as procommunist. They circulated "The Red Record of Senator Harley M. Kilgore" and attacked him as a "legislative water boy for communism." It was an attack in which even Senator McCarthy joined. Robert Franklin Maddox, *The Senatorial Career of Harley Martin Kilgore* (New York: Garland Publishing Co., 1981), pp. 310–12.

28. Undated typescript copy for "Good Morning" column in the *Fairmont Times,* C. E. Smith Papers, A. & M. 1604, 1606, WVU.

29. Joughin to Neely, Oct. 15, 1951 (copy), ACLU. Neely and Joughin spoke by phone on October 12 and exchanged letters in October and November. See Joughin to Neely, Oct. 18, 1951 (copy); Neely to Joughin, Nov. 6, 10, 1951, ACLU. See also Joughin to Himstead, Oct. 17, 1951, AAUP.

30. Neely to Joughin, Nov. 10, 1951, ACLU.

31. Memo, Joughin to Walter Gellhorn, Mar. 28, 1952, ACLU.

32. "Memorandum on the Civil Liberties and Academic Freedom Aspects of the Mundel Fairmont State College Case," Oct. 15, 1951, mimeograph, American Civil Liberties Union, ACLU. Also copies in JP and AAUP.

33. For Loudin's Americanism meeting, see *WV,* Oct. 17, 1951. To have yielded to the antisubversives' demands would have violated the American Library Association Council's "Library Bill of Rights," article 3 of which reads: "Censorship of

books [amended to include all materials and media of communication used or collected by libraries], urged or practiced by volunteer arbiters of morals or political opinion or by organizations that would establish a coercive concept of Americanism, must be challenged by libraries in maintenance of their responsibility to provide information and enlightenment through the printed word." See *A.L.A. Bulletin,* July–Aug. 1948.

34. Hand, "Report," pp. 8, 41–42. Five of the six members of the Anti-Subversive Committee were L. O. Bickel, George Parsons, Harry Cronin, Wayne Cornwell, and A. M. Darquenne. According to Jones, the president of West Virginia University and officials of accrediting bodies such as the North Central Association of Colleges and Secondary Schools wrote letters in defense of the right to freely read. Jones apparently placated the committee to a degree by demonstrating that the library's holdings included much anticommunist literature. Still, Jones had recognized that there was a problem in 1950 because radical groups, both right and left, sent free literature to libraries. Not to display them would have seemed like censorship. David K. Berninghausen to Jones, Aug. 21, 1950; Jones to Joughin, Oct. 12, 19, 1951 (copies), JP.

35. Hand, "Report," p. 42. In preparing this study the author was unable to locate copies of the *Worker* at any library in West Virginia.

36. Ibid., pp. 15, 43.

37. Hand, "Report," pp. 16, 43.

38. House to Himstead, Nov. 5, 1951; E. L. Lively to Himstead, Nov. 6, 1951, AAUP.

39. John C. Cort, "Jefferson in West Virginia," *Commonweal,* Dec. 7, 1951, pp. 225–28. The passage from the Virginia Statute of Religious Liberty (January 16, 1786) invoked by Cort reads: "*Be it enacted by the General Assembly,* that no man shall be compelled to frequent or support any religious worship, place or ministry whatsoever, nor shall be enforced, restrained, molested, or burthened in his body or goods, nor shall otherwise suffer on account of his religious opinions or belief; but that all men shall be free to profess, and by argument maintain, their opinion in matters of religion, and that the same shall in no wise diminish, enlarge or affect their civil capacities." Henry Steele Commager, ed., *Documents of American History,* 9th ed., vol. 1 (Englewood Cliffs, N.J.: Prentice-Hall, 1973), p. 126.

40. *Commonweal,* Dec. 7, 1951, pp. 227–28; Crosby, *God, Church, and Flag,* pp. 20–25.

41. See Helen C. White to Himstead, Dec. 15, 1951; Himstead to White, Dec. 20, 1951 (copy), AAUP. White was a University of Wisconsin English professor, AAUP chapter officer, and one of forty-three prominent women appointed to a commission to advise the government on women in the military. After reading Cort's article she inquired of Himstead if Mundel had indeed appealed to the AAUP and if so, what was being done. Obviously irritated, Himstead replied defensively. He charged that the Cort article was a deliberate misrepresentation of the facts and that the AAUP and AACTE were proceeding jointly to use the Mundel episode as a means of improving the tenure situation in teachers colleges.

What was currently delaying them, he claimed, was the trouble created by Mundel's suit against board member Loudin.

42. In a letter to Mundel's lawyers Jones reported that on Thursday, December 6, a "reporter or editor" from the *Baltimore Sun* had telephoned Hand after seeing the *Commonweal* article. The reporter, undoubtedly Manchester, was said to be enthusiastic about covering the case and Jones noted hopefully that it had been press coverage that had made the Scopes trial so well known. Jones to Morris and Meldahl, Dec. 11, 1951 (copy), JP. Reinforcing the Scopes analogy, the twenty-eight-year-old Manchester had recently published a biography of Mencken, *Disturber of the Peace* (New York: Harper, 1951).

43. Meldahl to Jones, Nov. 11, 1951, JP.

44. Memo to Executive Staff from L[ouis] J[oughin], Nov. 26, 1951; Joughin to Meldahl, Dec. 7, 1951, both ACLU.

CHAPTER 5

1. Manchester, "Mundel," pp. 54–61. See also Manchester's reports for the *Baltimore Evening Sun,* Dec. 19, 20, 1951. The first journalist to use the Scopes analogy was Marben Graham of the *Pittsburgh Post-Gazette* on December 14, 1951, under the headline "FAIRMONT HAS SCOPES CASE." Page 5 was as near as the Mundel story came to the front of the *New York Times.* The miscaptioned photo appeared on December 22, 1951. Manchester wrote in *Harper's* that the holiday season, the weather, and journalistic laziness limited coverage (p. 60).

Newspaper accounts are the best surviving trial records. No official transcript was prepared for the court because the case was not carried to the West Virginia Supreme Court of Appeals. Harold Jones tried on several occasions to obtain either the complete transcript or selected excerpts. He could not do so because court reporter Ruth Chartrand asked $775 for a complete transcript, not including Neely's opening address, and $1,030 for an original and a carbon. She refused to deliver just a jury summation on the grounds that part of it might be lifted out and distorted for partisan purposes. Chartrand to Jones, Mar. 6 and June 13, 1953, JP. Chartrand apparently carried her notes on the trial with her through many moves over many years before she discarded them in the early 1980s. Research is further complicated by the absence of a morgue or referenced back file at the Fairmont newspaper offices, by the destruction several years ago of most of the college records in a storage-facility fire, and by the unavailability of the correspondence of the state board of education.

2. Plaintiff's Bill of Particulars, *Mundel v. Loudin,* MCCC.

3. Defendant's Plea of Special Privilege; Defendant's Specifications of Defense, *Mundel v. Loudin,* MCCC.

4. See State Department of Education, *School Laws,* items 1730, 1731, 1738. These grant general supervisory powers to the board over teacher education but mention nothing about personnel evaluations of professors. Neither do they give the board jurisdiction over the loyalty or religious persuasion of faculty members.

5. *WV,* Dec. 19, 1951; *Polk's Greater Fairmont (Marion County, West Virginia) City Directory* (1952), 24 (Pittsburgh: P. L. Polk and Co., 1952). The jurors' surnames were: Rutherford, Downs, Leeper, Currey, Gracie, Higgs, Clayton, Stuck, Doak, Coughenour, Garrison, and Cover. Many of these names are still common in the area.

6. *WV,* Dec. 19, 1951; *FT,* Dec. 20, 1951.

7. *FT,* Dec. 20, 1951.

8. Manchester, "Mundel," p. 57; *FT,* Dec. 20, 1951; *WV,* Dec. 19, 1951.

9. Manchester, "Mundel," p. 57; *FT,* Dec. 20, 1951.

10. *FT,* Dec. 20, 21, 22, 1951; *WV,* Dec. 20, 1951; Manchester, "Mundel," p. 57. Meldahl answered Neely's tirade moderately and, one imagines, ineffectually by pointing out that religion and Russia were not germane to the case.

11. Stouffer, *Communism, Conformity, and Civil Liberties,* pp. 158–75.

12. *FT,* Dec. 20, 1951; *WV,* Dec. 19, 1951; Manchester, "Mundel," pp. 57–58.

13. Manchester, "Mundel," pp. 57–58; *FT,* Dec. 20, 1951.

14. Manchester, "Mundel," p. 58; ABC News, *American Inquisition,* p. 8; *FT,* Dec. 20, 1951.

15. *FT,* Dec. 20, 1951.

16. Ibid.

17. Ibid.

18. *FT,* Dec. 20, 21, 1951.

19. *WV,* Dec. 20, 1951; *FT,* Dec. 21, 1951.

20. Manchester, "Mundel," p. 58; *FT,* Dec. 21, 1951.

21. *FT,* Dec. 21, 1951. The newspaper account does not give a precise or complete quotation although it is substantively accurate. See *Commonweal,* Dec. 7, 1951, p. 225 for its entirety: " 'I avoid doctrinaire and dogmatic theories such as "atheism." I have no proof of the non-existence of a supreme being. On the other hand I have no proof of the existence of a deity; and so I wish to withhold an opinion on the matter. I am untrained in theology. However, I am the product of a Christian civilization and I believe in Christian ethics.' "

22. *Baltimore Sun,* Dec. 20, 1951; *FT,* Dec. 21, 1951.

23. *FT,* Dec. 21, 1951.

24. Ibid.; ABC News, *American Inquisition,* p. 8.

25. *FT,* Dec. 22, 1951; Manchester, "Mundel," pp. 58–59.

26. *FT,* Dec. 22, 1951.

27. Ibid.

28. Ibid.; Jones to Morris and Meldahl (copies), Dec. 13, 18, 1951, JP.

29. *FT,* Dec. 22, 1951.

30. Ibid.

31. Ibid.

32. Ibid.

33. Ibid.

34. *WV,* Dec. 27, 1951.

35. Lutz, "1952 Gubernatorial Election," pp. 211–12; Meldahl to Joughin, Dec. 24, 1951, ACLU.

36. *FT,* Dec. 28, 1951.
37. Ibid.
38. Ibid.
39. *FT,* Dec. 28, 1951.
40. Ibid.; Manchester, "Mundel," p. 59.
41. *FT,* Dec. 28, 1951; Manchester, "Mundel," p. 59.
42. *FT,* Dec. 28, 1951.
43. Ibid.
44. *FT,* Dec. 29, 1951.
45. Ibid.; *WV,* Dec. 28, 1951. During the discussion of her mental state Neely learned from the physician that Mundel had said during the night's stress that "Mr. Jones is happy with everything that has happened because he ruined me." The physician quickly added that the distraught Mundel was not to be held accountable for such a statement, but it surely reinforced the belief widespread in the Loudin camp that Jones was the éminence grise, in Neely's words, the "man who masterminded this case."
46. *FT,* Dec. 29, 1951; *WV,* Dec. 28, 1951.
47. *FT,* Dec. 29, 1951; *WV,* Dec. 28, 1951.
48. *FT,* Dec. 29, 1951.
49. Ibid.
50. Ibid.; *WV,* Dec. 31, 1951 (which reprinted a complete transcript of Mundel's deposition, given by Neely to the Republican paper after the mistrial).
51. *FT,* Dec. 29, 1951; *WV,* Dec. 31, 1951.
52. *FT,* Dec. 29, 1951; *WV,* Dec. 31, 1951.
53. *FT,* Dec. 29, 1951; *WV,* Dec. 31, 1951.
54. *FT,* Dec. 29, 1951; *WV,* Dec. 31, 1951.
55. *FT,* Dec. 29, 1951; *WV,* Dec. 31, 1951.
56. *FT,* Dec. 29, 1951; *WV,* Dec. 31, 1951.
57. *FT,* Dec. 29, 1951.
58. Ibid.
59. *FT,* Dec. 31, 1951; *WV,* Dec. 31, 1951.
60. *FT,* Dec. 31, 1951; *WV,* Dec. 31, 1951.

CHAPTER 6

1. *FT,* Dec. 31, 1951.
2. The ministers showed no reticence on January 4, when they formally urged Neely to oppose a State Department's plan to establish diplomatic relations with the Vatican. *FT,* Jan. 6, 1952.
3. *Baltimore Sun,* Dec. 21, 1951 (typescript copy), AAUP. *Louisville Courier-Journal,* Jan. 3, 1952. Jones also reported that papers in Milwaukee, Denver, Des Moines, and Baltimore published pro-Mundel editorials.
4. *Louisville Courier-Journal,* Jan. 3, 1952; *Grafton News,* Jan. 14, 1952; *Charleston Daily Mail,* Jan. 2, 6, 1952; Jones to Joughin (copy), June 8, 1952, JP. The college newspaper's silence was predictable, because its advisor was Hand opponent House. In March the paper broke its silence only to criticize the West Virginia

University student newspaper for publishing an editorial critical of the board of education. *Columns,* Mar. 18, 1952.

5. *FT,* Jan. 3, 4, 1952. The program was not seen in Fairmont, which, like much of the nation, lacked a local television station. At this time Neely was championing the cause of TV cameras at congressional hearings. See his insertions: "Is TV Winning the Fight for Equality?"; "Neely Inquiry Seems to Show Congress How Unobtrusive TV Can Be"; "TV Acquitted of Others' Sins," in the Appendix to the *Congressional Record,* 82d Cong., 2d sess., pp. A619, A603, A617. *FT,* Jan. 7, 1952; Joseph Wershba to author, Dec. 11, 1984. "See It Now," Jan. 6, 1952. (I am indebted to Mr. Wershba for an audio cassette of the dialogue of the three-minute Neely segment of the show.)

6. *FT,* Jan. 7, 1952; *WV,* Jan. 7, 1952; *Morgantown Dominion News,* Jan. 7, 1952; Lutz, "1952 Gubernatorial Election," pp. 211–14; Jones to Joughin, Jan. 14, 1952; Jones to Morris and Meldahl, Jan. 14, 1952 (copies), both JP.

7. Memo, Levy to Joughin and Alan Reitman, Jan. 3, 1952; Joughin to Meldahl, Jan. 9, 1952 (copy), both ACLU.

8. Meldahl to Jones, Jan. 9, Feb. 18, 1952; Jones to Meldahl, Jan. 13, 1952 (copy); Jones to Joughin, Jan. 14, 1952 (copy), all JP.

9. *FT,* Jan. 4, 1952; Jones to Joughin, Jan. 14, 1952 (copy), JP; Barnitz to Joughin, Jan. 29, 1952; Joughin to Meldahl, Jan. 9, 1952 (copy), ACLU; Jones to Meldahl, Jan. 29, 1952 (copy), JP. Mundel's friends tried for several weeks in January to contact Luckenbill, but he did not return their calls or meet with them. And he would say nothing more about the affair publicly.

10. Jones to Joughin, Jan. 14, 1952 (copy); same to Meldahl, Jan. 13, 1952, both JP; Barnitz to Ernst, Feb. 23, 1952; same to Joughin, Mar. 6, 11, 1952, all ACLU; Jones to M. W. Wilson, Apr. 9, 1952 (copy), JP.

11. Meldahl to Morris, Jan. 21, 1952 (copy), JP; author's interview with Jones (1984).

12. Barnitz to Joughin, Mar. 6, 1952; July 31, 1952, ACLU.

13. Barnitz to Joughin, Mar. 6, June 9, Aug. 11, 1952, ACLU; Jones to Morris, Jan. 29, 1952 (copy), JP; *FT,* July 11, 1952.

14. Jones to Morris and Meldahl, Jan. 29, 1952; Same to Dr. Wilson, Apr. 9, 1952; Same to Himstead, Feb. 14, 1952 (copies), all JP; Alan Reitman to Dean M. Kelly, Aug. 27, 1952 (copy); Kelly to Reitman, Sept. 1, 1952, both ACLU; Grant A. Butler [Church of the Larger Fellowship] to Jones, Feb. 6, 1952, JP.

15. See Jones to M. W. Wilson, Apr. 9, 1952 (copy), JP; *FT,* July 11, 1952.

16. *WV,* Mar. 10, 1952; *New Yorker,* Feb. 23, 1952, pp. 106–8.

17. *New Yorker,* Feb. 23, 1952, pp. 106–8.

18. *WV,* Mar. 17, 19, 20, 1952; Barnitz to Joughin, Mar. 11, 1952, ACLU.

19. *WV,* Mar. 19, 1952.

20. Meldahl to Joughin, Mar. 20, 1952 (copy), JP.

21. Meldahl to Morris, Mar. 20, 1952 (copy); Meldahl to Jones, Mar. 29, 1952; Jones to Meldahl, Mar. 21, 1952 (copy); Mar. 22, 1952 (copy), all JP; Barnitz to Joughin, Mar. 31, 1952, ACLU.

22. Hand, "Report," pp. 11–14, 47; Jones's correspondence.

23. Hand, "Report," p. 46. The college newspaper made do with a photograph of Rosier in its announcement of the scholarship. It is hard to see why the *West Virginian* could not have done the same. *Columns,* Mar. 18, 1952.

24. Hand, "Report," pp. 46–47.

25. Ibid. p. 47.

26. *WV,* Mar. 10, 11, 1952; Barnitz to Joughin, Mar. 11, 1952, ACLU; Depositions of Thelma Loudin (Mar. 14, 1952); M. N. Neely (Mar. 15, 1952), *Mundel v. Loudin,* MCCC; Hand, "Report," p. 45.

27. *Grafton News,* Jan. 14, 1952; Hand, "Report," pp. 16–16A, 47–48.

28. Hand, "Report," pp. 47–49.

29. Ibid., pp. 49–50.

30. Each of the five had more than three years' service at the college.

31. Board Minutes, Mar. 27, 1952.

32. Hand, "Report," pp. 17–18.

33. Ibid.; Warren B. Horner to George Pope Shannon, Apr. 1, 1952, AAUP.

34. Barnitz to Joughin, Mar. 31, 1952; June 9, 1952, both ACLU; Meldahl to Jones, Apr. 1, 1952; Jones to Meldahl, Apr. 9, 1952 (copy), both JP; Hand, "Report," pp. 18–19; Schrecker, *No Ivory Tower,* p. 308. *WV,* May 20, 1952, published the texts of the letters of resignation of Taylor and Lucker. As reasons for their decisions both cited the board's action toward Hand and the repressive atmosphere of the college. Lucker added that she was leaving because of the board's refusal to give Mundel a hearing.

35. *FT,* Apr. 3, 5, 26, 1952; *WV,* Apr. 2, 3, 4, 5, 7, 1952; *Fairmont Times-West Virginian,* Mar. 30, Apr. 6, 1952.

36. Board Minutes, Apr. 23, 24, 25, 1952; Radio script for 9:30 P.M., May 16, 1952, program on WVVW, JP. A partial list of periodicals that put out articles, notices, or letters about Mundel at this time is *Harvard Crimson, Commonweal, Christian Century, Harper's, Art News, Des Moines Register.* At other times the case was mentioned in *New Leader, Christian Register, New Republic, Churchman, Living Church, College and University Business,* and *Humanist.*

37. For Mundel's job hunting see Jones to Manchester (copy), Jan. 11, 1952, JP.

38. Barnitz to Joughin, May 3, June 9, 1952, ACLU; *Washington Post, Washington Evening Star, New York Times,* all Mar. 30, 1952; *Washington Post,* Apr. 10, 1952. Manchester's interpretation influenced the ABC News documentary in 1983 in which he narrated a portion of the Mundel segment.

39. Barnitz to Joughin, May 3, 1952, ACLU; Manchester, "Mundel," pp. 53–58. Fairmonters who read Manchester's later works could take comfort from the fact that he treated their city more gently than he would Korea, which he wrote "hangs like a lumpy phallus between the sprawling thighs of Manchuria and the Sea of Japan." *American Caesar: Douglas MacArthur, 1880–1964* (Boston: Little, Brown and Co., 1978), p. 545.

40. *WV,* May 2, 3, 7, 8, 9, 1952; *FT,* May 3, 1945. *WV,* May 22, 1952, reprinted *Morgantown Post* columnist Bob Mellace's defense of Fairmont. Fairmont State College students who, it will be remembered, were sympathetic to Hand and Mundel, showed their resentment of Manchester's article in the 1952 yearbook by

daringly for the time and place referring to Manchester's "sore-eyed houses" in a mock Socratic dialogue under a photograph of two students clowning next to men's room urinals. *Mound* (1952), p. 45.

41. Memo, Joughin to Gellhorn, Mar. 28, 1952, ACLU.

42. Mundel to Joughin, Mar. 29, 1952; Barnitz to same, Mar. 31, June 9, 1952; Meldahl to same, Mar. 31, 1952; Memo (by Joughin) on Fairmont State College Situation to P[atrick] M[urphy] M[alin] and W[alter] G[ellhorn], Apr. 14, 1952, all ACLU. Memo by Joughin on Fairmont State College Situation, Apr. 14, 1952, with Malin's penciled marginalia to Gellhorn dated the same, ACLU.

43. See McCarthy's remarks, U.S., Congress, Senate, *Congressional Record,* 82d Cong., 2d sess., May 27, 1952, pp. 5959–62; Anthony Marro's article in the *New York Times,* Aug. 4, 1977; William A. Donohoe, *The Politics of the American Civil Liberties Union* (New Brunswick, N.J.: Transaction Books, 1985), p. 182.

44. Memo, R[oger] N. B[aldwin] to Joughin, June 2, 1952, ACLU.

45. Joughin to Hand, Apr. 16, 1952 (copy); Himstead to Joughin, Apr. 25, 1952; Joughin to Barnitz, Apr. 24, 1952 (copy); Barnitz to Joughin, Apr. 26, May 3, 1952 (the May 3 letter encloses Barnitz's curriculum vitae); Bernice Solomon to Joughin, June 17, 1952; Joughin to Elsie Elfenbein, Feb. 20, 1952 (copy), all ACLU. The manuscript for the play by Solomon, who was assistant public relations director of the NCJW, is dated December 18, 1952.

46. Jones correspondence, JP; Barnitz to Joughin, Apr. 26, 1952, ACLU. A partial list of those who wrote on behalf of Mundel includes faculty members from the University of Wisconsin, Ball State University, the University of California Medical School (San Francisco), Syracuse University, the University of Buffalo, Michigan State University, and the University of Iowa. Himstead also received letters from an editorial writer for the *Denver Post* and a representative of the American Jewish Committee.

47. American Association of University Professors, *In Honor of Ralph E. Himstead, 1893–1955* (Washington, D.C.: American Association of University Professors, 1956), pp. 12–13, 21–23, 27–28. This publication is a respectful but frank appraisal of Himstead's stewardship of the AAUP by three of his colleagues, George Pope Shannon, William T. Laprade, and Mark H. Ingraham. For a more critical assessment of Himstead see Schrecker, *No Ivory Tower,* pp. 315–16, 319–32.

48. These letters will be found throughout the AAUP mss. Mundel's mentor, Meier, was particularly irate. He took the attack on Mundel's competence as an attack on the integrity of the graduate programs of the University of Iowa. See Meier to Himstead, Jan. 9, 19, Feb. 14, 1952, AAUP.

49. Hofstadter and Metzger, *Academic Freedom,* pp. 487, 491; Himstead to Meldahl, June 24, 1952, AAUP.

50. Night letter, Himstead to Pomeroy, Feb. 18, 1952 (copy); Pomeroy to Himstead, Mar. 5, 1952, both AAUP.

51. Charles W. Hunt to Carter V. Good, May 9, 1952; Hunt to Hand, May 9, 1952 (both copies), both AAUP. Good was a well-known and respected expert on educational research. Two of his more significant publications are, as author, *Essentials of Educational Research* (1966; reprint ed., New York: Appleton-Century-

Crofts, 1971) and as editor, *Dictionary of Education* (1945; reprint ed., New York: McGraw-Hill, 1973).

52. Good to Hunt, May 18, 1952 (copy); Taylor to Himstead, May 21, 1952; Schroder to Himstead, May 10, 1952; Night letter, Himstead to Dunn (copy), May 19, 1952; Good to Himstead, May 27, 1952, all AAUP.

53. Jones to Himstead, May 27, 1952; Good to Himstead, May 29, 1952; Night letter, Himstead to Mundel, June 5, 1952 (copy); Good to Hunt, Jan. 19, 1952 (copy); Joughin to Himstead, June 18, 1952; Himstead to Meldahl, June 24, 1952 (copy); Mundel to Himstead, June 28, 1952; Jones to Himstead, June 29, 1952; all AAUP.

54. *WV,* May 26, 1952; Barnitz to Joughin, June 9, 1952, ACLU; Himstead to Good, Aug. 11, 1952 (copy); Good to Himstead, Aug. 14, 1952; AAUP.

55. Board Minutes, Apr. 23, 24, 25, 1952; Hand to Himstead, June 16, 23, 1952, AAUP.

56. Telegram, Himstead to Hand, June 23, 1952 (copy), AAUP.

57. Himstead to Dunn, July 1, 1952 (copy), AAUP.

58. Jones to Meldahl, June 8, 17, 1952 (copies), JP.

59. U.S., Congress, Senate, *Congressional Record,* 82d Cong., 2d sess., pp. 109, 223, 225, 241–50, 986, 1704, 1962, 2033, 2889, 4127, 4881–83, A603, A3228; Hechler, *Working with Truman,* pp. 249–50. For Neely's political good tidings see *Congressional Record,* 82d Cong., 2d sess., pp. 6016–17.

60. *WV,* June 19, 1952; *New York Times,* July 6, 1952; Jones' correspondence with Meldahl; Meldahl to Jones, June 18, 1952, JP.

CHAPTER 7

1. As was true for the first trial, there is no formal transcript of the proceedings. So again I have relied on the Fairmont papers. *Fairmont Times* reporters covering the trial were Laura Ridenour and William D. Evans, Jr. Logan Carroll and Fanny Davis reported for the *West Virginian. FT,* July 7, 8, 1952; *WV,* July 7, 1952.

2. *FT,* July 8, 1952.

3. Ibid.; *Polk's Greater Fairmont... Directory* (1952). Disqualified as jurors were three active Legionnaires and several men who had witnessed the first trial or formed an opinion from it, one who had a "childhood prejudice," and one who had his mind made up based on Manchester's article.

4. *FT,* July 8, 1952; *WV,* July 7, 8, 1952.

5. *FT,* July 8, 1952; *WV,* July 7, 8, 1952.

6. *FT,* July 8, 1952; *WV,* July 7, 8, 1952.

7. *FT,* July 8, 1952.

8. Ibid.; *WV,* July 8, 1952. The judge would not allow Mundel's counsel to enter into evidence Hand's 2,200-word July 1951 report on Mundel to the board, the Marion County Anti-Subversive Committee's attempt to label library books, or Loudin's interference with college administration.

9. *FT,* July 8, 1952.

10. Ibid.

11. *FT,* July 9, 1952.

12. Ibid.

13. Ibid.

14. Ibid.

15. Ibid.

16. *FT,* July 9, 1952.

17. Ibid.

18. Ibid.

19. *FT,* July 10, 1952; *WV,* July 9, 1952.

20. *FT,* July 10, 1952. The story that Madelaine Hand allegedly told was of a different order of tastelessness than Mundel's. It was about Dr. Hand on a camping trip, who in the moonlight "apparently does not wear pajamas [while] chasing with a bow and arrow a porcupine in the garbage can" (*WV,* July 9, 1952).

21. *FT,* July 10, 1952.

22. Ibid.

23. Ibid.

24. Ibid. When Neely began to discuss her mental illness, Katherine Roberts rose from the audience to protest and had to be silenced by the judge.

25. Ibid.

26. Ibid.

27. Ibid.

28. Ibid.

29. Ibid.

30. *FT,* July 11, 1952; *WV,* July 10, 1952.

31. *FT,* July 11, 12, 1952.

32. *FT,* July 11, 12, 1952.

33. *FT,* July 11, 12, 1952.

34. *FT,* July 12, 1952.

35. Ibid.

36. Ibid.

37. *FT,* July 15, 1952; *WV,* July 14, 1952.

38. *FT,* July 15, 1952. Schroder told the AAUP that Mundel had said at a faculty meeting that because of students' unfavorable comments she wished her salary to be based totally on her degrees. Schroder to Himstead, Aug. 20, 1951, AAUP.

39. *FT,* July 15, 1952.

40. Ibid.

41. Ibid. Several witnesses were called back, including Jones and Katherine Roberts. When Neely tried to question Roberts about her treatment for mental illness more than a decade earlier, the judge would not allow it.

42. Ibid.

43. Ibid.

44. *FT,* July 16, 1952; *WV,* July 15, 1952; *CG,* July 16, 1952.

45. *FT,* July 16, 1952.

46. Ibid.

47. Ibid.

48. Ibid.

49. Ibid.

50. Ibid.

51. Ibid.

52. Ibid.; Plaintiff's Instructions, nos. 1–20 (July 15, 1952); Defendant's Instructions, nos. 1–19 (July 15, 1952); [Meldahl], Motion to Set Aside Verdict . . . (Aug. 2, 1952) in Case File, *Mundel* v. *Loudin,* all MCCC; Meldahl to Malin, Sept. 6, 1952, ACLU.

53. Case Files, *Mundel* v. *Loudin,* MCCC; Meldahl to Malin, Sept. 6, 1952, ACLU.

54. *FT,* July 17, 1952.

55. Ibid.; *CG,* July 17, 1952.

56. *FT,* July 17, 1952. After a bill to pay her legal costs failed to pass the state legislature, the board of education voted to reimburse Loudin an additional $2,500 to pay Neely for the second trial. Neely thus evidently received $5,000 for his efforts. *WV,* Feb. 17, 1953; *FT,* Aug. 21, 1953.

CHAPTER 8

1. Meldahl to Jones and Barnitz, July 17, 1952; same to Jones, July 24, 1952, both JP; *FT,* July 21–25, 1952; *WV,* July 21–24, 1952; and *CG,* July 21–25, 1952. The Fairmont Police Department has no copy of an arrest report on Mundel.

2. *CG,* Aug. 1, 1952.

3. *Denver Post,* Aug. 10, 1952.

4. William Manchester, "An Enemy of the People?" *Nation,* Aug. 9, 1952, pp. 111–13.

5. *WV,* Aug. 28, 1952, reprints the article in an "Off Main Street" column without citing its date of publication in the *Christian Science Monitor.*

6. Barnitz to Joughin, July 31, Aug. 6, 1952, ACLU.

7. Malin to Joughin, Aug. 13, 1952; Meldahl to Malin, Sept. 6, 1952; Malin to Meldahl, Sept. 15, 1952 (copy); Joughin to Alonzo F. Myers, Sept. 17, 1952 (copy); same to Barnitz, Jan. 29, 1954 (copy); all ACLU. Byse and Joughin, *Tenure,* pp. 98–103, 192–97. See also Joughin's *Academic Freedom and Tenure: A Handbook of the American Association of University Professors* (Madison: University of Wisconsin Press, 1967), pp. 136–37, 139–41, where in the unrestrained 1960s the AAUP advocated nearly absolute freedom of extramural utterance and freedom from religious tests for teachers.

8. Himstead to Good, Aug. 11, 1952 (copy), AAUP. For clipping service from the board to Himstead see Lynch to Himstead, July 25, 1952; Himstead to Baer, July 29, 1952 (copy), both AAUP.

9. Good to Himstead, Aug. 14, 1952, AAUP.

10. Ibid.

11. Ibid.

12. Ibid.

13. Schrecker, *No Ivory Tower,* pp. 314–32. For prodding of the AAUP to take action and queries about the Mundel case, see G. W. Martin to Himstead, Mar. 3,

1952; James H. Bell and Fred Rainsberry to same, Mar. 5, 1953; Leonard Towner to same, May 10, 1952; D. E. Kibbey to same, June 6, 1952; Stanton Peckham to same, Sept. 2, 1952; Edgar Jaynes [president of the Fairmont State AAUP] to same, Feb. 16, 1953, all AAUP.

14. *FT,* Oct. 7, 1952; Joughin to Meldahl (copy), Sept. 3, 1953; Meldahl to Jones and Barnitz, July 17, 1952; same to Jones, July 24, 1952; Sept. 5 and Oct. 27, 1953, all JP.

15. *CG,* Nov. 2, 4, 5, 1952. That the charge of extremism, right or left, was not a decisive factor in West Virginia politics in 1952 is suggested by Robert Byrd's victory in the Sixth Congressional District despite much being made in the campaign of his earlier Ku Klux Klan affiliation. For the Kilgore-Revercomb campaign, see Maddox, *Kilgore,* pp. 310–12.

16. *CG,* Nov. 2, 4, 5, 1952; Lutz, "1952 Gubernatorial Election," pp. 211, 218–24, 229–30; *FT,* Oct. 27, 1952; *Morgantown Dominion News,* Dec. 21, 1951; Jan. 4, 1952. Mollohan's 1952 victory began a small dynasty. He continued as First District representative until he turned his seat over to his son. For an uncomplimentary assessment of the elder Mollohan, see the Nader group study, Christopher Finch and Robert Fellmeth, *Robert H. Mollohan: Democratic Representative from West Virginia* ([n.p.]: Grossman Publishers, 1972). Marland is perhaps best remembered as the former West Virginia governor who after a precipitous fall from grace wound up driving a Chicago taxi. The Holts, elder and younger, were fascinating but dissimilar mavericks.

17. Lutz, "1952 Gubernatorial Election," pp. 218–24, 229–30; *FT,* Oct. 27, 1952; William Ellis Coffey, "Rush Dew Holt: 'The Boy Senator,' 1905–1942" (Ph.D. diss., West Virginia University, 1970), pp. 287–332, 374–91.

18. On the split among national liberals, see Pells, *Liberal Mind,* pp. 262–65, 285–300.

19. On the agrarian Jeffersonian republican ideology see Forrest McDonald, *Novus Ordo Seclorum: The Intellectual Origins of the Constitution* (Lawrence: University Press of Kansas, 1985), pp. 73–77.

20. A current school of thought contends that progressive, industrial America invented the concept of Appalachia in the late nineteenth century. While it is proper to call attention to the excessive and unfair stereotyping of Appalachian natives as a strange people inhabiting a strange land, as hillbillies, or as "our contemporary ancestors," this thesis is weakened by its failure to refute the abundance of evidence that in fact Appalachian culture *is* different and *does* incorporate values opposed to modern mass culture. Neither does it sufficiently account for the special problems that obviously persist throughout the region. See Henry D. Shapiro, *Appalachia on Our Mind: The Southern Mountains and Mountaineers in the American Consciousness, 1870-1920* (Chapel Hill: University of North Carolina Press, 1978), especially pp. 256ff.; David E. Whisnant, *All That Is Native and Fine: The Politics of Culture in an American Region* (Chapel Hill: University of North Carolina Press, 1983), pp. 3–16; Gaventa, *Power and Powerlessness,* pp. 65–66. Writing in 1984, Janet B. Welch found from interviewing West Virginians in two rural counties that traditional values had been reinforced rather than

weakened by the coming to the hills of television, interstate highways, and national mass culture. Many of the people she talked to wanted not to join the mainstream but to withdraw further from it. "Appalachian Cultural Values," pp. 166, 174–76.

21. U.S., Congress, House, Committee on Un-American Activities, *Annual Report for the Year 1953.* 83d Cong., 2d sess., H. Rept. 1192, pp. 8–22. See also Schrecker, *No Ivory Tower,* pp. 194–218. I have not found a source for the phrase "nest of vipers," although it may derive from the King James Bible, Matthew 3:7 — "But when he saw many of the Pharisees and Sadducees come to his baptism, he said unto them, O generation of vipers, who hath warned you to flee from the wrath to come?" Popular writer Philip Wylie used *Generation of Vipers* as the title of his 1942 tract against "momism."

22. See the case of the so-called Fairmont Seven who unsuccessfully sued the Fairmont State College president and the president of the state board of regents in U.S. District Court. *FT,* Mar. 16, Aug. 26, Oct. 13, 1972; Jan. 18, 1973; *WV,* Apr. 30, Oct. 12, 1972; Mar. 27, 1973.

23. West Virginia Education Association, *Annual Report* (1952), p. 58. In August 1952, just as Mundel's legal challenge was ending, the WVEA tenure and ethics committee did intervene in a similar case. It involved a well-qualified high-school teacher who was nonretained by a county school board because of the interference of a school board member and a private citizen. The committee managed to win for the teacher a hearing before the school board, but the board would not change its mind. The best the WVEA could do was help the teacher to find a job in another county, which it did. WVEA, *Annual Report* (1953), pp. 61–62.

24. *FT,* May 1, 1953. Among the dignitaries in the audience were presidents Oliver S. Eikenberry of Shepherd College and Kenneth L. Spaulding of West Liberty State College, both of whom were rumored to be having difficulty with the state board of education.

25. Ibid.

26. Ibid.

27. State Board of Education, *Biennial Report* (1950–52), p. 43; and (1952–54), p. 32.

28. In 1970 the author was advised against accepting employment at Fairmont State by a professor at an eastern university who had heard about the Mundel affair. However, by that time West Virginia state faculty were protected by ade-quate written tenure and academic freedom guidelines. Scholarly studies after 1952 usually made reference to the case. Robert M. MacIver, *Academic Freedom in Our Time* (1955; reprint ed., New York: Gordian Press, 1967), p. 143, called it deplorable. See also Caute, *The Great Fear,* pp. 420–21.

29. State Board of Education, *Biennial Report* (1950–52), p. 51; (1952–54), p. 40. According to the 1984 *Fairmont State College Catalog,* 23 percent of the permanent faculty held their baccalaureate degrees from Fairmont State College and 50 percent held their highest degrees from nearby West Virginia University.

30. "Elements of Strength and Weakness," (ditto copy) excerpt dated in pencil

1952 from North Central Association of Colleges and Secondary Schools on-site report, JP. Such reports are confidential and one cannot be absolutely certain of the excerpt's authenticity. Based upon what the author knows of the subject and the college, he believes it to be genuine.

31. Author's interview with Jones (1984); *Who's Who in Library and Information Services* (1982), p. 247.

32. *Traill County Tribune,* June 4, 1975; Interview with Jones (1984); Far happier was the academic fate of Dr. Helmut Schoeck, whose employment was questioned by the board of education in May 1951 along with Mundel. He was soon elected vice president of the West Virginia Philosophical Association and in late 1952 left the college, the recipient of a graduate scholarship to Yale. *Columns,* Dec. 18, 1952.

33. *New York Times,* June 10, 1955.

34. See n. 7 above for Joughin's AAUP publications.

35. *Columns,* Nov. 19, 1953; *Fairmont Times-West Virginian,* June 21, 1983. Loudin and former Legion Commander L. O. Bickel did not participate in the 1983 television documentary.

36. Carroll, *Energy of Physical Creation.*

37. *New York Times,* Jan. 19, 1958, and the outpouring of eulogies from many sources reprinted in Anon., comp., *Memorial Services . . . of Matthew Mansfield Neely. . . .* For the Brown quotation see ibid., p. 133. As might be expected, the local papers gave much attention to the memorial ceremonies and to Neely's career. Most of the information in this paragraph is drawn from them. See *FT,* Jan. 20, 21, 22, 1958; *WV,* Jan. 20, 21, 22, 1958; *Fairmont Times-West Virginian,* Jan. 19, 1958. The other participating counsel, Alfred Neely, eventually became a judge of the Marion County common pleas court before he, too, died.

38. See Meldahl's *Avenue of Abundance for All* (1971), an updated version of his 1934 *Maximum Welfare* and his obituary in *CG,* Oct. 8, 1983, which listed his membership in the American Legion, but not his books or sponsorship of the Maximum Welfare Society.

39. *Fairmont Times-West Virginian,* June 19, 1983.

40. Ibid.; *FT,* June 21, 1983.

41. *FT,* June 24, 1983; author's personal observations and conversations.

42. *Fairmont Times-West Virginian,* June 24, 26, 1983; *New York Times,* June 23, 1983.

43. *Fairmont Times-West Virginian,* June 24, July 3, 13, 1983. Lasky asked $9,000,000 in damages. See chapter 2 above for the causes. The case was decided in February 1988 after a ten-day trial in U.S. District Court, Southern District, New York. The jury determined that ABC had defamed Lasky but that its broadcast was not substantially false. See *Victor Lasky* v. *American Broadcasting Companies, Inc.* (83 Civ. 7438).

Bibliography

Manuscript Collections

Brooklyn, N.Y. Private Collection. Harold D. Jones Papers.

Charleston, W.Va. State Archives. Minutes of the West Virginia State Board of Education, 1945–53.

Morgantown, W.Va. West Virginia University. West Virginia and Regional History Collection. American Legion Mountaineer Post 127 Papers. Harley M. Kilgore Papers. Matthew M. Neely Papers. W. W. Trent Papers. Clarence Edwin Smith Papers. West Virginia Education Scrapbooks.

Princeton, N.J. Princeton University. American Civil Liberties Union. Archives. Mundel Case File.

Washington, D.C. American Association of University Professors. Luella Mundel Files.

Government Documents

Anon., comp., *Memorial Services Held in the Senate and House of Representatives of the United States, Together with Remarks Presented in Eulogy of Matthew Mansfield Neely, Late a Senator from West Virginia.* Washington, D.C.: U.S. Government Printing Office, 1958.

Baer, H.K., comp. *Annual Report of West Virginia Board of Education and the State Board of Vocational Education.* July 1, 1947, to June 30, 1948. Charleston: Jarrett Printing Co., 1948.

——, comp. *Annual Report: West Virginia Board of Education and the State Board of Vocational Education.* July 1, 1948, to June 30, 1949. Charleston: Jarrett Printing Co., 1949.

——, comp. *Annual Report: West Virginia Board of Education and the State Board of Vocational Education.* July 1, 1949, to June 30, 1950. Charleston: Rose City Press, 1949.

——, comp. *Biennial Report: West Virginia Board of Education.* July 1, 1950, to June 30, 1952. Charleston: Rose City Press, 1952.

——, comp. *Biennial Report: West Virginia Board of Education.* July 1, 1952, to June 30, 1954. [Charleston]: mimeograph, 1954.

Freer, R. H. *Reports of Cases Determined by the Supreme Court of Appeals of West Virginia from January 19, 1901 to September 7, 1901,* vol. 49. Charleston: Daily Mail Publishing Co., 1902 (Usually known as W.Va. *Reports* [49]).

President's Commission on Higher Education. *Higher Education in American Democracy.* 6 vols. New York: Harper and Brothers, [1948].

State Department of Education. *The School Laws of West Virginia, 1947.* Charleston: State Department of Education, 1947.

——. *The School Laws of West Virginia* (Reprinted from Michie's *West Virginia Code of 1949* and 1953 Cumulative Supplement). Charlottesville, Va.: Michie Co., 1954.

Strayer, George D. *A Report of a Survey of Public Education in the State of West Virginia.* Legislative Interim Committee, State of West Virginia, 1945.

U.S., Congress. *Congressional Record.*

U.S., Congress, House, Committee on Un-American Activities. *Annual Report for the Year 1953.* 83rd Cong., 2d sess, H. Rept. 1192.

U.S., Department of Commerce, Bureau of the Census. *City and County Data Book* (1952). Washington, D.C.: U.S. Government Printing Office, 1953.

——. *Statistical Abstract of the United States* (1951). Washington, D.C.: U.S. Government Printing Office, 1952.

U.S., Department of Justice. "FBI American Legion Contact Program." comp. Athan Theoharis. Wilmington, Del.: Scholarly Resources, 1984 (microfilm copy of FBI documents released under provisions of the Freedom of Information Act/Privacy Act).

U.S. Government. *Proceedings of the Thirty-first National Convention of the American Legion. Philadelphia, Pa., Aug. 29–Sept. 1, 1949.* 81st Cong., 2d sess., House Doc. 447.

——. *Proceedings of the Thirty-second National Convention of the American Legion. Los Angeles, Calif., Oct. 9, 10, 11, 12, 1950.* 81st Cong., 2d sess., House Doc. 734.

——. *Proceedings of the Thirty-third National Convention of the American Legion. Miami, Fla., Oct. 15, 16, 17, 18, 1951.* 82d Cong., 2d sess., House Doc. 313.

——. *Proceedings of the Thirty-fourth National Convention of the American Legion. New York, N.Y., Aug. 25, 26, 27, 28, 1952.* 83d Cong., 1st sess., House Doc. 76.

——. *Proceedings of the Thirty-fifth National Convention of the American Legion. St. Louis, Mo., Aug. 31, Sept. 1, 2, 3, 1953.* 83d Cong., 2d sess., House Doc. 284.

West Virginia State Government. *Annual Report of the Department of Mines* [1948–52]. Charleston: Jarrett Printing Co., [1946–52].

——. *The West Virginia Code of 1949.* Charlottesville, Va.: Michie Co., 1949.

Maps

Sanborn Fire Insurance Maps. City of Fairmont (9403), reel 3, West Virginia, 1894–1950. Alexandria, Va.: Chadwyck-Healy (microfilm).

Newspapers

Columns (The Fairmont State College student newspaper).

Fairmont [W.Va.] *Times.*

Fairmont [W.Va.] *West Virginian.*

Fairmont Times–West Virginian (In the 1950s the two papers put out a combined Sunday paper under this title. They merged in the early 1970s and since then have published a single daily morning paper).

Charleston [W.Va.] *Daily Mail.*
Charleston [W.Va.] *Gazette.*
Morgantown [W.Va.] *Dominion News.*
New York Times.

Theses and Dissertations

Adler, Leslie K. "The Red Image: American Attitudes toward Communism in the Cold War Era." Ph.D. diss., University of California at Berkeley, 1970.

Carrico, William E. "Political Party Strength in West Virginia, 1920–1968." M.A. thesis, West Virginia University, 1972.

Casdorph, Paul D. "Legislative Politics and the Public Schools of West Virginia, 1933–1958: A Twenty-five Year History." Ph.D. diss., University of Kentucky, 1970.

Coffey, William Ellis. "Rush Dew Holt: 'The Boy Senator,' 1905–1942." Ph.D. diss., West Virginia University, 1970.

Holmes, Thomas M. "The Specter of Communism in Hawaii, 1947–1953." Ph.D. diss., University of Hawaii, 1975.

Johnson, Gerald Woiblet. "West Virginia Politics: A Socio-Cultural Analysis of Political Participation." Ph.D. diss., University of Tennessee, 1970.

Lanham, Robert E. "The West Virginia Statehouse Democratic Machine: Function and Process." Ph.D. diss., Claremont Graduate School and University Center, 1971.

Lord, Charles A. "The West Virginia Education Association, 1865–1961." Ph.D. diss., West Virginia University, 1963.

McKinley, Wayne Edwin. "A Study of the American Right: Senator Joseph McCarthy and the American Legion, 1946–1955." M.S. thesis: University of Wisconsin, 1962.

Pinnell, William G. "A Survey of the Economic Base of Marion County." M.A. thesis, West Virginia University, 1953.

Sorenson, Dale R. "The Anticommunist Consensus in Indiana, 1945–1958." Ph.D. diss., Indiana University, 1980.

Vicars, Bobby Lee. "Changes in College Presidents' Role under a Centralized State Board." Ed.D. thesis: West Virginia University, 1976.

Welch, Janet Boggess. "A Study of Appalachian Cultural Values as Evidenced in the Political and Social Attitudes of Rural West Virginians." Ph.D. diss., University of Maryland, 1984.

Williams, John Alexander. "Davis and Elkins of West Virginia: Businessmen in Politics." Ph.D. diss., Yale University, 1967.

Yaremchuk, William A. "The Congressional Speaking of Matthew Mansfield Neely in Behalf of Cancer Research Legislation." M.A. thesis: West Virginia University, 1964.

Bibliographies

Forbes, Harold M. *West Virginia History: A Bibliography and Guide to Research.* Morgantown: West Virginia University Press, 1981.

Haynes, John Earl, ed. *Communism and Anti-Communism in the United States: An Annotated Guide to Historical Writings.* New York: Garland Publishing, 1987.

Books and Articles

ABC News. *The American Inquisition.* New York: Journal Graphics, 1983 (television documentary script).

Alinsky, Saul. *John L. Lewis: An Unauthorized Biography.* New York: G. P. Putnam's Sons, 1948.

Ambler, Charles H. *A History of Education in West Virginia.* Huntington, W.Va.: Standard Printing and Publishing Co., 1951.

American Association of University Professors. *In Honor of Ralph E. Himstead, 1893-1955.* Washington, D.C.: AAUP, 1956.

Anon. "The Propaganda Program of Our Academic Hucksters." *American Legion Magazine* (Dec. 1952): 18–19, 56–58.

Asimov, Isaac. *A Whiff of Death.* New York: Fawcett-Crest, 1958.

Baarslag, Karl. "How to Spot a Communist." *American Legion Magazine* (Jan. 1947): 9–11, 44–47.

Barrett, Edward L. *The Tenney Committee: Legislative Investigation of Subversive Activities in California.* Ithaca, N.Y.: Cornell University Press, 1951.

Barzun, Jacques. *Teacher in America.* Boston: Little, Brown and Co., 1945.

Bayley, Edwin R. *Joe McCarthy and the Press.* Madison: University of Wisconsin Press, 1981.

Belknap, Michal R. *Cold War Political Justice: The Smith Act, the Communist Party, and American Civil Liberties.* Westport, Conn.: Greenwood Press, 1977.

———, ed. *American Political Trials.* Westport, Conn.: Greenwood Press, 1981.

Beth, Loren P. *The American Theory of Church and State.* Gainesville: University of Florida Press, 1958.

Bontecou, Eleanor. *The Federal Loyalty-Security Program.* Ithaca, N.Y.: Cornell University Press, 1953.

Bouscaren, Anthony. *A Guide to Anti-Communist Action.* Chicago: Henry Regnery Co., 1958.

Bremner, Robert H., ed. *Children and Youth in America: A Documentary History.* 3 vols. Cambridge, Mass.: Harvard University Press, 1971.

Buckley, William F., Jr. *God and Man at Yale.* Chicago: Henry Regnery Co., 1951.

Budenz, Louis Francis. "Do Colleges Have to Hire Red Professors?" *American Legion Magazine* (Nov. 1951): 11–13, 40–43.

Burke, Colin B. *American Collegiate Populations: A Test of the Traditional View.* New York: New York University Press, 1982.

Burnham, James. *The Coming Defeat of Communism.* 1949–50. Reprint. Westport, Conn.: Greenwood Press, 1968.

Byse, Clark, and Louis Joughin. *Tenure in American Higher Education: Plans, Practices, and the Law.* Ithaca, N.Y.: Cornell University Press, 1959.

Caplow, Theodore, and Reece J. McGee. *The Academic Marketplace.* New York: Basic Books, 1959.

Carleton, Don E., "McCarthyism in Houston: The George Ebey Affair." *Southwestern Historical Quarterly* 80 (Oct. 1976): 163–76.

——. *Red Scare! Right-Wing Hysteria, Fifties Fanaticism and Their Legacy in Texas.* Austin: Texas Monthly Press, 1985.

Carter, Paul A. *Another Part of the Fifties.* New York: Columbia University Press, 1983.

Carroll, Robert L. *The Energy of Physical Creation.* Columbia, S.C.: Carroll Research Institute, 1985.

Casdorph, Paul D. "Clarence W. Meadows, W. W. Trent and Educational Reform in West Virginia." *West Virginia History* 41 (Winter 1980): 126–41.

Caudill, Harry M. *Theirs Be the Power: The Moguls of Eastern Kentucky.* Urbana: University of Illinois Press, 1983.

Caute, David. *The Great Fear: The Anti-Communist Purge under Truman and Eisenhower.* New York, N.Y.: Simon and Schuster, 1978.

Chafe, William H. *The American Woman: Her Changing Social, Economic, and Political Role, 1920–1970.* New York: Oxford University Press, 1972.

Cochran, Bert. *Harry Truman and the Crisis Presidency.* New York: Funk and Wagnalls, 1973.

——. *Labor and Communism: The Conflict That Shaped American Unions.* Princeton, N.J.: Princeton University Press, 1977.

Commager, Henry S. et al. *Civil Liberties under Attack.* Philadelphia: University of Pennsylvania Press, 1951.

——, ed. *Documents of American History.* 9th ed., in 2 vols. Englewood Cliffs, N.J.: Prentice-Hall, 1973.

Cook, Fred J. *The Nightmare Decade.* New York: Random House, 1971.

Cort, John C. "Jefferson in West Virginia." *Commonweal,* Dec. 7, 1951, pp. 225–28.

Crosby, Donald F. *God, Church and Flag: Senator Joseph R. McCarthy and the Catholic Church, 1950–1957.* Chapel Hill: University of North Carolina Press, 1978.

Cutting, Gary, ed. *Paradigms and Revolutions: Appraisals and Applications of Thomas Kuhn's Philosophy of Science.* Notre Dame, Ind.: Notre Dame University Press, 1980.

Davis, David B., ed. *The Fear of Conspiracy: Images of Un-American Subversion from the Revolution to the Present.* Ithaca, N.Y.: Cornell University Press, 1971.

Demos, John P. *Entertaining Satan: Witchcraft and Culture in Early New England.* New York: Oxford University Press, 1982.

Donohoe, William A. *The Politics of the American Civil Liberties Union.* New Brunswick, N.J.: Transaction Books, 1985.

Donovan, Robert J. *The Tumultuous Years: The Presidency of Harry S Truman, 1949–1953.* New York: W. W. Norton and Co., 1982.

Ellis, Evelyn. "Social Psychological Correlates of Upward Social Mobility among Unmarried Career Women." *American Sociological Review* 17 (Oct. 1952): 558–63.

Ernst, Morris L., and David Loth. *Report on the American Communist.* New York: Holt, Rinehart and Winston, 1952.

Fenton, John H. *Politics in the Border States.* New Orleans: Hauser Press–Galleon Books, 1957.

Finch, Christopher, and Robert Fellmeth. *Robert H. Mollohan: Democratic Representative from West Virginia.* [n.p.]: Grossman Publishers, 1972.

Fisher, William. "Progress and Demise of Teachers Colleges." *School and Society* (1951): 149–51.

Franklin, Samuel F., and William P. Tucker. "The Postwar Liberal Arts College Faculty." *School and Society* (1947): 397–98.

Fried, Richard M. *Men against McCarthy.* New York: Columbia University Press, 1976.

———. "Communism and Anti-Communism: A Review Essay." *Wisconsin Magazine of History* (1980): 309–21.

Gaventa, John. *Power and Powerlessness: Quiescence and Rebellion in an Appalachian Valley.* Urbana: University of Illinois Press, 1980.

Gellhorn, Walter, ed. *The States and Subversion.* Ithaca, N.Y.: Cornell University Press, 1952.

Gellermann, William. *The American Legion as Educator.* New York: Columbia University Press, 1938.

Genauer, Emily. "Still Life with Red Herring." *Harper's Magazine* 199 (Sept. 1949): 88–91.

Goldman, Eric F. *The Crucial Decade — and After: America 1945-1960.* New York: Alfred A. Knopf, 1966.

Goodman, Walter. *The Committee: The Extraordinary Career of the House Committee on Un-American Activities.* New York: Farrar, Straus, and Giroux, 1964.

Gosnell, Harold F. *Truman's Crises: A Political Biography of Harry S. [sic] Truman.* Westport, Conn.: Greenwood Press, 1980.

Graham, Patricia Albjerg. *Progressive Education: From Arcady to Academe.* New York: Teachers College Press, 1967.

Gray, Justin. *The Inside Story of the Legion.* New York: Boni and Gaer, 1948.

Griffith, Robert. *The Politics of Fear: Joseph R. McCarthy and the Senate.* Lexington: University Press of Kentucky, 1970.

Griffith, Robert, and Athan Theoharis, eds. *The Specter: Original Essays on the Cold War and the Origins of McCarthyism.* New York: New Viewpoints, 1974.

Gutek, Gerald L. *George S. Counts and American Civilization: The Educator as Social Theorist.* Macon, Ga.: Mercer University Press, 1984.

Hamby, Alonzo L. *Beyond the New Deal: Harry S. [sic] Truman and American Liberalism.* New York: Columbia University Press, 1973.

Handy, Robert T. *A Christian America: Protestant Hopes and Historical Realities.* 2d ed. New York: Oxford University Press, 1984.

Harper, Alan D. *The Politics of Loyalty: The White House and the Communist Issue, 1946-52.* Westport, Conn.: Greenwood, 1969.

Hauptman, William, "The Suppression of Art in the McCarthy Era," *Artforum* 12 (Oct. 1973): 48–52.

Hechler, Ken. *Working with Truman.* New York: G. P. Putnam's Sons, 1982.

Henige, David. *Oral Historiography.* New York: Longman, 1982.

Hoffmann, Joseph E., comp. *Marion County Centennial Yearbook, 1863–1963.*

Hofstadter, Richard. *The Paranoid Style in American Politics and Other Essays.* New York: Alfred A. Knopf, 1965.

Hofstadter, Richard, and Walter Metzger. *The Development of Academic Freedom in the United States.* New York: Columbia University Press, 1955.

Hoover, John Edgar. "Civil Liberties and Law Enforcement: The Role of the F.B.I." *Iowa Law Review* (Winter 1952): 175–95.

Hughes, Everet C. *Men and Their Work.* London: Collier-Macmillan, 1958.

Hyman, Harold M. *To Try Men's Souls: Loyalty Test in American History.* Los Angeles: University of California Press, 1960.

Iverson, Robert W. *The Communists and the Schools.* New York: Harcourt, Brace and Co., 1959.

Jackameit, William P. "The Evolution of Higher Education Governance in West Virginia: A Study of Political Influence." *West Virginia History* 36 (Jan. 1975): 97–130.

Jencks, Christopher, and David Riesman. *The Academic Revolution.* Garden City, N.Y.: Doubleday and Co., 1968.

Jezer, Marty. *The Dark Ages: Life in the United States, 1945–1960.* Boston: South End Press, 1982.

Joughin, Louis, ed. *Academic Freedom and Tenure: A Handbook of the American Association of University Professors.* Madison: University of Wisconsin Press, 1967.

Keely, Joseph C. "Let's Have More Schools Like This." *American Legion Magazine* (Aug. 1951): 26–27, 57–58.

Kelly, Alfred H., Winfred A. Harbison and Herman Belz. *The American Constitution: Its Origins and Development.* 6th ed. New York: W. W. Norton and Co., 1983.

Komarovsky, Mirra. "Cultural Contradictions and Sex Roles." *American Journal of Sociology* 52 (Nov. 1946): 184–89.

Kozloff, Max. "American Painting during the Cold War," *Artforum* 12 (Oct. 1973): 39–41.

Kuhn, Irene Corbally. "Why You Buy Books That Sell Communism." *American Legion Magazine* (Jan. 1951): 53–55, 58–63.

———. "Your Child Is Their Target." *American Legion Magazine* (June 1952): 18–19, 54–56.

Kuhn, Thomas S. *The Structure of Scientific Revolutions.* 2d ed. Chicago: University of Chicago Press, 1969.

Kutler, Stanley I. *The American Inquisition: Justice and Injustice in the Cold War.* New York: Hill and Wang, 1982.

Lantz, Herman R. *People of Coal Town.* 1958. Reprint. Carbondale: Southern Illinois University Press, 1971.

Latham, Earl, ed. *The Meaning of McCarthyism.* 2d ed. Lexington, Mass.: D. C. Heath and Co., 1973.

Lattimore, Owen. *Ordeal by Slander.* Boston: Little, Brown and Co., 1950.

Lazarsfeld, Paul F., and Wagner Thielens, Jr. *The Academic Mind: Social Scientists in a Time of Crisis.* Glencoe, Ill.: Free Press, 1958.

Levenstein, Harvey A. *Communism, Anticommunism, and the CIO.* Westport, Conn.: Greenwood Press, 1981.

Levine, David O. *The American College and the Culture of Aspiration, 1915-1940.* Ithaca, N.Y.: Cornell University Press, 1986.

Lipset, Seymour M., and Earl Raab. *The Politics of Unreason: Right Wing Extremism in America 1790-1970.* New York: Harper and Row, 1970.

Lipsitz, George. *Class and Culture in Cold War America: "A Rainbow at Midnight."* South Hadley, Mass.: Praeger, 1981.

Lord, Charles A. *Years of Decision: A History of an Organization.* Charleston: West Virginia Education Association, 1965.

Lundberg, Ferdinand, and Marynia Farnham. *Modern Woman: The Lost Sex.* New York: Harper and Brothers, 1947.

Lutz, Paul F. "The 1952 West Virginia Gubernatorial Election." *West Virginia History* 39 (Jan.–Apr. 1978): 210–35.

Lyons, Eugene. "Our New Privileged Class." *American Legion Magazine* (Sept. 1951): 11–13, 37–40.

McCarthy, Mary. *The Groves of Academe.* New York: Harcourt, Brace and World, 1952.

MacIver, Robert M. *Academic Freedom in Our Time.* New York: Columbia University Press, 1955.

McWilliams, Carey. *Witch Hunt: The Revival of Heresy.* Boston: Little, Brown and Co., 1950.

Maddox, Robert F. *The Senatorial Career of Harley Martin Kilgore.* New York: Garland Publishing, 1981.

Manchester, William. "An Enemy of the People?" *Nation,* Aug. 9, 1952, pp. 111–12.

——. "The Case of Luella Mundel." *Harper's Magazine* (May 1952): 54–61.

Manion, Clarence. *The Key to Peace.* Chicago: Heritage Foundation, 1953.

——. "We Can Win on These Terms." *American Legion Magazine* (July 1951): 9, 48.

Manwaring, David R. *Render unto Caesar: The Flag Salute Controversy.* Chicago: University of Chicago Press, 1962.

Marsden, George. *Reforming Fundamentalism: Fuller Seminary and the New Evangelicalism.* Grand Rapids, Mich.: William B. Eerdmans Publishing Co., 1987.

——. ed. *Evangelism in Modern America.* Grand Rapids, Mich.: William B. Eerdmans Publishing Co., 1984.

Mason, Medora. "Joseph Rosier, Teacher-Senator." *West Virginia School Journal* (Sept. 1946): 5–6.

Mathews, Jane De Hart. "Art and Politics in Cold War America." *American Historical Review* 81 (Oct. 1976): 762–87.

Matthews, J. B. "Communism and the Colleges," *American Mercury* (May 1953): 111–44.

Mauldin, Bill. *Back Home.* New York: William Sloane Associates, 1945.

Meldahl, Horace. *Avenue of Abundance for All.* Jericho, N.Y.: Exposition Press, 1971.

——. *Maximum Welfare.* Charleston, W.Va.: Hood, Hiserman-Brodhag Co., 1934.

Miller, Merle. *The Judges and the Judged.* Garden City, N.Y.: Doubleday and Company, 1952.

Navasky, Victor S. *Naming Names.* New York: Viking Press, 1980.

Neely, Matthew Mansfield. *State Papers and Public Addresses.* Charleston, W.Va.: Mathews Printing and Lithographing Co., n.d.

Neier, Aryeh. "Adhering to Principle: Lessons from the 1950s." *Civil Liberties Review* (Nov.–Dec. 1977): 26–32.

Nelson, Steve, James R. Barnett and Rob Ruck, *Steve Nelson: American Radical.* Pittsburgh: University of Pittsburgh Press, 1981.

Newcomer, Mabel. *A Century of Higher Education for American Women.* New York: Harper and Brothers, 1959.

O'Reilly, Kenneth. *Hoover and the Un-Americans: The F.B.I., H.U.A.C., and the Red Menace.* Philadelphia: Temple University Press, 1983.

Pells, Richard. *The Liberal Mind in a Conservative Age: American Intellectuals in the 1940s and 1950s.* New York: Harper and Row, 1985.

Phillips, Cabell. *The Truman Presidency: The History of a Triumphant Succession.* New York: Macmillan Co., 1966.

Powers, Richard G. *Secrecy and Power: The Life of J. Edgar Hoover.* New York: Free Press, 1987.

Pritkin, R. B. "The Legion's New Commander." *American Legion Magazine* (Apr. 1952): 20–21, 54–55.

Rascoe, Burton. "You Should Know about This Book." *American Legion Magazine* (May 1951): 28, 52.

Ravitch, Diane. *The Troubled Crusade: American Education, 1945–1980.* New York: Basic Books, 1983.

Reeder, Edwin H. "The Quarrel between Professors of Academic Subjects and Professors of Education: An Analysis." AAUP *Bulletin* (Autumn 1951): 506–21.

Ribuffo, Leo P. *The Old Christian Right: The Protestant Far Right from the Great Depression to the Cold War.* Philadelphia: Temple University Press, 1983.

Rice, Otis K. *West Virginia.* Lexington: University Press of Kentucky, 1985.

Riesman, David. *Faces in the Crowd.* New Haven, Conn.: Yale University Press, 1952.

——. *The Lonely Crowd.* New Haven, Conn.: Yale University Press, 1950.

Rogin, Michael Paul. "Kiss Me Deadly: Communism, Motherhood, and Cold War Movies." *Representations* 6 (Spring 1984): 1–35.

——. *McCarthy and the Intellectuals.* Cambridge, Mass.: Harvard University Press, 1967.

Salisbury, Harrison E. "The Strange Correspondence of Morris Ernst and John Edgar Hoover, 1939–1964." *Nation* 239 (Dec. 1, 1984): 575–89.

Schrecker, Ellen W. *No Ivory Tower: McCarthyism and the Universities.* New York: Oxford University Press, 1986.

Schroder, Fridtjof. "The Nature and Meaning of Art." Fairmont, W.Va.: Privately published, 1955.

Selcraig, James T. *The Red Scare in the Midwest, 1945–1955.* Ann Arbor, Mich.: UMI Research Press, 1982.

Shapiro, Henry D. *Appalachia on Our Mind: The Southern Mountains and Mountaineers in the American Consciousness, 1870–1920.* Chapel Hill: University of North Carolina Press, 1978.

Sizer, Leonard M. *Estimates of the Population of West Virginia Counties, July 1, 1950–1962.* Morgantown: Office of Research and Development Appalachian Center, West Virginia University, 1969.

———. *Population Change in West Virginia with Emphasis on 1940–1960.* Morgantown: West Virginia University Agricultural Extension Station Bulletin no. 563 (May 1968).

Solomon, Barbara M. *In the Company of Educated Women: A History of Women and Higher Education,* New Haven: Yale University Press, 1985.

Starobin, Joseph R. *American Communism in Crisis, 1943–1957.* Berkeley: University of California Press, 1972.

Stouffer, Samuel A. *Communism, Conformity, and Civil Liberties: A Cross-Section of the Nation Speaks Its Mind.* Garden City, N.Y.: Doubleday and Co., 1955.

Sturm, Albert L. *State Administrative Organization in West Virginia.* Morgantown: West Virginia University, Bureau for Government Research, Publication no. 7, 1952.

Theoharis, Athan. "The FBI and the American Legion Contact Program, 1940–1966." *Political Science Quarterly* 100 (Summer 1985): 271–86.

———, ed. *The Truman Presidency: The Origins of the Imperial Presidency and the National Security State.* Stanfordville, N.Y.: Earl M. Coleman Enterprises, 1979.

Thompson, Francis H. *The Frustration of Politics: Truman, Congress and the Loyalty Issue.* Rutherford, N.J.: Fairleigh Dickinson University Press, 1979.

Trumbo, Dalton. *The Time of the Toad: A Study of the Inquisition in America and Two Related Pamphlets.* New York: Harper and Row, 1972.

Turner, William P. *A Centennial History of Fairmont State College.* Fairmont, W.Va.: Fairmont State College, 1970.

Ungar, Sanford J. *FBI.* Boston: Little, Brown, and Co., 1976.

Vinocour, S. M. "The Veteran Flunks the Professor: A G.I. Indictment of Our Institutions of Higher Education!" *School and Society* 66 (1947): 289–92.

Weinstein, Allen. "The Symbolism of Subversion: Notes on Some Cold War Icons." *Journal of American Studies* 6 (Aug. 1972): 165–80.

West, Rebecca. *The Meaning of Treason.* New York: Viking Press, 1947.

———. *The New Meaning of Treason.* New York: Viking Press, 1964.

West Virginia Education Association. *Annual Report of the Secretary* [1950–53] (Charleston: WVEA, 1950–53).

Whisnant, David E. *All That Is Native and Fine: The Politics of Culture in an American Region.* Chapel Hill: University of North Carolina Press, 1983.

White, Lynn, Jr. *Educating Our Daughters.* New York: Harper and Brothers, 1950.

Wiebe, Robert H. *The Segmented Society: An Introduction to the Meaning of America.* New York: Oxford University Press, 1975.

Williams, John Alexander. *West Virginia: A Bicentennial History.* New York: W. W. Norton and Co. and American Association for State and Local History, 1976.

Wilson, Logan. *The Academic Man: A Study in the Sociology of a Profession.* New York: Oxford University Press, 1942.

Woltman, Fred. "Race-Religion." *American Legion Magazine* (May 1952): 15, 44–45.

Zilversmit, Arthur. "The Failure of Progressive Education, 1920–1940" in *Schooling and Society,* edited by Lawrence Stone, pp. 252–63. Baltimore: Johns Hopkins University Press, 1976.

Index

Note on the Author

Charles H. McCormick is Professor of History at Fairmont State College.